Aligning National Approaches to Digital Preservation

Nancy Y. McGovern, Volume Editor

Katherine Skinner, Series Editor

EDUCOPIA INSTITUTE PUBLICATIONS
Atlanta, Georgia

EDUCOPIA INSTITUTE PUBLICATIONS
Atlanta, Georgia
www.educopia.org/publications

Publication and Cataloging Information:

ISBN: 978-0-9826653-1-2

Volume Editor: Nancy Y. McGovern

Series Editor: Katherine Skinner

Publisher: Educopia Institute Publications
                 Atlanta, GA 30309
                 USA

TABLE OF CONTENTS

ACKNOWLEDGEMENTS

This volume emerged out of a digital preservation conference held in Tallinn, Estonia, in May 2011: "Aligning National Approaches to Digital Preservation." We are grateful to the many people who helped bring that conference to life, especially the conference organizers—Martha Anderson, Michelle Gallinger, Martin Halbert, Mari Kannusaar, Abigail Potter, Matt Schultz, Katherine Skinner, and Aaron Trehub—and the keynote speakers— Laura Campbell and Gunnar Sahlin—and the panel chairs—Inge Angevaare, Joy Davidson, Maurizio Lunghi, Adrienne Muir, Raivo Ruusalepp, and Michael Seadle—all of whom brought a wealth of experience, passion, and intellectual engagement to this endeavor.

We would like to extend a special thanks to all of the presenters and delegates (from more than 20 countries!) who participated in the conference. We look forward to our continued work with you all in the growing community of cultural stewardship that we will collectively foster.

We also want to take the opportunity to thank the wide range of memory institutions that provided various kinds of support to enable this publication. Topping that list are the National Digital Information Infrastructure and Preservation Program (NDIIPP) of the Library of Congress and the University of North Texas Libraries, both of which provided financial support for this volume's production.

Finally, we want to express our gratitude to Laura Campbell, whose vision, strength, and determination has contributed so substantially to the establishment and evolution of the field of digital preservation in ways far too numerable to recount here. We dedicate this volume to her.

Nancy Y. McGovern, Volume Editor
Katherine Skinner, Series Editor
August 2012

Prologue

On May 23-25, 2011, more than 125 delegates from more than 20 countries gathered in Tallinn, Estonia, for the "Aligning National Approaches to Digital Preservation" conference. At the National Library of Estonia, this group explored how to create and sustain international collaborations to support the preservation of our collective digital cultural memory.

Organized and hosted by the Educopia Institute, the National Library of Estonia, the US Library of Congress, the University of North Texas, and Auburn University, this gathering established a strong foundation for future collaborative efforts in digital preservation. Using a combination of plenary panels and hosted discussions, the convened group studied a range of opportunities and barriers to alignment in areas such as technology, law, education, economics, organizational frameworks, and standards.

This publication contains a collection of peer-reviewed essays that were developed by conference panels and attendees in the months following ANADP. Rather than simply chronicling the event, the volume intends to broaden and deepen its impact by reflecting on the ANADP presentations and conversations and establishing a set of starting points for building a greater alignment across digital preservation initiatives. Above all, it highlights the need for strategic international collaborations to support the preservation of our collective cultural memory.

The digital preservation field is still in an early stage of emergence and development, and we know that the techniques and technologies that early adopters are exploring today will be, at best, building blocks for a still unimaginable future environment. We also are aware that the digital content we are called to curate increasingly confounds national boundaries. We publish this volume in hopes that it will help our field continue to imagine and bring into being the strong international alliances we need to support the persistence of our digital memory.

We were honored to have President Toomas Hendrik Ilves of the Republic of Estonia address the ANADP attendees as the conference's opening event. We are likewise honored to reproduce his timely address here as a foreword to this volume.

-Katherine Skinner (Educopia Institute)

Foreword

The President of the Republic of Estonia at the opening of the international conference, "Aligning National Approaches to Digital Preservation," at the National Library of Estonia on 23 May 2011.

Dear Friends,

I am pleased to welcome you to Estonia, a country that has been an innovative pioneer in a range of areas involving the application of information technologies to provide new services to the public. Estonia pioneered the e-government cabinet, computerized tax returns (already in 1994), mobile phone parking, as well as online elections. All of a person's health records are available to him and his personal doctor on computer; the same holds true for dentistry, and seventy percent of pharmacy prescriptions are digital. So, with that background it should come as no surprise that our host today, the Estonian National Library, is also a leader in digitization with its digital archive, DIGAR, which now contains a significant part of our cultural heritage.

But while we are proud of what we have done, we also are keenly aware how important it is to keep up with current developments. As the speed of progress cranks up, so too does the speed of obsolescence.

As I noted, Estonia has invested a good amount of energy in innovation and modern technologies. Yet we also have perhaps exceptionally strong ties to institutions that serve as a repository for historical memory. Indeed, the formation of the nation in the Karl Deutsch sense of social communication was inextricably intertwined with archivization.

In the second half of the 19th century, a Lutheran pastor here, Jakob Hurt, organized a nationwide folklore collection campaign in which more than 1,400 people took part. This is an impressive figure, considering that Estonia's population was less than a million in those days.

This imposing compendium of the Estonian psyche is laid out in 162 thick volumes totaling 114,696 pages. This folklore collection is one of the most important compilations of information on 19th century folk culture anywhere in the world.

Through Hurt's project, Estonians came to understand the value of our traditions. What had been a primarily peasant culture came to understand that we too have a history and our own stories, and this realization, I would argue, in turn helped lay the foundations for eventual statehood in 1918.

One reason the campaign begun by Hurt was so successful was that it was volunteer-driven. It was a grassroots effort; today we would say it was a civil society initiative. Similarly, a hundred years later, our awareness of our history and our memories of statehood helped in restoring our independence. The occupation forces of the Soviet Union and Nazi Germany had tried to erase the memory of a free Estonia and supplant it with some rather bizarre fairy tales, but memories lived on in homes, at dinner table discussions, in student dormitories, nurturing the hope that one day the country would be free again. But the occupation was brutal and the efforts to erase an entire nation's memory were not small. In the first years after being re-occupied by the Soviets, an estimated 10 million books were destroyed. Ten million. That's roughly 10 books for every Estonian.

As Estonia moved closer to independence we faced new issues; people who did not want a record of their own acts to be known began to pilfer our archives. We know of cases where priceless material simply vanished from archives in Estonia or otherwise did not survive. During the "Singing Revolution" era, there were those who wanted to hide their earlier words and deeds, who wanted to erase or distort our own common past and allowed much valuable archive material to be misplaced. Fortunately, this would no longer be possible with digital materials, especially if many people have free access to them.

That is why I am glad that a major part of the Radio Free Europe archive has been preserved, and that thanks to the Hoover Institute, more and more of it is being digitized. This record helps us keep alive events that were difficult for many Eastern European peoples. It allows us and our descendants to understand how people were actually governed back then, and how they lived.

Yet even still, great swathes of our experience tend to disappear and fade. Some archives are lost for good, other materials, for example the archives and files of the KGB were spirited out of the country. This is why I established the Estonian Memory Institute to research and document the era under the occupations and how things actually worked, what really happened. After all, ignorance presents an opportunity for tampering with and manipulating history and knowledge. Since newspapers did not report the news, unless they were reporting sports victories or communist party plenum speeches, it is quite a formidable task to determine *Wie es eigentlich gewesen ist*, as Leopold von Ranke defined the guiding principle of the historian: what really was, or what really took place.

What can we conclude from this? Knowledge and memory help people stand against totalitarian societies. It is important to preserve historical memory and ensure that it remains freely accessible. This is what separates totalitarianism from liberty: dictatorships fear unrestricted remembrance and public disclosure, for there is so much to conceal. For democracies, remembrance is a strength.

We must make sure that as much as possible of the material in the repositories remains freely accessible. Digitization is what allows us to do this. Our task is to preserve and to protect access to these archives, while we entrust the job of interpreting our past to researchers and scholars.

Dear friends, I am proud that the Jakob Hurt folklore collection I spoke of earlier—an important repository of our national memory—will become digitally available in the near future, along with all of the primary Estonian documents from the 16th century to the beginning of the 20th century. This is being made possible through the collective effort of our memory institutions, archives, and libraries. All copyright and data protection issues are being addressed in the same spirit—in cooperation.

Digitizing our national memory is a cornerstone of liberty and the better we understand that, I think, that freer we all shall be.

-President Toomas Hendrik Ilves (Republic of Estonia)

Aligning National Approaches to Digital Preservation: An Introduction

Nancy Y. McGovern (Massachusetts Institute of Technology)

Introduction

The accumulation of standards and good practice for digital preservation has been emerging and consolidating since the release of the 1996 report, *Preserving Digital Information.*[1] As we advance towards twenty years of progress and the establishment of an international community of practice, there is an opportunity to measure our progress in response to the original set of challenges delineated in the 1996 report and to consider opportunities for achieving a future desired state. This volume considers the accomplishments, remaining challenges, and next steps in considering the alignment of national approaches to digital preservation (ANADP).

Envisioning an International Community of Practice

Since the release of the 1996 report, "Preserving Digital Information," the digital preservation community has been progressing through the stages of group formation: *forming*, coming together; *storming*, considering competing perspectives; *norming*, agreeing upon common outcomes; and *performing*, working together effectively.[2] This volume marks the maturation of the digital preservation community as a growing portion of the community embraces norming and seeks to identify the means for performing—or aligning in this context. The objective of the ANADP conference that was held in Tallinn, Estonia, in May

---

[1] Don Waters, and John Garrett, "Preserving Digital Information: Report of the Task Force on Archiving of Digital Information" (Washington, DC: The Commission on Preservation and Access and The Research Libraries Group, 1996.

2 Bruce Tuckman (1965). "Developmental sequence in small groups." *Psychological Bulletin* 63 (6): 384–99. DOI:10.1037/h0022100 (last accessed 07-20-2012).

2011, and this complementary volume is to better understand core aspects of alignment to inform the further development of the digital preservation community.

Emergence of the Digital Preservation Community

Another way to review the emergence of the digital preservation community to date is to adapt a model that is used by sociologists to study emerging groups. That model defines four attributes of a group that enable a group to be identified and studied: *membership, interaction among members, goals shared by members*, and *norms held by members*.[3] The following brief review applies these attributes of an emerging group to the digital preservation community at this point in its development.[4]

Membership

For a group to demonstrate *membership*, "a person must think of himself or herself as belonging to the group and must also be recognized by other members as belonging to the group."[5] There are indicators that the digital preservation community has an increasing membership of digital curators who would self-identify as members of the community and who can also be identified readily by the community as members. For example, a growing number of practitioners have a job title or description that references digital preservation, which explicitly marks them as members of the digital preservation community. Using this indicator, it is possible today to identify a set of authors, conference attendees, researchers, and practitioners who are engaged in digital preservation.

Interaction Among Members

Interaction among members specifically requires that "group members communicate with one another and influence one another."[6] The maturation of the digital preservation community is increasingly reflected in a growing body of relevant literature. The

---

[3] H. Andrew Michener, John D. DeLamater, and Daniel J. Myers, *Social Psychology*, Fifth Edition, (Belmont, CA, USA: Thomson-Wadsworth, 2004): 324.

[4] This review is adapted from a more extensive discussion that appears in *Technology Responsiveness for Digital Preservation: A Model*, a doctoral thesis submitted by Nancy Y. McGovern to meet the PhD requirements at University College London, 2009.

[5] Michener, et al., *Social Psychology*, 324.

[6] *Ibid.*

domains that compose the digital preservation community have included periodic articles in their literature about the challenges of preserving digital content—since the late 1960s in the case of archival literature.[7] The issue of the longevity of digitized content emerged as a topic in the literature of the library domain in the 1980s.[8] The literature of museum curatorship has included digital preservation articles since the 1990s.[9] In addition to the mainstream publications in the professions that compose the digital preservation community, increasing numbers of publications since 1996 either highlight or are devoted to digital preservation issues, e.g., the *International Journal of Digital Curation* that was launched in 2006.[10] This accumulation represents a step towards formal literature for the digital preservation community.

Interaction among members is also supported by professional conferences—formal, scheduled events for exchanging current information by members. Several relevant professional conferences have come into being within the past five years. The Society for Image Science and Technology (IS&T) Archiving Conference has been held since 2004.[11] This conference series was initiated by the digital imaging domain and includes both general digital preservation sessions and image-specific preservation sessions. The Digital Curation Centre (DCC) has hosted conferences that include digital preservation topics on the program, with international attendees since 2004.[12] The International

---

[7] For an early example in the archival community see: Morris Rieger, "Archives and Automation," in Technical Notes, *American Archivist* 29, no.1 (1966): 109-111; and for an example of emerging archival practice see: Margaret L Hedstrom. *Archives & Manuscripts: Machine-Readable Records.* (Chicago, IL: Society of American Archivists), 1984.

[8] For example, an early article in the literature of the library community noted that developments in new technology, e.g., videodiscs, may be used to conserve precious and fragile materials. Nancy Jean Melin, "Serials in the '80s: A report from the field, " *Serials Review* 7, no. 3 (1981): 80.

[9] In the museum literature, an interesting discussion of the issues is: Cynthia Goodman, "The Digital Revolution: Art in the Computer Age," *Art Journal* 49, no. 3 (1990): 248.

[10] *International Journal of Digital Curation* is an open access journal. *International Journal of Digital Curation (IJDC)*, UKOLN, http://www.ijdc.net/index.php/ijdc/index (last accessed 06-20-2012).

[11] There is a Website for all IS&T conferences that includes the archiving conferences. Society for Imaging Science and Technology (IS&T), "IS&T Meetings Calendar," http://www.imaging.org/ist/conferences/archiving/ (last accessed 06-20-2012).

[12] Digital Curation Centre, "DCC Events," http://www.dcc.ac.uk/events/ (last accessed 06-20-2012).

Conference on the Preservation of Digital Objects (iPres) has been held annually since it began in 2004.[13] This was the first regularly held international conference devoted entirely to digital preservation. The ongoing occurrence of these conferences since 2004 suggests measurable progress towards formalizing the digital preservation community through an exchange of developments and practice.

Shared Group Goals

Shared group goals require that "group members are interdependent with respect to goal attainment, in the sense that progress by one member towards his or her objectives makes it more likely that another member will also reach his or her objectives."[14] There have been ongoing efforts to define and encourage good practice that reflect shared goals for digital preservation since the mid-1990s.[15] Three community documents have formalized digital preservation practice. The OAIS Reference Model was developed with broad participation by digital curators and approved by the International Standards Organization (ISO) in 2003.[16] OAIS was developed to be applicable in any organizational context in which digital content is managed for the long-term. The *Attributes of a Trusted Digital Repository: Roles and Responsibilities* report addressed the implementation of OAIS by identifying prerequisites for an organization to conform to OAIS.[17]

---

[13] International Conference on Digital Preservation (iPres), http://ipres-conference.org/ipres/ (last accessed 06-20-2012).

[14] Michener, et al., *Social Psychology*, 324.

[15] Examples include: Neil Beagrie and Maggie Jones, *Preservation Management of Digital Materials – the Handbook* (London: British Library, 2001) [now maintained online by the Digital Preservation Coalition, http://www.dpconline.org/advice/preservationhandbook (last accessed 06-20-2012)]; and *Best Practices Guides: A Typology*, Canadian Heritage Information Network (CHIN, 2004), http http://www.pro.rcip-chin.gc.ca/index-eng.jsp?Ne=8109&N=8109 (last accessed 06-20-2012).

[16] ISO 14721:2003:*OAIS Reference Model*, 2003. Institutions that participated in the development of OAIS include the Arts and Humanities Data Service (AHDS) of the UK, the Cedars Project, National Library of Canada, and the US National Archives and Records Administration. As an example, see the full list of participants: Archival Workshop on Ingest, Identification, and Certification Standards (AWIICS), October 13-15, 1999, http://nssdc.gsfc.nasa.gov/nost/isoas/awiics/ (last accessed 06-20-2012).

[17] Research Libraries Group (RLG) and Online Computer Library Center (OCLC), "Trusted Digital Repositories: Attributes and Responsibilities," (Mountain View, CA: RLG, May 2002 [now maintained by OCLC]), http://www.oclc.org/programs/ourwork/past/trustedrep/repositories.pdf (last accessed 06-20-2012).

Together, the trusted digital repositories document and OAIS define a holistic context for digital preservation, explicitly addressing for the first time both the organizational and technological aspects of digital preservation management. In 2003, the OAIS working groups released the *Producer-Archive Interface – Methodology Abstract Standard* (PAIMAS) that was approved as an ISO standard in 2006.[18] PAIMAS delineates in detail the interaction between the producer that submits the digital content and the archive that accepts responsibility for preserving this digital content. These documents represent community guidance that increasingly defines shared goals in the form of prevailing practice for digital preservation.

Primary funding sources for a community's activities influence the focus and direction for the research and developments undertaken by that community. There have been ongoing and ad hoc funding programs for digital preservation research and development since the mid-1990s. The funding programs of the Joint Information Systems Committee (JISC) fund digital preservation research and development.[19] The US Library of Congress collaborated with the US National Science Foundation (NSF) to establish the National Digital Information Infrastructure and Preservation Program (NDIIPP) in 2002. The NDIIPP program funded projects intended to create a national network of preserved digital content.[20] In 2002, the European Union collaborated with the National Science Foundation (NSF) in the USA to develop a joint research agenda for digital preservation and the NSF hosted a workshop with the Library of Congress to develop a research agenda for digital preservation.[21] Those research agendas and

---

[18] ISO 20652:2006: International Standards Organization, *Producer-Archive Interface – Methodology Abstract Standard* (Geneva, Switzerland: International Standards Organization, 2006), http://www.iso.org/iso/iso_catalogue/catalogue_tc/catalogue_detail.htm?csnumber=39577 (last accessed 06-20-2012).

[19] JISC, "Digital Preservation and Records Management Programme," http://www.jisc.ac.uk/whatwedo/programmes/programme_preservation.aspx (last accessed 06-20-2012).

[20] National Digital Information Infrastructure and Preservation Program (NDIIPP), Library of Congress, http://www.digitalpreservation.gov/ (last accessed 06-20-2012).

[21] NSF and DELOS, *Invest to Save: Report and Recommendations of the NSF-DELOS Working Group on Digital Archiving and Preservation,* 2003, prepared for the National Science Foundation's (NSF) Digital Library Initiative and The European Union under the Fifth Framework Programme by the Network of Excellence for Digital Libraries (DELOS), 2003,

community efforts since were in part developed to help define and encourage funding programs for digital preservation.

Shared Norms

Shared norms require that "group members hold a set of normative expectations (that is, norms or rules) that place limits on members' behavior and provide a blueprint for action."[22] The certification requirements for digital archives and development of shared curriculum for digital preservation are two examples of norms for the digital preservation community. The 1996 *Preserving Digital Information* report and the OAIS Reference Model both included a call for a certification process for digital archives to demonstrate the effectiveness of the implementation of an OAIS system for preserving digital content. In January 2007, the certification of digital archives became the focus of an international working group to develop an ISO standard via the ISO TC20/SC13 technical committee.[23]

The working group used the *Trustworthy Repositories Audit & Certification (TRAC): Criteria and Checklist* that was published in 2007 as a starting point for its work.[24] The work on the certification standard is also informed by the Digital Repository Audit Method Based on Risk Assessment (DRAMBORA) toolkit developed by the Digital Curation Centre and Digital Preservation Europe (DPE), and the work of the nestor project in Germany.[25]

---

http://eprints.erpanet.org/94/01/NSF_Delos_WG_Pres_final.pdf (last accessed 06-20-2012); and NSF and NDIIPP, *It's About Time: Research Challenges in Digital Archiving and Long-term Preservation,* Final Report Workshop on Research Challenges in Digital Archiving and Long-term Preservation, April 12-13, 2002, sponsored by the National Science Foundation, Digital Government Program and Digital Libraries Program, Directorate for Computing and Information Sciences and Engineering, and the Library of Congress National Digital Information Infrastructure and Preservation Program (NDIIPP), 2003, http://www.digitalpreservation.gov/documents/about_time2003.pdf (last accessed 06-20-2012). Seamus Ross and Margaret L. Hedstrom chaired the *Invest to Save* group and Hedstrom chaired the *It's about Time* group.

[22] Michener, et al., *Social Psychology*, 324.

[23] The Digital Repository Audit and Certification Working Group, http://wiki.digitalrepositoryauditandcertification.org/bin/view (last accessed 05-10-2008).

[24] The TRAC document was developed between 2003 and 2007 by the RLG / NARA Task Force on Digital Repository Certification. It defines criteria that should be addressed for a digital repository to be certified. http://www.crl.edu/PDF/trac.pdf (last accessed 06-20-2012).

[25] DRAMBORA uses an evidence-based and risk management approach. "Digital Repository Audit Method Based on Risk Assessment (DRAMBORA)," Digital

Standards for audit and certification of good practice define measurable norms for digital preservation.

Applying these attributes of an emergent group, i.e., membership, interaction of members, common goals, and shared norms, provides a useful starting point for considering the current state of the digital preservation community as we work towards realizing its future state. The digital preservation community has begun to exhibit examples of each of the four group attributes discussed in this section. Cumulatively, these indicators document the emergence, increasing cohesion, and ongoing maturation of the digital preservation community. Progress towards the terminology needed for developing digital preservation as a domain, the development and promulgation of standards and good practice, and understanding the nature of the sound investments of resources for sustainability are good indicators of the maturation of the digital preservation community. These results suggest that the community is ready to engage in the development of strategies for aligning national approaches.

Stages of Development Applied to Community Building

Having explored the current state of the digital preservation community using the attributes of emergent groups as a metric, there are other models that may be useful in understanding the implications of that community view and developing a framework for community-based action. Since 2003, the curriculum of the Digital Preservation Management (DPM) workshop series has featured a maturity model for any organization to use in developing a digital preservation program that is holistic and sustainable.[26] The DPM model consists of two interlocking core concepts: the five stages of development and the three-legged stool

---

Curation Centre (DCC) and DigitalPreservationEurope (DPE), http://www.repositoryaudit.eu/ (last accessed 11-10-2007). The nestor project uses a coaching approach to help bring organisations into conformance with standards. nestor Working Group Trusted Repositories - Certification, *Catalogue of Criteria for Trusted Digital Repositories*, studies 8, Version 1(Frankfurt am Main : nestor c/o Deutsche Nationalbibliothek, 2007). http://www.langzeitarchivierung.de/Subsites/nestor/EN/Standardisation/standardis ation.html?nn=16918 (last accessed 06-20-2012).

[26]More than 1,000 managers with responsibility for long-term management of digital content who represent more than 350 organizations have attended the DPM workshop since 2003. See the Digital Preservation Management workshop at: http://dpworkshop.org (last accessed 06-20-2012).

for digital preservation.[27] The model adapts easily to a consideration of alignment opportunities for national approaches to digital preservation because the five stages progress towards effective inter-institutional and international collaboration. This brief overview of the DPM model demonstrates how the concepts apply to international alignment activities.

The five stages for an organization to use in developing a digital preservation program as defined in the DPM model are:[28]

- *Acknowledge*: Understand that digital preservation is a local concern;

- *Act*: Initiate digital preservation projects;

- *Consolidate*: Segue from projects to programs;

- *Institutionalize*: Incorporate the larger environment; and

- *Externalize*: Embrace inter-institutional collaboration and dependency.

In 2003 when the DPM model was first applied, there were very few examples of organizations that had achieved a stage three or four and no stage five organizations. Now, there are an increasing number of collaborative initiatives that reflect the digital preservation community's natural progression towards stage five behaviors, many of which are discussed in the six chapters of this volume. The five DPM stages could also be applied to the stages of community development for aligning national approaches to digital preservation like this:

- *Acknowledge*: Understand that alignment of national approaches is a desirable outcome;

- *Act*: Initiate projects, e.g., conferences like ANADP, that encourage alignment;

---

[27] Anne R. Kenney and Nancy Y. McGovern, "The Five Organizational Stages of Digital Preservation," in *Digital Libraries: A Vision for the Twenty-first Century*, a festschrift to honor Wendy Lougee, 2003. Available from the University of Michigan Scholarly Monograph Series Website:
http://quod.lib.umich.edu/cgi/t/text/text-idx?c=spobooks;idno=bbv9812.0001.001;rgn=div1;view=text;cc=spobooks;node=bbv9812.0001.001%3A11 (last accessed 06-20-2012).
[28] The characteristics of the five stages are defined and discussed in Kenney and McGovern, 2003.

- *Consolidate*: Segue from projects to programs by engaging sustained alignment initiatives;

- *Institutionalize*: Incorporate the larger environment by establishing an international presence; and

- *Externalize*: Embrace international collaboration and interdependency.

Current collaborative examples often occur at a regional or national level, but could be extended to an international level. All of these kinds of stage five initiatives represent examples of alignment. Within collaborative efforts of any kind, the three-legged DPM stool frames a balanced approach for working together. The three legs of the stool are *organizational*, *technological*, and *resources*. They represent core components of a sustainable digital preservation program.

The *organizational leg* is best framed by the community document, *Attributes of a Trusted Digital Repository: Roles and Responsibilities* (TDR).[29] The seven attributes of the organizational infrastructure for a TDR are:

1. *OAIS Compliance*, an intention to develop a digital preservation program in accordance with the concepts and principles laid out in the Open Archival Information System (OAIS) Reference Model;

2. *Administrative Responsibility*, an explicit commitment to develop a digital preservation program that adheres to community standards;

3. *Organizational Viability*, the wherewithal to engage in digital preservation, e.g., requisite legal status, relevant skills, policies, and plans;

4. *Financial Sustainability*, designated funding to sustain a digital preservation program and the demonstrated intent to appoint an heir to continue the program if needed;

5. *Technological and Procedural Suitability*, the identification and implementation of appropriate technologies and

---

[29] Research Libraries Group (RLG) and Online Computer Library Center (OCLC), "Trusted Digital Repositories: Attributes and Responsibilities," (Mountain View, CA: RLG, May 2002 [now maintained by OCLC]), http://www.oclc.org/programs/ourwork/past/trustedrep/repositories.pdf (last accessed 06-20-2012)

documented practice to meet community-defined requirements, e.g., the requirements defined in Audit and Certification of Trustworthy Digital Repositories (ISO 16363: 2012*);*

6. *System Security*, protocols and practice sufficient to control and protect digital content identified as within the scope of responsibility for a digital preservation program; and

7. *Procedural Accountability*, a commitment to continuously document and demonstrate good practice in accordance with prevailing community standards.

The *technology leg* is best framed by the OAIS Reference Model, an ISO standard approved more than a decade ago that encompasses the roles, functions, and states of digital content as managed over time and that has informed technical developments for most major digital preservation programs since. Components of requisite technological infrastructure for digital preservation include hardware and software, file formats and storage media, tools and workflows, platforms and networks, and skills, both technical and archival. The *resources leg* is best framed by the *Final Report of the Blue Ribbon Task Force on Sustainable Digital Preservation and Access*, which is being supplemented by the development of an economic sustainability reference model.[30] Cumulatively the three legs are addressed in the six chapters of the volume.

Aspects of Alignment

This review of the emergence of the digital preservation community and the stages of development for communities provides context and background for the entirety of this volume, which addresses six core aspects of alignment for national approaches to digital preservation. These six aspects of alignment can be said to parallel the three legs of the DPM stool, as described below.

---

[30] *Final Report of the Blue Ribbon Task Force on Sustainable Digital Preservation and Access* (Washington, DC: the National Science Foundation, 2010). http://brtf.sdsc.edu/ (accessed 06-20-2012). The first community meeting to review the BRTF economic sustainability reference model was held in conjunction with the ANADP conference in May 2011. Updates about the reference model being developed by Brian Lavoie and Chris Rusbridge can be found at: http://unsustainableideas.wordpress.com/economic-sustainability-ref-model-page/ (last accessed 06-20-2012).

There are two alignment aspects for the organizational leg, *legal* and *organizational*:

- *Legal Alignment*: The lead essay in this chapter addresses the alignment of legal issues for digital preservation and access, covering issues that arise at various stages in the lifecycle of digital material. There is an emphasis on legal deposit, copyright exceptions for preservation and access, and multi-partner and cross-border working and rights management. In addition to the essay on alignment, this chapter includes an informative review of the current state of legal deposit and Web archiving by Adrienne Muir.

- *Organizational Alignment*: This essay discusses and demonstrates why digital preservation is not only a technical issue by enumerating the many organizational implications that must be addressed. The essay's authors present a series of illustrative case studies from across the international community.

And two alignment aspects for the technological leg, *standards* and *technical*:

- *Standards Alignment*: This essay defines the term "standard" then provides an in-depth analysis of standards that are relevant to digital preservation and places digital preservation standards within the broader context of standards development.

- *Technical Alignment*: This essay selects from the array of technical issues two core topics: the importance of infrastructure and of robust testing protocols to enable digital preservation services to demonstrate reliability, transparency, and accountability. It argues for devising and applying agreed-upon metrics that will enable the systematic analysis of the technical infrastructure for digital preservation.

And two alignment aspects for the resources leg, *economic* and *education*:

- *Economic Alignment*: The lead essay in this chapter presents an overview of the economic issues that define, promote, or inhibit effective national and international programs for preserving digital cultural heritage materials. In addition to the essay on alignment, this chapter includes two case studies by two of the lead essay's authors. Aaron Trehub discusses community implications of three community-owned and community-governed digital preservation networks in "Economic Sustainability and Economic Alignment: Examples from North America." Bohdana Stoklasová and her colleagues discuss lessons learned from their experiences in developing their digital preservation programs in "Czech National Digital Library: Economic, Strategic, and International Aspects of Digital Preservation."

- *Education Alignment*: This essay reviews the community's progress in incorporating data management and curation skills into information technology, library and information science, and research-based postgraduate courses within national contexts. The essay also addresses the need and the means to bridge formal education with professional development training opportunities more coherently.

Within each chapter, the lead essays highlight opportunities for alignment. An insightful set of observations and recommendations by Clifford Lynch close the volume as they closed the conference, both framing and supplementing the cumulative list of alignment opportunities that are summarized there. This final chapter of the volume is intended to provide a framework for next steps in moving towards an international community of practice.

A Tale of Two Countries

Two examples of efforts to encourage and sustain digital preservation at the national level were featured during the ANADP conference through keynote addresses. The first example, presented by Laura Campbell from the US Library of Congress, highlights factors that encourage community building and lessons learned over more than a decade. The second example, presented by Gunnar Sahlin from the Royal Library - National Library of Sweden, emphasizes the role and impact of national leadership in collaborating and coordinating across institutions to achieve common goals. The remainder of this Introduction showcases these two national programs, drawing from the transcripts of the presenters' talks.

A Tale of Two Countries: Part I

Laura Campbell (Library of Congress)

Introduction

Today I'd like to begin a conversation in the spirit of exploring an alignment of our various natural approaches to digital preservation. I'd like to tell you about the NDIIPP program, our national preservation program that began in the year 2000, and to focus on some lessons learned over the last decade and some considerations and ideas for international collaboration.

NDIIPP: A Brief History

For over 10 years now, the NDIIPP network has been effectively leveraging the strengths of a very diverse set of partners and has proven resilient in the face of technological volatility, economic downturn, and explosive growth in digital creation. We now have saved more than 1,400 collections and more than four billion Web pages in our born digital archive.

This program was created in response to a congressional mandate in the year 2000 to establish a national strategy to meet the challenge of preserving materials that only exist in digital form and are at risk of loss. There was no particular pathway forward; we received this legislation in December out of the regular cycle as a surprise special appropriation of a hundred million dollars. And believe me, those of us who were on the ground that day started to get very nervous. We'd had some experience with digitizing but now we were tackling completely unknown territory—capturing, preserving, and handling born digital creations.

The library began this effort, wisely I think, by conferring with hundreds of stakeholders in diverse content creator and distributor communities—music, movies, e-journals, maps, digital TV—about what the overall approach should be.

There was wide consensus in this early convening dialog about a decentralized distributed strategy with many participants. Over the last decade, the library has developed and tested a distributed preservation network to answer this original charge. I'm going to focus on some of the lessons that we've learned.

We grew from an initial planning process that engaged stakeholders in every phase of the digital preservation lifecycle, including content creators, owners and distributors in the private sector, legal and technical advisors, subject matter experts and librarians, and archivists from state and local entities, as well as participants from higher education, particularly big research libraries.

They all told us about their barriers to digital preservation and I think one of the most remarkable "take-homes" for me was how ill-understood the copyright law was with regard to digital preservation. In fact, many participants in the group thought because the Library of Congress includes the U.S. copyright office, we ought to be able to just step out of the room, make some edits and come back having fixed those parts of the law that happen to be challenging. We had a battle ahead of us and we had a lot of education to do.

Researchers and leading technologists worked early on to define the basic technical infrastructure for preservation that the NDIIPP program would model and test. Our program model was to learn by doing—that was essentially to establish the notion of taking early action and evaluating progress iteratively, making adjustments as appropriate. The model encourages experimental action to help the partners ensure access over time to a rich body of at-risk content. No one thought we had a perfectly clear pathway forward; we needed to constantly evaluate our direction.

In 2003, we actually began collecting material with preservation partners working in eight consortial projects. It was very important that from the beginning we worked in teams. These were diverse teams that combined a range of skills and a variety of organizations and domains. To date the library has recruited more than 185 digital preservation partners in 45 states and 25 countries to collect and preserve a very broad spectrum of high value digital content, with special attention to user needs in the areas of public policy, education and research, and cultural heritage. Over the last 10 years, we've learned a lot.[1]

---

[1] A report about this decade of cumulative progress, "Preserving Our Digital Heritage: The National Digital Information Infrastructure and Preservation Program 2010 Report," is available:

NDIIPP Strategic Goals

NDIIPP organized its initiatives and investments around four strategic goals; I'll try to summarize the key outcomes and findings associated with each of these—a collaborative network, a national collection, technical infrastructure that supports both, and public policy work.

First, the collaborative network. Building distributed network capacity for digital preservation and long-term stewardship is a complex undertaking. Supporting the growth of that network capacity requires sustained dedicated coordination. Intentionally, NDIIPP engaged a diverse set of preservation partners and brokered relationships with complex interactions between networks of partners rather than individual parties. As a consequence, partners formed groups around mutual interests— geospatial interests, harvesting the Web, public broadcasting, music, movies, e-journals, research data, and technical tool development.

Thus, natural networks within the larger group formed. The library service is a central node in this network of networks, articulating and coordinating roles and responsibilities. Essentially, the library's role is to be a team leader. We're a part of the team— we're not directing all the activities, but we're trying to help shape success.

Through regular meetings, strategy sessions, issue-based groups, and digital preservation research projects, partners regularly shared their outcomes and lessons learned from their local preservation programs. All NDIIPP participants learn from one another. Some things worked, some things did not work; we cultivated an atmosphere where people felt free to try new things.

For example, early on we thought we would just exchange a digital collection among four fairly sophisticated institutions to test various aspects of what we called at that time "interoperability"— remember we were all trying to figure out what that word meant way back then. Well, we were stopped at the very first step, "ingest

---

http://digitalpreservation.gov/multimedia/documents/NDIIPP2010Report_Post.pd f (last accessed 06-29-2012).

of the content," learning it is not so easy to transfer data from one archive to another and get the same results. [2]

There is a great heterogeneity among partners. The network brings together small and large organizations with digital preservation staff of one and two people in some cases, as well as organizations with preservation staff in the dozens, as well as great diversity of organizational focus. Our partners include universities; professional societies; associations—like the photographers association; commercial businesses; universal music; the academy of motion pictures; government agencies—including those at the federal, state and local level; libraries; museums; and archives. Each participating institution brings to the network its own resources, interests, and strengths as well its own culture that contributes to areas of interest common to organizations throughout the network.

We tend to work in six key areas. Let me say a few words about each.

- *Content*. We've worked hard to try to identify at-risk content. Take for example, the changing face of news today—we need to engage with citizen journalism to capture their work as it becomes a more important part of delivering timely news; or harvest political Websites as more information about candidates and elections happen online today; or, determine how to handle geospatial mapping, given how vastly this field is changing.

- *Infrastructure.* We work together to identify the best technical means to share content and to create specific tools to aid our digital preservation activities. Anything that can help us do this more efficiently and at less cost is of high value for investment for us.

- *Innovation*. This is an important area where we are conducting basic digital preservation research in new and ground-breaking areas that produce exciting projects such Memento with its Web-versioning capabilities. We all need to

---

[2] For a brief synopsis of the Archive Ingest and Handling Test, please see Clay Shirky. (2005). "AIHT: Conceptual Issues from Practical Tests" *D-Lib Magazine* Vol. 11, No. 12, available at: http://www.dlib.org/dlib/december05/shirky/12shirky.html (last accessed 06-29-2012).

cultivate new ideas that will become solutions to make preservation easier.

- *Education and Outreach.* A new area for us is education and outreach, finding ways to help the broader archival community outside of the network with training and establishing guidelines for what is digital preservation, how do you do it.

- *Standards and Best Practices.* These are of major interest to all of us. Developing standards, such as WebARChive (WARC) for Web archiving and Public Broadcasting Core (PBCore) for TV broadcasting, have been community-based activities because of a recognized need for information about effective methods for selecting, organizing, describing, and preserving digital content.

- *Sustainability.* This is an area where we all struggle for ongoing funds, particularly in these tough times. We are working on how to maintain open source tools in absence of direct funding, for example.

Together we are covering more ground than any one of us could do alone. Our common values are part of what makes this diverse mix of organizations come together in a successful network. Almost all participants represent an archival responsibility of some kind, be it a big research library, a state archive or the archiving responsibilities in the universe of music.

So, archival network partners are committed actors, they're "doers" working together, learning by doing and making or trying to make digital preservation work in changing conditions and often challenging situations.

Among the commonly held values of the preservation network is *stewardship*—all partners are committed to managing the content for current and long-term use, emphasis on the long term. Organizations in the network actively ensure sustained access to digital content that constitutes our national legacy. Individually, these organizations support management of digital resources. Together, they commit to protecting the United States' national, cultural, scientific, scholarly, and business heritage. It's a major responsibility and individuals and organizations have stepped up to accept this long-term responsibility.

Collaborative work is a practice shared by all our members. Approaching digital stewardship collaboratively allows partners to maximize their own work, learn new practices, share or adopt new tools, and essentially, to flexibly respond to the changing landscape. There is an increasing recognition that NDIIPP partners were early crowd-sourcers of a sort, learning to build capacity to manage content beyond their institutional boundaries.

NDIIPP: Lessons Learned

From the early test on how to exchange and ingest content to the PeDALS state government records project, we've provided practical experiences that help define which aspects of digital preservation are institution specific and which are more general and can be applied more broadly.

In every project, collaboration has been identified by NDIIPP partners as a key to success in keeping up with and managing a changing set of digital preservation responsibilities. Inclusiveness is a value for our network partners. They embrace and understand the advantages of including all committed partners in the dialog. You do not learn new ideas from taking time to talk to people you are most familiar with, think about that. Engaging across different communities strengthens the nation's digital preservation results by increasing the likeliness for new ideas and solutions to emerge, now and into the future.

I mentioned that we learned a few things over the years. There are some considerable differences between when we started this program—then and now—and I want to say a few things about those differences.

Atoms vs. Bits.

Physical materials require care and conservation, digital materials require maintenance of the bits that comprise them as well as the physical media on which they are stored. Not only are there new issues to solve in the preservation of bits, but the associated atoms we're conserving are now servers, tapes and discs and require significantly different expertise than the atoms of historic collections—books, maps, photographs, and films. More to the point, after two decades of trying to build a digital library, it is clear that the skills necessary to manage the atoms are very different than the skills needed to manage the bits.

Trying to integrate the two worlds is complex and slow. My experience in a leadership role reinforces the need to separate the two worlds and integrate digital and physical worlds at the point of access through a catalog or a common index. Early on we used to talk about seamless integration. I will tell you, you can try it but it's going to take you forever to get there.

High Level of Curation vs. Bulk Download.

Digital offerings online were initially highly curated publications like the *American Memory*, whereas today users express more interest in having access to the raw content or to bulk downloads of data. Users now have tools to mine large bodies of digital data that many didn't have before.

Ownership vs. Shared Access.

It's not enough for institutions to hold interesting and important materials and significant collections in the current environment. Shared access to these materials is as critical as having and preserving them in the first place. No user today cares about the institution as owner.

Consumers vs. Discoverers.

Users no longer are content to consume static information prepared for them. Today's users engage with collections as explorers, looking to discover new connections and use them creatively. Again, new navigation tools have become more widely accessible.

Watching vs. Creating.

We're moving from a culture of passive consumers to one of engaged creators. I learned a disturbing figure recently that the average American spends 50,000 hours watching television in their lifetime, that's five and a half years! Whooh! But already in 2007, an IBM online survey demonstrated that television sets are losing ground to the Internet when it comes to personal leisure time; 19% of all respondents stated that they spent six hours or more per day on the Internet vs. 9% of respondents spending the same amount of time in front of the television.[3]

---

[3] IBM (2007) "IBM Consumer Survey Shows Decline of TV as Primary Media Device." *Marketwire*. See http://www.marketwire.com/press-release/ibm-consumer-survey-shows-decline-of-tv-as-primary-media-device-nyse-ibm-762949.htm (last accessed 06-29-2012).

Institutional Identity vs. Loose Collaboration.

It is not enough to have a strong institutional identity with a mandate to preserve cultural heritage material in the digital environment. The scale and manner of digital preservation requires loose collaborations of committed organizations that are willing to work together. Memory institutions will get material in many different ways, not just traditional forms of acquisition and donation. We all know that in previous times these institutions were reluctant to share their treasured assets for fear of losing institutional identity.

Systematic Planning vs. Fluid Cooperation.

No amount of deliberate planning is going to address the complexities of digital preservation. True discovery and advancement within the field comes from handling the digital objects throughout their lifecycle. Cooperative lifecycle experiences help spread the know-how faster and further. So, over-planning the function may be counterproductive.

Push vs. Pull.

The Library of Congress started its digital library by pushing highly curated content out to its users. Now the user prefers to pull content down from the Library of Congress Website and creatively combine it with other content and re-share the new creation.

Closed vs. Open Platforms.

Trying to create and maintain a competitive advantage through secrecy via proprietary systems does not result in leadership or long-term innovation. As Google has officially blogged, "Open systems win, they lead to more innovation, value, and freedom of choice for consumers, and a vibrant, profitable, and competitive ecosystem for businesses."[4]

Expert Vetting vs. Cognitive Surplus.

Libraries and archives have historically vetted all collections via experts. This has yielded high-value descriptions and compilations, but at a high cost. Currently many people are using their free time for creative acts rather than passive consumption. A

---

[4] Google (2009). "The Meaning of Open." See http://googleblog.blogspot.com/2009/12/meaning-of-open.html (last accessed 06-29-2012).

challenge ahead will be to engage people and leverage this cognitive surplus via social tools to improve our collections and collecting strategies.

Clay Shirky in his book *Cognitive Surplus* estimates that there are over one trillion hours of free time annually that can be devoted to online sharing, problem solving, and crowd sourcing; that's a phenomenal figure. Ultimately, we have the opportunity to improve understanding in many fields and endeavors.

Let me say a few things about the big trends and drivers of the future. There is something in long-term planning called scenario-planning, where different and even divergent future states are examined, where you look at the big drivers of the future. In future scenario planning we ask questions like "what are the big trends for the future," or "what will impact digital libraries and digital preservation in the future?" So what are some of these "big drivers" and how can we expect them to affect our field?

- *Cognitive surplus* is a big driver and perhaps the biggest; as just mentioned it will supply the brain power to let many contributors shape digital content. Users can add metadata, share content, create new works, help link works to other content, and make new discoveries by deriving associations and new insights from digital creations.

- *Shared learning*, another big driver, is changing the way we have traditionally done research in academic institutions. This generation of researchers is far less proprietary than those of the past and is moving to develop academic research in teams, shaking that hallowed ground. It is more prevalent than ever in K through 12 programs to study and report in groups. The digital age allows us all to share what we know. It provides the opportunity for new interactions that may hold the greatest promise for big results. An online generation is a big driver. 2011 marks the first undergraduate community that has never been without the Internet. Think about all those traditional professors out there who are going to have to deal with this Internet savvy classroom. Hats off to those guys, it's not going to be easy.

- *Innovation* happens at the margins of diversity and interaction. More and more businesses and governments are recognizing that innovation happens by communicating and working with people you do not normally work with. Creative collaboration can result in innovation. Has anyone here heard the story of

Goldcorp? Just quickly, this is a Canadian gold mining company, privately held, that was looking to make a major investment in improving the infrastructure in their mine. When the president went to his managers and asked what they thought Goldcorp should do, nobody had any ideas. Then he set the managers aside and he went to the staff, who also had no new ideas. So, in great frustration, he did the unthinkable— he said we're going to take all of our proprietary mining data and we're going to put it out there on the Internet for free and we are going to invite geologists and scientists worldwide to help us figure out whether it's important and worthwhile to make an investment in this mine. And they offered a monitory price, not a huge price, but a price. Well today they've gone from a 10 billion dollar company to a 50 billion dollar company because the top eight ideas were complete winners and they invested in the infrastructure they needed to grow their mine. That was revolutionary. You see better use of such methods as Goldcorp—the X Prize, competitive awards, and challenges to stimulate new discoveries. Sharing content makes a lot of new discovery possible. Everyone is a creator of content now, another big driver. It is now possible to publish and distribute without going to a big music distributer or a large publishing house. More of our cultural heritage is online for free and easily distributed.

- *Mobile distribution.* Cell phones are now the most widely dispersed mobile device, with over five billion in use worldwide. That's pretty amazing when the worldwide population is only 6.9 billion. Smart phones are adding greater capacity to be connected any time to content.

- *Discovery tools* are another big driver. We mentioned that ways to search and navigate content that have been greatly improved by the creation of tools to let you tag, share, match up, compare, and extract from large bodies of content. As open source development continues to expand, there will be more and more ways to analyze and discover data quickly.

- *Storage capacity.* We're all familiar with this one. Storage is nowhere near the cost it once was and it'll soon be possible to think about collecting everything. A wild idea? Maybe.

- *Security* will continue to be a growing concern to protect both users and content. Malicious attacks will only get more sophisticated and an increasing amount of budget will be spent on securing data and networks. Not all these trends are good news.

- *Economic efficiency through shared infrastructure.* We're seeing that now. The institutional economics of managing and preserving digital content are such that shared infrastructure will be more attractive for collecting institutions—whether it's in the cloud or through a networked approach to a national collection such as NDIIPP. There will be a need for shared solutions.

- *Energy.* This is a big rising cost as well as a huge risk. Given the growing demand for computing power and the availability of affordable energy, this may become our single biggest driver.

- *Incentives* for digital preservation are limited. Most businesses do not see an investment in long-term preservation as a top priority; it's really quarterly results we're looking for, particularly if you've got shareholders.

- *Public policy* lags behind the need to motivate creators and distributors to save the national patrimony for future generations. In the US, most state and local governments have no budget for digital preservation, yet most of their documents, legislations, land maps, and other vital records are now in digital form. Should there be tax incentives to preserve? Should government demand that federally funded research be preserved by researching entities?

- *Education and a productive workforce.* You heard the President of the Republic of Estonia talk about this. A productive workforce will be an educated workforce. Skills to navigate the digital landscape, to find the information needed, and to know how to use it will be basic core competencies for the next generation of students and workers.

These are only some of the big forces that will impact any decision that we—as individual organizations or collectively—take with our digital libraries and our digital preservation programs. They're all major considerations.

Current Challenges

Finally, there are always some wicked problems to consider and I'll just say a couple of words about those. These, I guess, we probably all know the best. The road ahead is not without challenges; there are intractable problems that we face. The biggest one is finding and maintaining funding in these difficult economic times.

Top management in all kinds of organizations has begun to understand the importance of digital preservation. The fact that we're studying and planning how best to bring national approaches together, I consider a huge milestone. This shows real foresight, it is a milestone.

Many of us face intellectual property restrictions that impede our ability to properly steward information that we are attempting to save. The sheer volume of digital content continues to increase and the standards and formats in which they come are quickly changing—even staff that are skilled in handling the current preservation techniques struggle to keep ahead of the changing landscape. And I would submit that we're going to lose this battle unless we get very smart about how we do it.

Having said all this, what is necessary to make international collaboration successful? The qualities that have strengthened and made national collaborations such as NDIIPP successful over the last decade can be applied to ensuring success in an international collaboration.

I think some of the key elements are (briefly):

- *Planning*. Together, we must plan out our broad goals for collaboration. It's not enough to have good intentions; we must create a framework by which international collaboration can flourish.

- *Build on existing relationships*. We must build upon those that are already in place and ultimately leverage the strengths of each of the participants for the benefit of the entire collaborative network. Conferences like this one, *Aligning National Approaches to Digital Preservation,* provide opportunities for us to discuss and hopefully extend existing relationships.

I'm looking forward to hearing your ideas. Actively working together to make things happen encourages future achievement. So I ask you, what are some of the priority efforts that you think that we can undertake together?

Conclusions

I have a few ideas that may have potential to serve our collective interests:

One, we might establish an international preservation body or association that would focus on policy aspects of digital preservation. Such a coordinating body might be aided by an advisory groups of experts to help identify what is most at risk and most important to preserve. This group could focus on content and changing forms of communication or trends in certain disciplines. Establishing a common index of already preserved content in a virtual international collection, regardless of where it is housed, could be a valuable service of such a coordinating body. It's not about the preservation body itself, it's about the results.

Second, we might expand the notion of a national digital collection to an international digital collection, I think it's worth talking about how such a collection might be made accessible broadly.

And finally, we might encourage support for standards and tools that make the world of digital preservation more efficient and ultimately cost effective.

In conclusion, I look forward to exploring your ideas. Together we may be able to discover the best avenues for sharing and strengthening international relationships while producing concrete results. Together we can light up the world.

A TALE OF TWO COUNTRIES: PART II

Gunnar Sahlin (Royal Library - National Library of Sweden)

Introduction

I'm going to talk about international and national collaboration in the digital age, though I will focus on Sweden and Europe. I hope you will excuse me for that limitation, but there are things to learn about Europe and so on and we are more or less in the same position. I'm going to talk about some general views from a library perspective, but these issues also apply to museums, archives, and other cultural heritage institutions. In each of these environments, collaboration is essential to progress. In different ways and with the users' needs always in mind, we are all in the process of building a comprehensive digital library, as well as digital museums and digital archives.

We have a long way to go in providing digital copies of all library collections; some are already available in digital form and some are still awaiting digitization. For example, research journals in medicine or in natural science already exist in electronic version and that work occurred at the end of the 1990s. I was responsible for this work at Stockholm University. In two years, we moved from the print version to the digital version. It was different for e-books in medicine and natural science, but now there has been progress there, too.

In the humanities, we still have a lot of print versions of research journals. Of course, even if we worked together to digitize a significant amount of books, film, etc., it would take many years to digitize all of that material. For example, a user might find one manuscript on the Web, but will have to go to the archive to locate other manuscripts he or she needs.

We are transforming our national libraries, research libraries, and public libraries into digital libraries with the help of the Web, with the digital influx of born digital material, and with countless digitization projects. Of course, digital libraries are a responsibility for national libraries in quite a different way than for university libraries and public libraries.

This development process demands new ways of collaborating and coordinating nationally and internationally, such as the Preservation EU project and other digitization projects in the library sector; and for archives and museums projects like Europeana, the European Library (TEL), ATHENA, and ATNET. We also have national labs in New Zealand, Australia and Singapore, and the World Digital Library, a very interesting project at the Library of Congress, for example.

As an example of collaboration in Europe, many countries contribute actively as aggregators for Europeana, though we are doing so in very different ways. In Sweden, for example, we are not going to have a common portal for the whole ALM sector as they are going to have in Finland and in some other countries, but we do support aggregation and a portal for libraries, archives, and museums for access to digital material.

The situation in Sweden is not an exception compared with the whole of Europe. Here, I am focusing on how national libraries and federal institutions have participated in the Swedish University Network as well as in the regional and municipality infrastructures as they have been authorized to do. I will also address collaboration in general; the ways in which the integration of collection management has altered the way archives, libraries, museums and various media agencies interact; and my views on the intersection of national and international issues.

It is crucial in collaborations to retain sight of common goals and joint purpose. This involves creating structures that allow participating institutions to share their experience and coordinate their efforts. Experience has shown that a precondition for success with large scale and diverse collaborations is consensus on things like digitization requirements and preservation issues, including metadata options and technical solutions.

Consensus can be achieved only if the institutions collaborate closely with one another and show a readiness to change course for the sake of the common course. Collaboration on a large scale can make the work cost effective.

With the growing complexity and diversity of digital collections, collaboration is more important than ever—in our effort to find solutions to difficult technical problems as well as to meet the demands of current and future users.

It is necessary to find new ways to collaborate. We are now aware of the important role of international collaboration, though we are only at the beginning of establishing effective international collaborations. Not long ago, national libraries worked in isolation from institutions in other sectors. Today, a national library works much closer to other sectors. Similarly, in the 1990s, the university library shifted from being a closed and very separate organization on campus to becoming more involved in research and education at the university. And it's a challenge for public libraries to find new roles inside and outside the cultural sector. Sometimes I think we in archives, libraries, and museums are not aware how important we can be for economical reasons for the whole society. We have to be more proud of what we are doing. It's not only a cultural question or educational question, it's also important for the whole economy.

Here we're talking very much about international collaboration. We can say that we have moved from the exchange of experience to joint projects. International recession is of course one of the most important challenges for our libraries, as it is for the rest of the society. Within the library world and also for the other sectors—museums and archives—national boundaries have ceased to exist and users want to find information as easily as possible, regardless of region. And there I think it's very important that we make closer collaborations with researchers because we have to form new teams around the world, for example, you don't have to have a team only in your own university. I think it's the same with archives and museums and I know it very well from the library world. We have to work closer with researchers so they can use the material we have, but also find new ways to work together in research.

It is against this public interest background that we have to view library organizations such as IFLA, LIBER, Bibliotheca Baltica as well as the Museum and Archive association. As we are in Tallinn for this conference, it is worth noting the increasing awareness of the value of cooperation in the Baltic Sea region. Our institutions can directly influence societal development. The national libraries have moved to closer cooperation based on common projects. In the Nordic countries for example, the national libraries have always lived in close contact, but I think it's an exception because of the same language and cultural heritage.

I will now talk a little about the libraries' collaboration and cooperation and coordination in Sweden, but I will also give it an international perspective, because for me it's very important how national collaboration also has an influence on international collaboration. If we don't have very good national collaboration, we cannot work effectively on an international level.

The National Library of Sweden

The traditional task of the National Library of Sweden is to collect, preserve, describe, and provide access to Swedish printed and digital materials. This is a traditional role for all national libraries around the world, but most have other tasks. These broader roles include integrating other material types and serving in a coordinating and regulating role. There are no two national libraries that are identical.

Our functions and tasks in Sweden are comprehensive and diverse. This year the National Library of Sweden celebrates 350 years with a Deposit Law; from 2012, we will have a new law for gathering e-material. We started collecting Web pages on a regular basis as early as 1997, and we are partnering in the International Internet Preservation Consortium (IIPC). As a research library, we make the collection of books, manuscripts, pictures, and maps available to the public. Even if we move to a digital platform of this type of material, we can still regard it as part of the traditional role for the Swedish National Library, but this role is changing and more change is about to happen.

Two years ago, in 2009, the National Library merged with the National Archive of Recorded Sound and Moving Pictures. This means that we now also collect and preserve, catalog, and provide access to material from radio, television, films, videos, and multi-media, as well as music and other sound recordings.

This development is in line with the Swedish government policy to use resources more effectively and to provide users with better service. It has followed a trend in the last few years to reduce the number of government agencies in Sweden. The merger also felt quite natural because it was becoming increasingly difficult to separate the various types of materials we handle. What is the newspaper of today? Is it a paper edition that you read at the breakfast table? Is it a Web version? What is the difference between the digital version of printed material and the material produced by radio and television stations? Very often in Sweden and other countries, the same editor owns a TV station, radio station, and a newspaper edition and it's important to put these organizations together.

To merge two organizations with different corporate cultures, different technical backgrounds and different uses is a hard task and it takes time. We want to shape something quite new. We have different production lines for text material and other visual materials, but from the beginning of this year we have created a new common public area for all types of materials.

It's also natural that the audio/visual organizations have more technical experience and this is very useful when we now develop our digital preservation approaches. From this year, we have quite a new digital preservation system and we have invested several million euros in this new system. I'll come back to how we work together with the National Archives on this.

The National Library of Sweden is an agency under the ministry of education and is part of the national infrastructure for research. For more than 20 years our task has been to support university libraries and special libraries in their efforts to improve library services for research and students, to serve as a link between public resource institutions and to develop all encompassing solutions.

By providing multiple options we are advised to reduce redundancy, while at the same time guaranteeing access to national network and solutions. I shall provide a number of examples. We produce the Swedish National Bibliography and we are responsible for LIBRIS, the national online search service and the union catalog for all Swedish research libraries. It contains records for more than 6.5 million books and periodicals held by nearly 200 Swedish university libraries, special libraries and some public libraries. It contains information of printed books, periodicals and articles.

This catalog is of course related to international databases and catalog systems and just now we are running a project to merge a catalog for the public library and LIBRIS and we will have a union catalog for all of the Swedish material—in public, university, and research libraries.

Closely related to providing bibliographical data, as in the LIBRIS national union catalog, is the need to continually adapt and develop metadata. This enhanced bibliographical work is unthinkable without international collaboration, mostly in IFLA.

To give you an example of how everything is connected, our bibliographic coordinator in the National Library had a distinct role in our own civilization, a similar one on the national level, and faces challenges even on the international stage.

Since the middle of the 90s, we have been heading a consortium of Swedish research libraries for licensing e-journals and databases. The National Library negotiates with the publisher and each member of the consortium has to pay their part of the contract. In this task, we also have international partners beyond the publisher with whom we negotiate—difficult negotiations, such as consortia in other countries and the international coalition of library consortia (ICOLC).

To make it easier for researchers, students and teachers to locate research publications, which are at times difficult to find, a special search service has been developed as part of the LIBRIS system. This system was inaugurated in 2005, and now, six years later, we have to upgrade it by developing a new system. We can do it ourselves or buy an existing one.

We have heard at this conference about the importance of open access for global information. Open access is important on a lot of levels—for publication, for metadata and for the system. The National Library of Sweden is promoting open access, publishing and open linked data. We coordinate a program—OpenAccess.se —in Sweden that is run in partnership with Swedish universities, the Swedish Research Council and other research founders, as well as with the Royal Swedish Academy of Science.

All universities have their repositories for e-publishing. Together we have developed a common search tool called SwePub, which harvested all the research publications produced at the universities in the form of metadata but also increasingly as full text. Our ambition is that this database will be used by governmental agencies for allocating research funding. Furthermore, the National Library has been entrusted the task of preserving and maintaining the integrity of these materials.

We have been actively engaged in promoting open access within IFLA, which recently adopted a statement that clarifies IFLA's position and strategy concerning open access. Also, the Nordic countries have invested one million Euros for a program focusing on open access, the Nordbib program—it is run by the five national libraries in the five Nordic countries.

Our LIBRIS department is very active in the field of opened linked data and this is very important for us. I think we can more-or-less agree about open access, but for open linked data this is not easy, because there are companies that are not willing to provide data for free—I just had a very heated discussion with a company about this. Therefore, we strongly support Europeana and TEL in their engagement for open linked data.

As I said before, we have 20 years of experience in coordinating research libraries. The parliament of Sweden had recently commissioned us to coordinate policy even for public libraries, school libraries, and special libraries. From the first of January this year, the National Library has a central regulating authority for the entire Swedish library system. This will facilitate convergence between different library roles and traditions even though the various types of libraries will continue to have different areas of concentration and specialty different user groups.

But even there we see a great change. For example, when we have e-learning the students not only go to the university libraries, they go to the public library and so on and don't have a close connection with one university or one library—we can imagine one big digital library in the future.

There is a strong support for our new task in both the political and the library worlds. Of course there are complications, for example financing. As part of our new assignment, we will develop national guidelines and strategies for publicly financed libraries. We would like to develop collective library statistics, promote bibliographic development; work with accessibility, copyright, and national development issues; and create forums for collaboration among different types of libraries. Also, we will be responsible for monitoring the practical application of the Swedish Acts on Library Services.

And now we have very important and difficult issues of how to manage the introduction of e-books in the library, because it's not easy; we have the reader, we have the publisher, we have the library and we have the user. How we use e-books in the future is not an easy question, I can talk for an hour about it so I'll leave it for now.

Not many national libraries have such a broad coordinating role. You can find some examples around the world, but each has a different philosophy. In Finland and Norway, the National Libraries also have broad coordinating roles as in Sweden, but the rules are nonetheless very different. Even the Nordic National Library will need to coordinate their coordinating roles.

As coordinator, the National Library cannot be despotic. It must give every library and university the possibility to make their opinions known and make their own decisions. All areas mentioned above and some others have an independent expert group and we have an advisory board for all overriding issues. We try to support them on high-level strategic and infrastructural issues.

We are currently engaged in planning for the future—what should we do and what is more important, what could we let go. This last is a very difficult question; we can always find new things to collaborate and coordinate, but what could we let go?

How far will our financial resources take us, and should we produce our own systems or buy them? One of the big issues we are discussing at the moment is how we, together with the universities, can manage metadata mining programmatically. Another important issue is e-science, scientific data from universities, because the universities have no idea—I have been chair of the IT council in one university and I know that in science and in medicine they have some international organizations to address e-science, but for humanities and social science, they have no idea and for this I think national archives, national museums, or other organizations have a role in the future.

In this process, the National Library has high ambitions to work even more closely with the research community and to increase our support to researchers, teachers, and students in the digitization process and in the preservation process. We have agreements of cooperation with the Swedish Law and Information Research Institute at the Stockholm University about legal matters, the Institution for Digital Preservation and the National Archives for preservation, and we are also involved in research and digitization carried out at universities.

Collaborating with Public Sector Partners

In this section, I will talk about collaborating with public sector partners. We have worked very closely with universities and with municipalities, but we also have worked very closely inside the archive, library, and museum (ALM) sector. We have expanded partnerships outside the ALM sector as well with other government agencies. For these, we have extended cooperation, for example, in IT issues and preservation. I am going to talk about ALM cooperation.

In Sweden, we are striving to streamline the whole ALM and the National Library is playing an active role in this. Archives, museums, and libraries have joined forces in most areas of digitization, electronic access, and digital preservation. Until last autumn, we collaborated under the auspices of what we call the ALM Center, financed by the members, and the National Library was responsible for its administration. But from this year we have a new coordinating institution in the ALM sector, the National Archives, which is responsible for the office and has just started. I think it can be fruitful to have closer cooperation through this office.

Nearly all government agencies in the ALM sector report to the ministry of culture, but the National Library reports to the ministry of education. The center was established as a response to Swedish government's enquiry concerning a national strategy for digitization, electronic access, and digital preservation. Several EU states already have such strategies in place or are working towards that goal, but not in Sweden. We work very differently in Sweden compared to some other countries because the governments of some countries might decide "now you will do this." It's not this way in Sweden because cooperation or collaboration among government agencies, whether the government supports it or not, is initiated by the government agencies.

An important duty of this office is to further internationalize the digitization and preservation processes. For example, Swedish ALM institutions already collaborate very closely as aggregators for Europeana and the other portals. We don't have a common portal. The National Library aggregated for TEL, for EUScreen for visual material and for museums and archives like APEnet and ATHENA.

We collaborate with a large number of museums but first and foremost the National Library collaborates with Swedish Archives and Swedish National Heritage Board. We are developing a common platform and taking on jointly the difficult financial and technical problems we will be facing in the coming years.

The National Archives and the National Library have, for several years, worked together to find a way to a common system of preservation of digital material. In this matter, cooperation with research institutes for long-term digital preservation is of vital importance.

Furthermore, and this is very interesting I think, we have developed a common search interface—we call it Sondera—which makes it easier for users to find material from both libraries and archives. We have the Swedish media database with audio/visual material, we have LIBRIS for text material, and we have NAD for archive material. So when you are looking for an author for example, you can see which books he or she has produced, what has been written about the author, you can see manuscripts found in different archives, and you can also TV and radio programs about the author.

For the audio/visual sector, our partner is a Swedish film institute, Swedish television and Swedish radio. In our effort to increase the level of service for users and reduce the cost for digitization and preservation, we have started closer collaboration.

The National Library migrates huge quantities of radio and television programs to digital files using transfers systems developed by our own technicians. We are currently transferring about 2,500 hours of broadcast material per day. More than one million three hundred thousand hours have been transferred so far.

The National Library is acquiring high-quality Swedish television content; and now we are digitizing Swedish radio's local programs. What's important for us when we talk about preserving this digital material—radio material, music—is that it is large and therefore we have completely changed our preservation system to accommodate it.

"Leadership in the Digital Age," I think that was the topic of an online conference in London two or three years ago. This is one the big problems when you are the director or leader of an organization. You need to communicate about technical solutions, you have to negotiate. In the past, you knew everything about the system, but today you have to regain a level where you can negotiate and talk and know what you are talking about. This is one of the greatest problems for leadership in our sector in the digital—how deep can you go? Are you going too deep and can't think of anything but the technical solution? If you don't know anything and leave everything out on the cloud, that's not possible, you can't negotiate and you can't communicate about it. This is also a very interesting matter when we talk about the digital age.

A problem today is that the National Library as well as Public Service Institution and Film Institute preserve the material. We have different standards, which is not cost efficient. Swedish television and the National Library have the ambition to build a common audio/visual archive, which also in the future should include radio and film material. Our ministers agree with that idea but haven't made a final decision.

Together with the Swedish Film Institute, we recently have started a common film site on the Internet with more than 300 short films. We intend to increase and develop to expand this film site. We also have plans for cooperation in digital preservation of films. This is going to be an enormous problem in the future.

With the spread of digitization, commercial enterprises and libraries are implementing new business models for both parties. Creative entrepreneurs and other participants are welcome to develop new products and services. Public/private partnership has high priority today in our country as it has in other countries. For example, when we have a big digitization project, we work on this jointly with the National Archives with money from EU, but we also spend money ourselves; also, newspaper editors are partners in this digitization project.

The National Library explores opportunities for public/private partnership and advocates new business models. I will also say that open linked data is a possibility for helping companies to use this material we put on the Web.

By establishing viable business models and agreements, we can launch new partnerships with commercial institutions. Collaboration with the private sector, publishing IT companies. etc., is important for development of new technical solutions, digital production and presentation, and preservation of the material. We have agreements mostly with newspapers and publishers, but also with other commercial enterprises. For example, one of the editors will digitize their material and we'll share the cost for this.

The National Library also is engaged in ongoing negotiation with representatives of organizations that administer copyrights and collect royalties, such as the Swedish Writers' Union.

I will also mention—and this is very important for us as a Nordic country—we are confident that these issues can be resolved by extended collective licensing. The five Nordic national libraries as well as copyright organizations have worked closely together for developing this collective licensing. We have different opinions about this in Europe, but I'm talking from my perspective.

There are also discussions in the EU commission and we'll see what happens in the future, but the ministry of justice in Sweden is preparing a new law and I hope they are going to make a decision later this year in the parliament on a new copyright law about collective licensing.

International Collaboration

Finally, I will mention something about my own experience of international collaboration. I'll mention two things. My own experience is from library organizations, IFLA, CENL, TEL, CDNL, Bibliotheca Baltica and so on. I have served on several boards around the world and also here in the Baltic Sea region. Experience has shown that there were differences between national and international organizations.

International endeavors require merging different perspectives, taking into account both what's good for the whole library sector and what is good for the nation or your own library. These interests are not always easily combined. Nordic collaboration has been an exception because we are working very close together, but it's because we have a common history and cultural heritage and for the most part a common language and there we can see what's good for one national library is also good for all the Nordic library system.

When we talk about the ALM sector, there's also close collaboration there between the Nordic countries. If you are a member of the IFLA governing board, it's different. In this position you need to have a common perspective. In organizations such as Bibliotheca Baltica, we have yet another perspective—a societal one, which I mentioned before.

What can organizations in general and libraries in specific do for closer cooperation among the states around the Baltic Sea and how will this benefit all of society? As I said before, we should be proud of what we can do and what we have done.

Secondly, I would like to underscore that we have moved from exchanges of experience in conferences and other kinds of meetings to a situation where we're actually working side-by-side and this is very interesting with this conference because we are talking about common projects, not only to exchange experience.

We need both a theoretical framework and the practical experiences that common projects offer. Collaborative projects like the EU's Europeana project with broad participation are an important part of digital development. At the same time, we also need bilateral projects—projects with few countries involved. It can be a common project like the one we had in Finland and Sweden, digitizing Swedish newspapers from northern parts of the country, written in the Finnish language.

In the five Nordic countries, we have a common project to digitize and preserve Nordic research journals. The Nordic National Library has initiated a closer IT collaboration with digital preservation as a high priority in this collaboration. Some of the national libraries also are partners in preservation, for example in PLANETS. So collaboration comes from the country perspective, Nordic perspective and European perspective—and we widen it to the global perspective.

In the continuing process towards the technical development of digital libraries, difficult strategic choices and large investments will be necessary, as well as concrete collaborative projects conducted nationally and internationally. Moving forward will require significant economic and personal resources in the years to come. The challenges are immense and require that institutions collaborate more closely than ever before.

Legal Alignment

Adrienne Muir (Loughborough University)
Dwayne Buttler (University of Louisville)
Wilma Mossink (SURFfoundation)

Abstract

This essay discusses the current state of play with regard to alignment of legal issues for digital preservation and access. A range of legal issues arises at various stages in the lifecycle of digital material. Our focus is on the key issues: legal deposit, copyright exceptions for preservation and access, and multi-partner and cross-border working and rights management. The essay is not a comprehensive survey but focuses on prominent initiatives and useful examples. The order in which the issues are presented should not be taken as a reflection of their relative importance, rather as an attempt to impose a logical order on issues that are heavily intertwined. The implications of the current lack of alignment are identified. Suggestions are made on what is required and how progress can be made to facilitate digital preservation at a national and international level. The content of this essay is based on presentations written by members of the Legal Alignment panel and discussions which took place in the panel, breakout, and plenary sessions at the Aligning National Approaches to Digital Preservation conference.

Introduction

Acquiring, storing, preserving, and providing access to digital material involves actions that are restricted acts under national copyright regimes. This makes copyright a dominant issue to consider when thinking about alignment of digital preservation practices. Preservation of traditional "library" material, such as books, periodicals, and musical and dramatic works, has been facilitated mainly by two legal mechanisms: legal deposit and preservation exceptions to copyright law. Legal deposit is a legal obligation on publishers to deposit publications with designated preservation institutions that provide limited access to those publications. Preservation exceptions to copyright law generally provide for limited copying by certain types of institutions for preservation or replacement purposes.

Copyright and legal deposit laws originate in a pre-digital world and need to be adapted to continue to fulfill their purpose in a digital one. For example, legal deposit provisions need to take developments in digital publishing, including Web publishing, into account. Preservation of digital material may also require disabling technological protection mechanisms or providing access to manuals or software applications. Digital material is often provided to libraries under license agreements and these agreements often have not allowed for preservation by the purchasing or subscribing library. Digitization of analog material can be used to create surrogates for rare or fragile originals as well as to improve access to this material. However, it may not be possible to digitize if existing copyright laws do not allow it and if rights owners are untraceable. These "orphan" works are then at risk of being lost.

Other developments, such as the use of information and communications technologies in research, have hugely increased the amount of raw digital data available for analysis and made it possible to link or integrate disparate data collections. This data can be stored and made available for further analysis or other use. Increasingly, digital research data is being stored and preserved in research institutions or specialist data centers. Preservation, access, and use of digital data raises more than copyright and database rights issues. For example, in the case of research involving human subjects, these actions raise data protection and privacy issues.

Providing access to preserved digital material may also raise liability issues for the preservation institution. Automated Web harvesting operations are likely to result in the acquisition of large amounts of material, some of which could be illegal in some way. Given the lack of quality filtering mechanisms on the Internet, content may be libelous, offensive or obscene, or fall foul of blasphemy or anti-terrorism laws. Providing access to such material may expose the preservation institution to liability for the material, not only in its own country but also in other jurisdictions. The Internet transcends national and jurisdictional boundaries, and there are cultural differences between what is and is not acceptable, which is reflected in national laws.

Alignment in digital preservation includes the development of common approaches, which typically requires some implicit or explicit understanding among the interested parties. That shared understanding may exist informally through common challenges and efforts or more formally through legal agreements. In either event, the arrangement would typically identify shared goals and relevant work necessary to address the common challenges. The common approach may also reveal a desire to standardize efforts and systems in order to manage the effort and improve outcomes. Some efforts to align shared approaches through cooperation and standardization rely on informal arrangements driven by network effects, interoperability needs, market dominance, or other practical social, and pragmatic considerations. These arrangements are sometimes loosely called "agreements" but might not have the force of law. Conversely, other efforts to cooperate may rely far more heavily on law and formal legal agreements that are typically called contracts or licenses. These legal instruments directly reflect and record the shared responsibilities and obligations of the parties involved. Their consequences may flow to third parties who benefit directly from the contract itself as beneficiaries, or more indirectly as participants in a standardized or aligned approach to solve a social concern.

That apparent split of possible approaches to cooperative endeavors is in fact overly simplistic. The law *writ large* ultimately governs all realms of interaction by acting as an overarching layer of preferred social policy applied to all, or at least the policy of a governing majority or a geographical location. Social policy preferences are displayed in common, statutory, treaty, and constitutional law. They also occur in agreements between parties who avail themselves of contract law to develop and enter into legally binding and judicially enforceable agreements among themselves. "The law" at times displays a broader meaning of "all law" and, at other times, the lesser meaning, concentrated on a specific area of law, such as contract or copyright law.

The fact that digital preservation activities take place within broader legal and policy frameworks makes it more difficult to effect alignment between national responses to the legal issues arising from digital preservation. Stakeholders in digital preservation include the preservation community, the beneficiaries of preservation, rights holders, and legislators and policy makers at institutional, national, and international levels. When it comes to making legislative changes, these stakeholder groups may or may not agree on the policy goal to be achieved. Even if they do agree on the goal, they may not agree on the means to achieve this goal. Disagreement may exist between or even within nations.

Even where there is a will, or a need, to cooperate across jurisdictional boundaries, different legal approaches may make this difficult or even impossible. Still, there is potential for alignment in national approaches. There is potential for learning from each other on how to address legal issues in digital preservation and applying that learning within a particular legal jurisdiction. There are already groups of states working together on harmonization of legal arrangements for managing rights and examples and lessons available from attempts to draft agreements or amend legislation. A prominent example is the European Union Member States.

Current Status and Challenges for Alignment

Legal Deposit

Legal deposit is the legal obligation on publishers to deposit their publications in designated depositories. The aim of legal deposit is the preservation of a country's published output for posterity. Legal deposit is usually implemented at a national level. In some cases, national arrangements are accompanied by federal arrangements, for example in the case of Australia. For the last twenty or so years, governments have been updating legal deposit provisions to take into account developments in digital publishing. UNESCO produced an updated version of its guidelines on legal deposit in 2000, which included a legal framework for national legal deposit schemes and discussed requirements for the deposit of digital material. Despite this, there are still differences between national approaches, with some countries adopting comprehensive and/or technology-neutral provisions, expanding regulation on a piecemeal basis, or relying on a wholly voluntary approach to deposit. Other countries are currently taking a hybrid approach with formal regulations for some types of material and voluntary or no deposit arrangements for digital material. There may be a variety of reasons for differences, including national policy priorities, or relationships between stakeholders.

The question is whether these differences have a negative impact on the preservation of the world's intellectual heritage. The key issue is the scope of digital legal deposit approaches. Some countries include all kinds of digital material, going beyond traditional library material to include software, for example. However, this is not the case in all countries. For example, in the UK, film and sound recordings, analogue or digital, are explicitly excluded from legal deposit. The potential consequences of such differences go beyond the inevitable gaps in national collections to gaps in the world's digital archive of the outputs of the human mind over the long-term. Whilst legal deposit arrangements may be supplemented by voluntary schemes, ensuring compliance over the long-term is more difficult than through a statutory approach, although this is not always perfectly satisfactory either. In countries where legislation has been updated, there are examples of how to deal with challenging issues, such as how to frame definitions of publications and publishers, inclusion of preservation provisions, and limited protections against liability for unlawful material.

Recognizing the potential implications of divergence between national approaches to deposit, the European Commission issued a *Recommendation*[1] that advised Member States, when establishing policies and procedures for the deposit of material originally created in digital format, to take into account developments in other Member States in order to prevent a wide divergence in depositing arrangements. The recommendation also suggested making provision in legislation for the preservation of web content by mandated institutions using techniques for collecting material from the Internet such as Web harvesting.

An interesting complementary approach was suggested in 2011 by The "Comité des Sages" (a Reflection Group on bringing Europe's cultural heritage online). The Comité reiterated the importance of long-term preservation and that it is the responsibility of cultural heritage institutions to take care of the preservation of digitized and born digital cultural material. The Comité also suggested that a copy of the material should be archived at Europeana.[2] For works in copyright, the deposit site would be a dark archive functioning as a safe harbor. Preservation should be backed by copyright and related legislation to enable

---

[1] See Commission Recommendation 2006/585/EC of 24 August 2006 on the digitization an online accessibility of cultural content and digital preservation: http://eur-lex.europa.eu/LexUriServ/LexUriServ.do?uri=OJ:L:2006:236:0028:0030:EN:PDF (last accessed 04-16-2012).

[2] The Europeana project is a portal to digitized content in European libraries, see: http://www.europeana.eu/portal/aboutus_background.html (last accessed 04-10-2012).

this.[3] To avoid duplication of copies of material, the members of the Comité proposed a system (including a workflow for passing on the copy to any institution that has a right to it under national deposit legislation) by which any material that now needs to be deposited in several countries would only be deposited once. Whether this approach is acceptable to relevant stakeholders, or even feasible, is debatable.

Digital Preservation and Copyright

There has been some alignment activity in this area, particularly on copyright exceptions, approaches to dealing with orphan works, and improving access to the digital cultural heritage. There has also been some research in this area that has identified issues that are a cause for concern, including provision of digital material being regulated by license agreements that hamper the ability of institutions to preserve or provide perpetual access to digital material. There has been exploration of ways to address issues, through legislative change, development of principles to guide approaches to identifying orphan works, and model license agreements.

An international study on the impact of copyright law on digital preservation surveyed the situation in Australia, the Netherlands, the United Kingdom, and the United States.[4] The 2008 report of the study concluded that copyright was a significant barrier to digital preservation in these jurisdictions. Although all of the countries surveyed had relevant copyright exceptions, they were inadequate for digital preservation and there was inconsistency between the provisions. A number of joint recommendations were made, including revising exceptions so that they apply to all types of copyright materials in all formats. The exceptions would apply to authorized non-profit institutions, which should be able to preserve at risk material, according to current best practice, rather than waiting for it to become obsolete

---

[3] The New Renaissance, Report Comité des Sages p. 6, Brussels January 2011, see: http://ec.europa.eu/information_society/activities/digital_libraries/doc/refgroup/fi nal_report_cds.pdf (last accessed 04-16-2012).

[4] Besek, J. et al. (2008) International study on the impact of copyright law in digital preservation: a joint report of the Library of Congress National Digital Information Infrastructure and Preservation Program, the Joint Information Systems Committee, the Open Access to Knowledge (OAK) Law Project and the SURFfoundation. See: http://www.digitalpreservation.gov/documents/digital_preservation_final_report2 008.pdf (last accessed 04-16-2012).

or deteriorate. The report recognized the need to protect the interests of rights holders and recommended investigating how preservation institutions could work together to preserve and provide access to digital material, including the scope for private arrangements. The report also recommended investigating national approaches to the interaction between contractual arrangements between institutions and rights holders and copyright exceptions. The findings of the study were presented at a WIPO workshop in July 2008.

Preservation Exceptions

Preserving digital content will require actions that potentially infringe copyright in the material. The main issue is copying:

- It may be necessary to make copies of material for ingest into a digital archive;

- Several copies may need to be made for redundancy purposes;

- Material may need to be copied from its original medium onto a different medium and this may need to happen periodically over time;

- Migration strategies will require conversion to new file formats and conversions may have to be carried out periodically; and

- Emulation strategies will require actions that may considered to be adapting copyright works.

Unless these actions fall within the scope of exceptions to copyright law, preservation institutions have to seek permission to carry out preservation. Because technology changes faster than the law, technical legal solutions are often outdated in application by the time they are passed. For example, any exceptions to copyright laws in Berne Convention countries have to be in line with the Berne three-step test. This only allows for exceptions and limitations in certain special cases, which do not conflict with a normal exploitation of the work or other subject matter, and do not unreasonably prejudice the legitimate interests of the rights holder.[5] Copyright law in some countries includes preservation exceptions for libraries and archives. However, these exceptions may have been introduced before the advent of digital publishing

---

[5] Berne Convention for the Protection of Literary and Artistic Works, article 9.

and may therefore not allow for reformatting and multiple copying of works. Other countries have made changes to their exceptions to take digital preservation into account, but whether these exceptions will allow preservation institutions to carry out all the required activities for digital preservation is debatable. For example, Canadian copyright law allows reformatting, but only when the original format is already obsolete.[6] Despite the existence of numerous studies and reviews of copyright laws[7] that have identified the need to include or update preservation exceptions, many countries have not yet made such changes.

In the European Union, the European Commission has been involved in trying to make progress on harmonizing copyright laws in EU Member States for at least the last ten years. The InfoSoc Directive[8] introduced a non-mandatory exception to the reproduction right under article 5.2.(c), which allows publicly accessible libraries, educational establishments, museums, or archives, which are not for direct or indirect economic or commercial advantage to conduct specific acts of reproduction. As the possible exceptions and limitations contained in the InfoSoc Directive are not mandatory, they are not consistent throughout the European Union. EU Member States have different conditions under which preservation is allowed. For example, UK provisions are currently limited to making single copies of analogue material in reference collections. Under UK law, a librarian or archivist of a prescribed library or any archive is allowed to make a single copy of literary, dramatic, and musical works in permanent reference collections that cannot be acquired by other means.[9] The implementation of the InfoSoc Directive created an exception in the Dutch Copyright Act which allows libraries, museums, and archives to make reproductions of works in their collection for the sole purpose of restoring them or, in the case of threatening deterioration, to preserve a reproduction for the institution, or to keep such works in a condition in which they can be consulted if there is no technology available to render them.[10] A

---

[6] Copyright Act (R.S.C., 1985, c. C-42), s. 30.1(1).

[7] For example, in the UK, both the Gowers and the Hargreaves reviews of the copyright regime have recommended updating preservation exceptions; this has not yet happened.

[8] Directive 2001/29/EC of the European Parliament and of the Council of 22 May 2011 on the harmonization of certain aspects of copyright and related rights in the information society.

[9] Copyright, Patent and Design Act 1988, s42.

[10] Dutch Copyright Act, article 16.

later European Commission Recommendation suggested that there should be provisions in legislation for multiple copying and migration of digital cultural material by public institutions for preservation purposes, whilst fully respecting Community and international legislation on intellectual property rights.

The difficulties of adapting copyright exceptions to address the above issues are not limited to the harmonization efforts of the narrowly prescribed provisions in European Union Member States' laws. US copyright law, for example, also requires change. Section 108[11] in US law applies to some facets of preservation but offers little support for widespread digital preservation. The US Copyright Office hosted a Section 108 Study Group in the late 2000s. Despite a thorough discussion of possible approaches to updating Section 108, the Study Group's report[12] thus far has spurred no new legislative efforts to make Section 108 more amenable to digital technologies and resolving contemporary challenges in the library, archive, and digital preservation efforts.

However, US copyright law includes "fair use" which excuses otherwise infringing acts, depending on the merits of a particular case, and it is possible that preserving institutions can rely on fair use in situations where the section 108 libraries and archives exceptions do not provide for the activities necessary for preserving digital content, such as making multiple copies over time. The benefit of fair use is that it provides an equitable set of factors that are balanced around important public policy concerns.

License Agreements

Without appropriate exceptions to copyright, preservation institutions have to obtain permissions to preserve digital material. This also applies to other preservation-related activities such as Web harvesting and digitization. Tracing rights holders and obtaining their permission is a time consuming and expensive activity. In the case of preserving digital material that is acquired from vendors, even if appropriate exceptions were available, these could be overridden by license agreements in jurisdictions where contract law trumps copyright provisions.

---

[11] 17 USC Sec. 108

[12] See the 2008 Section 108 Study Group report: http://www.section108.gov/docs/Sec108StudyGroupReport.pdf (last accessed 4-10-2012).

"Agreement" is theoretically and functionally the foundation of contract law. Courts and legal scholars often refer to this necessity, albeit inaccurately in some cases, as a "meeting of the minds." This meeting-of-the-minds theory assumes equal bargaining power among the parties even if equality is lacking in actual practice. Historically, a license is focused on delineating a right to do something—to cross my property, for instance. The term now embodies more than the right to do something and often creates a binding agreement limiting other conduct, such as agreeing that "all applicable laws" bind the licensee.

Freedom-to-contract principles are deeply ingrained in the legal community. Consequently, in theory (and often practice), persons and other entities are generally free to agree to nearly any contract terms. This may be the case even if those contract terms might prove detrimental to them and there is unequal bargaining power between the parties. The only limits on that freedom are typically legislative influences, such as consumer protection, commercial uniformity, and other narrow refinements or judicial interventions. Judicial limits in some broad sense typically find the contract untenable for public policy reasons or because the contract violates some basic sense of "fairness." Such interventions in contract review are rare. As a practical matter, regardless of whether the parties have read or understood the contact, they are bound by its terms and conditions.

Individual preservation institutions may lack the bargaining power to greatly influence license agreements with suppliers of digital content. However, there has been progress on creating model license agreements incorporating archival provisions that have been accepted by many publishers. The UK's Model NESLi2 license[13] is a good example that could be adapted in other jurisdictions. NESLI2 is a national electronic journal licensing initiative for higher and further education. The model license includes provisions for access to previously subscribed-to material when current subscriptions are terminated. The arrangements for archiving material for preservation purposes can also be specified within the license.

---

[13] See the Model NESLi2 license: http://www.jisc-collections.ac.uk/nesli2/NESLi2-Model-Licence-/ (last accessed 4-10-2012).

Orphan Works

One reason for digitizing analog material is to improve and widen access to the material. Another reason is to create digital surrogates for fragile and rare material, such as early films and sound recordings that are at risk of being lost. The creation of digital libraries from existing analogue holdings raises copyright issues. The European Digital Library[14] concentrated on works in the public domain because otherwise a substantial change in copyright legislation would be required. The other possibility, i.e., making agreements on a case-by-case basis between the rights holders and preservation institutions, requires establishing the copyright status of a work. In the case of so-called orphan works, the copyright holder in the work cannot be traced. It may, therefore, not be possible to establish whether the work is still in copyright. However, the costs of determining the status of a work, particularly as to whether a work is an orphan or not[15] and where mass digitization is envisaged, are much higher than the costs of digitizing material and making it available online.

If preservation institutions cannot find the rights holder, even after a diligent search, the institution has to decide whether to digitize and make the work accessible online or not. Proceeding with digitization raises the risk of complaints of infringement, take-down orders or even litigation. Not going ahead means that a productive and beneficial use of the work may be forestalled, which is not in the public interest.[16] Several possible solutions have been identified to solve the problem of orphan works, varying from measures to promote voluntary supply of

---

[14] See the European Digital Library Project:
http://www.theeuropeanlibrary.org/portal/organisation/cooperation/archive/edlproject/ (last accessed 4-10-2012).

[15] An orphan work can be defined as a copyright protected work (or subject-matter protected by related rights), the rights owner of which cannot be identified or located by anyone who wants to use of the work in a manner that requires the rights owner's consent.

[16] U.S. Copyright Office. "Report on orphan works." Library of Congress, 2006: http://www.copyright.gov/orphan/orphan-report.pdf (last accessed 4-16-2012). See also Agnieszka Vetulani. "The Problem of orphan works in the EU: an overview of legislative solutions and main actions in this field." European Commission, 2008:
http://ec.europa.eu/information_society/activities/digital_libraries/doc/reports_orphan/report_orphan_v2.pdf (last accessed 4-16-2012).

information, to strictly legal solutions, or solutions that support some sort of contractual arrangement by law.[17]

Again, there has been activity in this area in the European Union. The European Digital Libraries Initiative High Level Expert Group Copyright Subgroup concluded unanimously in December 2009 that a solution to the issue of orphan works was desirable, at least for literary and audiovisual works.[18] Member States could chose different solutions[19] but on a European level, defining relevant criteria for generic due diligence guidelines as one practical and flexible tool to facilitate the identification and location of right holders for the lawful use of orphan works[20] was a first step in addressing the problem. This resulted in a Memorandum of Understanding establishing that a work can only be considered orphaned, and consequently be used, if due diligence according to relevant criteria, including the documentation of the process, have been followed.[21]

A mechanism to facilitate the use of orphan works was initiated by the European Commission Internal Market and Services Directorate at the end of 2010. Since then, stakeholders (including rights holders) have been involved in a dialogue to formulate a Memorandum of Understanding (MOU) containing key principles regarding digitization and making available works not currently being commercially exploited. Compliance with the

---

[17] Van Gompel, S, & P.B.Hugenholtz, The Copyright conundrum of digitizing large-scale audiovisual archives, and how to solve it, *Popular Communication: The International Journal of Media and Culture, 8(1 2010), pp. 61-7;* Elferink, M, H & A. Ringnalda."Digitale Ontsluiting van historische archieven en verweesde werken: een inventarisatie". Utrecht: Universiteit Utrecht, Centrum voor Intellectueel Eigendomsrecht (CIER), WODC July 2008; U.S. Copyright Office. "Report on orphan works." Library of Congress, 2006: http://www.copyright.gov/orphan/orphan-report.pdf (last accessed 4-16-2012).

[18] i2010 Digital Libraries Initiative High Level Expert Group on Digital Libraries. "Digital libraries: recommendations and challenges for the future." December 2009: http://ec.europa.eu/information_society/activities/digital_libraries/doc/hleg/report s/hlg_final_report09.pdf (last accessed 4-16-2012).

[19] For examples, see: i2010; Digital Libraries High Level Expert Group, ibid.

[20] See Memorandum of Understanding on Diligent Search guidelines for Orphan Works at: http://ec.europa.eu/information_society/activities/digital_libraries/doc/hleg/orpha n/memorandum.pdf (last accessed 4-10-2012).

[21] See the European Digital Libraries initiative, Sector-specific guidelines on Due Diligence Criteria for Orphan Works: Joint Report at: http://ec.europa.eu/information_society/activities/digital_libraries/doc/hleg/orpha n/guidelines.pdf (last accessed 4-10-2012).

key principles allows cultural institutions to digitize and make available books and journals, including embedded works, which are "out of commerce." Under the MOU, cultural institutions can negotiate agreements on a voluntary basis. The contracting parties will agree on the type and number of works covered by their agreement and if those works are covered by the MOU. Agreements will specify authorized uses and the licenses will be granted by collective rights management organizations. Articulating guiding principles emphasized certain problems of a soft law approach. Regulating cross-border access to works that are not part of the repertoires of collective management organizations is proving to be a difficult topic that might need to be addressed by legislation.

The Comité des Sages mentioned the need for speedy adoption of a European legal instrument for orphan works. Whilst the Comité did not specify the nature of the instrument, the European Commission issued a Proposal for a Directive on certain permitted uses of orphan works.[22] The legal instrument brought forward by the Comité has to cover all the different types of material and includes eight steps to concurrently comply with:[23]

1. Ensure that a solution for dealing with orphan works is in place in all the Member States. Where no national instrument is in place, national legislation needs to be implemented;
2. Cover all the range of works: audiovisual, text, visual arts, sound;
3. Ensure cross-border recognition of orphan works;
4. Ensure the cross-border effect of this recognition;
5. Be compatible with the implementation of PPPs for digitization;
6. Foresee, in the case of commercial use, remuneration for the rights holders if after some time they are traced or make themselves known;

---

[22] European Commission, Proposal for a Directive of the European Parliament and of the Council on certain permitted uses of orphan works, Brussels 24.5.2011, COM (2011) 289 final.
http://ec.europa.eu/internal_market/copyright/docs/orphan-works/proposal_en.pdf (last accessed 4-16-2012).

[23] See The New Renaissance, *Report Comité des Sages* p. 18, Brussels (January 2011), at:
http://ec.europa.eu/information_society/activities/digital_libraries/doc/refgroup/final_report_cds.pdf (last accessed 4-16-2012).

7. Ensure reasonable transaction costs for dealing with orphan works, commensurate with the commercial value of the work; and

8. Be supported by rights information databases, such as the Arrow system,[24] which is currently under construction.

The US Congress has also indicated some willingness to resolve the orphan works problem. One cornerstone principle for any orphan work solution is recognizing that vital information about many works has simply vanished from the historical record. Requiring a "reasonable search" to limit liability for the use of such works must acknowledge that defining "reasonable" is directly proportional to availability of information about the work. That equation has been lacking thus far.

The Commission's proposal encompasses the steps the Comité des Sages had mentioned in its report. Furthermore, it builds on the European Commission's 2006 *Recommendation* on the digitization and online accessibility of cultural content and digital preservation.[25] With the proposed Directive, the Commission intends to create a legal framework to ensure lawful, cross-border access to orphan works through a system of mutual recognition of the orphan status of a work. The proposal specifies the institutions that are protected when they use orphan works in the pursuance of their public missions. Libraries, educational establishments, museums, and archives can use orphan works that are published in the form of books, journals, newspapers, magazines, or other writings, including photographs and illustrations embedded in them. Film heritage institutions are allowed to use audiovisual and cinematographic collections and finally public service broadcasting organizations can use the latter works and audio works produced by them. The special position of public service broadcasters as producers has led to providing a cut-off date for works that are within the scope of the proposal to limit the phenomena of orphan works.

---

[24] See Accessible Registries of Rights Information and Orphan Works (ARROW) http://www.arrow-net.eu/ (last accessed 4-10-2012).

[25] See Commission Recommendation 2006/585/EC of 24 August 2006 on the digitization and online accessibility of cultural content and digital preservation at: http://eur-lex.europa.eu/LexUriServ/LexUriServ.do?uri=OJ:L:2006:236:0028:0030:EN:PDF (last accessed 4-16-2012).

To establish the status of a work the specified institutions need to carry out a prior good faith and reasonable diligent search in line with the requirements set out in the proposed Directive and its annex, in the country where the work is first published. For each category of works the appropriate, thus different, sources need to be consulted. These sources shall be determined in each Member State in consultation with rights-holders and users. To avoid costly duplication, Member States shall ensure that the results of the diligent searches carried out in their territories are recorded in a publicly accessible database. Once the orphan work status is established, the institutions covered by the proposal can make that work lawfully available online under certain conditions and for specific purposes. The Directive only applies to works that are first or broadcast in a Member State.

A work is considered as an orphan if the rights-holder in the work is not identified or, even if identified, is not located or traced after a diligent search. Where a work has more than one rights-holder, and only one of the rights-holders has been identified and located, that work shall not be considered an orphan.

Orphan works can be used in several ways: making a work available within the meaning of the Copyright Directive, by acts of reproduction for the purposes of digitization, making available, indexing, cataloguing, preservation, or restoration. These acts can only be performed by the specified institutions as they seek to achieve their public interest missions. Furthermore Member States may permit institutions to use orphan works for additional purposes under specified conditions.

It is not clear whether the proposed Directive will solve the orphan works problem if it is adopted. The requirement for diligent search hampers mass digitization due to the human and financial resources required. The Directive does not provide for an efficient and streamlined rights clearance system that will facilitate copyright clearances on a larger scale.

Access to Preserved Digital Material

There is no point in investing in digital preservation without access of some sort to the preserved material. It may be necessary for preservation institutions to make access copies of material, depending on user needs and available technology. For example, access copies may involve making copies in compressed file formats. This would require permission from rights holders. Legal and voluntary deposit arrangements usually specify restricted conditions for access to deposited material and wider access has to be negotiated with rights holders. Giving maximum accessibility to the preserved material requires the permission of the author(s) or rights holder(s) of the work(s) for works that are still in copyright, or, alternatively, focusing on out of copyright works. Without the consent of rights holders, the result is that the public has no online access to recent material—the reason libraries identified the concept of the 20th (and now 21st) century black hole.[26]

A fair balance between the legitimate rights of creators and other rights holders and the interests of the public to access digital materials should be reaffirmed and promoted, in accordance with international norms and agreements.[27] Recent developments have arguably tipped the balance very much in favor of rights holders when it comes to digital resources. For example, rights-holder groups have lobbied policy makers on the extension of the term of copyright and related rights. The US Congress regressed in a recent amendment and purposefully limited the dissemination of some digital copies to the "premises of the library." Some communities fear revisiting (or reopening) Section 108 in the legislative arena because of the possibility of further limitations, not greater empowerment. Those fears may be warranted given that the trend in recent legislation has been less-than-supportive of viable use opportunities. This trend has left the judiciary to look more closely at fair use opportunities to make the copyright system work at all in some situations.

In its 2005 policy paper on the Digital Libraries Initiative: "i2010: digital libraries,"[28] the European Commission designated preservation and online accessibility as two of the strands to focus on in the process of building a digital European library.[29] The

---

[26] Boyle, J. "A copyright black hole swallows our culture," *Financial Times*, September 6, 2009. http://www.ft.com/cms/s/0/6811a9d4-9b0f-11de-a3a1-00144feabdc0.html#axzz1LgCBWo5A (last accessed 4-10-2012).

[27] Charter on the Preservation of Digital Heritage: http://portal.unesco.org/en/ev.php-URL_ID=17721&URL_DO=DO_TOPIC&URL_SECTION=201.html (last accessed 4-16-2012).

[28] Communication from the Commission to the European Parliament, the Council, the European Economic and Social Committee and the Committee of the Regions i2010: Digital Libraries, Brussels, 30.9.2005 COM (2005) 465 final.

[29] A digital library is defined as an organized collection of digital content made available to the public. Such a library can consist of material that has been digitized and other "physical" material from libraries and archives, or based on information originally produced in digital format.

policy paper started diverse activities to create mechanisms, frameworks, and regulations to enable further digitization and dissemination of digital material. The subsequent *Recommendation*[30] proposed to establish national strategies for the long-term preservation of, and access to, digital material.

These findings are consistent with those in the final report of the High Level Expert Group on Digital Libraries (HLEG).[31] In 2006, the Commission established a committee to advise on how best to address the organizational, legal, and technical challenges of a digital library at European level. The HLEG set up several subgroups, including one to deal with the issues of intellectual property rights. Regarding digital preservation, the HLEG mentioned the problems of multiple copying, migration, and technical protection devices; web harvesting was especially mentioned.

Voluntary Deposit Schemes and Cooperative Agreements

Hybrid deposit systems consist of a mix of legal deposit and voluntary arrangements between parties. The intention can be to use voluntary schemes as a stop-gap measure until legislation can be passed. The level of compliance achieved in a voluntary scheme can inform a decision on whether a more formal regulatory approach is required. Voluntary schemes can also provide a means of understanding the practical issues in digital deposit and therefore inform the framing of laws. Alternatively, voluntary arrangements may work better for certain types of material than others. In the UK, films and sound recordings have been deposited on a voluntary basis and this approach seems to work reasonably well. In the Netherlands, all deposit of print and non-print material is carried out on a voluntary contractual basis between the national depository and publishers without requiring statutory enforcement. However, this is not the case in all jurisdictions.

---

[30] Commission Recommendation 2006/585/EC of 24 August 2006 on the digitization an online accessibility of cultural content and digital preservation at: http://eur-lex.europa.eu/LexUriServ/LexUriServ.do?uri=OJ:L:2006:236:0028:0030:EN:PDF (last accessed 4-16-2012).

[31] See High Level Expert Group on Digital Libraries (HLEG): http://ec.europa.eu/information_society/activities/digital_libraries/other_groups/hleg/index_en.htm (last accessed 4-16-2012).

The UNESCO guidelines[32] advise against voluntary deposit arrangements, recommending that deposit should be a statutory obligation. In 2001, the Conference of European National Libraries (CENL) and the Federation of European Publishers (FEP) made a declaration advocating the immediate implementation of voluntary schemes for digital material.[33] The declaration recognized that it takes time to update legal deposit legislation. The declaration included a model voluntary code for local adaptation. The model code was based on the then UK scheme for offline digital material[34] and included both offline and online digital publications.

In terms of alignment, the current UK self-regulated code for offline publications[35] has been endorsed by all of the libraries benefitting from UK legal deposit, including Trinity College Dublin library in the Republic of Ireland. The elements of the code include the scope of the arrangement, or the publications to be deposited; exclusions from deposit; the number of copies to be deposited; access and use arrangements; and copying for preservation purposes. The original 1999 agreement between the KB and the Dutch Publishers Association[36] covers both offline and online digital publications and addresses the same issues as the UK Code. The Dutch agreement provided more detail on how the KB would store and provide access to deposited publications and warranties against third-party claims against the publications. The Agreement was revised in 2005,[37] the revisions mainly related to the "availability" clauses, particularly interlibrary loans (ILLs),

---

[32] Larivière, J. "Guidelines for legal deposit legislation." (Rev., enl. and updated ed.) Paris: Unesco, 2000: http://archive.ifla.org/VII/s1/gnl/legaldep1.htm (last accessed 4-16-2012).

[33] Conference of European National Libraries & Federation of European Publishers. "International declaration on the deposit of electronic publications." CENL & FEP, 2001:
http://deposit.ddb.de/ep/netpub/85/61/78/967786185/_data_dyna/_snap_stand_20 00_10_12/Web/Archiv/Server_neu/Server_20001012/aktuell/epubstat.htm (last accessed 4-16-2012).

[34] See the "Code of practice for the voluntary deposit of non-print publications:" http://www.bl.uk/aboutus/stratpolprog/legaldep/voluntarydeposit/ (last accessed 4-10-2012).

[35] See UK self-regulated code for offline publications:
http://www.bl.uk/aboutus/stratpolprog/legaldep/offlinevoluntary/offline.html (last accessed 4-10-2012).

[36] See 1999 agreement between the KB and the Dutch Publishers Association:
http://www.kb.nl/dnp/overeenkomst-nuv-kb-en.pdf (last accessed 4-10-2012).

[37] See the 2005 agreement (Dutch): http://www.kb.nl/dnp/overeenkomst-nuv-kb.pdf (last accessed 4-16-2012).

which are not usually permitted under legal deposit arrangement. The 2005 revision allowed making printouts to send to users and downloading is now permitted "for private study and use." Although the Dutch agreement in theory covers "all electronic publications," in reality the terms were drafted with journal articles in mind. Publishers now wish to renegotiate the terms of the 2005 agreement in response to developments in the e-book market. This may result in withdrawal of downloading provisions with access restricted to on-site perusal. Voluntary deposit agreements can be more flexible than statutory provisions, so issues such as access provision can potentially be tailored to different categories of material and the needs for different types of publisher if desired. On the other hand, as can be seen in the Dutch example, parties to voluntary agreements may wish to change these agreements over time to the potential detriment of the preservation of digital material.

Various cooperative approaches to digital preservation have developed in recent years. The purpose and scope of cooperative groups vary, as do governance arrangements and legal underpinnings. Purposes include advocacy, awareness and training, for example the Digital Preservation Coalition in the UK. Others include developing approaches to preservation, such as the International Internet Preservation Coalition. Some cooperative groups exist for the practical purposes of sharing carrying out preservation activities using centralized or distributed models. Initiatives are regional or national in scope; others extend across national boundaries.

The Council of Library and Information Resources' 2006 report on e-journal archiving programs[38] identified the governance structures for each program. These included various consortial or membership arrangements. For example, the HathiTrust focuses on preserving and providing access to digitized content and is a university-led arrangement. All members sign agreements with a lead institution, University of Michigan, and each member is thus bound to the institution where the core infrastructure, technical, and organizational, is located. Another example, the MetaArchive Cooperative, is organized on a distributed model; all members are on an equal footing and knowledge and infrastructure is embedded

---

[38] Kenney, A. et al. *E-Journal Archiving Metes and Bounds: A Survey of the Landscape.* (CLIR, 2006). http://www.clir.org/pubs/abstract/pub138abst.html (last accessed 4-10-2012).

within the member sites. The MetaArchive members sign agreements with a non-profit host institution, the Educopia Institute, which was founded for that purpose.

Whatever the nature of the cooperative venture, success is likely to be dependent on the degree of clarity in the objectives and benefits of the venture, how the venture will be managed, the roles and responsibilities of participants, and resource implications. This could involve a statement of purpose, such as a charter as well as an agreement between participating partners. Access to legal counsel is driven by resource availability, but not all institutions and cultural memory organizations have ready resources to expend on legal guidance. Nevertheless, all participants are bound by the terms of the agreement under contract principles. A generic source of guidance on the legal issues to consider and address in cooperative agreements would provide a degree of alignment even if specific legal provisions differ between jurisdictions. It would also help cooperative groups to articulate their requirements to legal advisers.

Need for Alignment

It is clear from the foregoing discussion that copyright and related rights are key issues in digital preservation. Current regulatory frameworks are not supportive of digitization or digital preservation efforts and need to be changed. Exceptions for preservation are either non-existent or are not appropriate for digital material. The digitization of orphan works is hindered because of a lack of applicable exceptions in most jurisdictions and time and resource intensive approaches to clearing rights which do not scale well for mass digitization efforts. There is a need to better understand how to manage copyright and advocate copyright provisions that can facilitate preservation. There is also the issue that in many jurisdictions, although Ireland is a notable exception, contractual arrangements can override copyright exceptions.

There should be alignment in the scope of legal deposit to reduce the potential for loss of digital heritage over the long term. Broadening the coverage of legal deposit in terms of type of work reduces the risk of uneven coverage. Statutory obligations improve compliance. It is clear, at least in some jurisdictions, that there is resistance to extending legal deposit to digital material and in particular to material emanating from the digital media industry. The reasons for this need to be clearly identified and understood before any meaningful actions can be taken. It may be that the issue is lack of understanding on the part of the industry, or there could be genuine concerns around the risks and/or costs to the industry.

Digital preservation activities are increasingly international in scope. Alignment between preservation provisions in different jurisdictions would facilitate cooperative preservation activities. Progress on legal issues in digital preservation has been relatively slow, due to jurisdictional issues but also due to different stakeholders' interests in digital preservation and lack of political will to change the situation. An examination of developments in recent years reveals some factors that contribute to this state of affairs. There is an imbalance of lobbying power between prominent stakeholders and a lack of a compelling case for the value and impact of opening up access to works through the digitization and preservation of digital material. Preservation institutions may devote more effort and resources to lobbying for change, but they cannot hope to compete with the resources of digital content and information technology industries.

There is a need for the preservation community to develop a position or positions in order to strengthen and amplify the messages to be conveyed. The preservation community may have the same overarching goal of preserving access to digital material, but it is not a homogenous group. The specific objectives of archives, legal deposit and national libraries, academic libraries and other preservation organizations may differ to a greater or lesser degree. It may be a case of groups within the community developing their own coherent positions. There is also a need for evidence, perhaps in the form of case studies, to demonstrate the value and impact of preservation and access. Valuable lessons may be gleaned from examining examples of successful projects to identify the key elements of that success.

There is a need to engage more meaningfully and constructively with stakeholder groups, such as the general public and creators, who have hitherto not been directly involved in discussions and lobbying efforts. Whilst engagement should be more widespread it can take place at different levels and be targeted to specific groups. It may be that a combination of approaches—international, national and regional—are adopted. It may be that efforts are targeted for particular stakeholder groups and sub-groups, for example users of digital material include researchers and scholars in different disciplines, members of the general public with different interests, and creators and authors with different motivations for creation, including making a livelihood and disseminating knowledge for the public good.

Increased understanding of the motivation for digitization and digital preservation and the benefits it could bring for stakeholders, including rights holders, may well reduce indifference or opposition to the changes that are needed. The balance between protecting the interests of rights holders and the public good could be redressed if policy makers could make more informed and balanced policy decisions and these decisions could be enacted by legislative change. Where an internationally coordinated non-legislative approach is required, existing international groups can take the lead in developing and testing practical and sensible solutions that may be taken up in other regions. As far as cooperative working is concerned, the agreements and arrangements already made should be evaluated and lessons learned more effectively disseminated.

Possibilities for Alignment

It is reasonably clear that there is a need for legislative change as far as preservation exceptions to copyright and legal deposit is concerned. The key issue is how to make the case to rights holders and policy makers. Where preservation exceptions exist, they should be framed in such as way as to allow preservation institutions to do whatever is necessary to ensure preservation. More needs to be done to clarify how the digitization orphan works exceptions could be implemented, whether this would be through legislative change, agreements or both. Whilst legislative change may be the ultimate goal, this will take time. In the shorter term, a first step is to start with agreements and risk management approaches. Whilst the nature of agreements between partners in preservation organizations will depend on various factors, we suggest some questions to consider when making agreements. A key point is that agreements, at whatever level, should not be too complex and difficult to understand or they will not be used.

Making the Case for Change

It may be possible to overcome resistance to legal deposit for digital material by identifying, articulating, and disseminating case studies demonstrating the benefits and impact of legal deposit to different stakeholder groups. Legal deposit institutions are likely to be able to identify suitable cases, but it may also be necessary to engage with users, as value and impact may occur in ways that are not obvious to the institutions. A further approach to collecting evidence to help inform lobbying efforts may be to identify and examine cases where voluntary deposit schemes are in place to identify the extent to which they succeed in terms of compliance and to examine the reasons for this. It may be that where there is strong resistance to legal deposit, voluntary deposit schemes may be a less threatening and therefore more acceptable alternative that may, in turn, increase trust and provide useful evidence to support the introduction of more formal approaches.

The International Federation of Library Associations and Institutions (IFLA) is an international body that has an interest in national libraries and legal deposit. IFLA can engage with international publishing agencies and national governments. UNESCO has already shown support for legal deposit through updating its guidelines. UNESCO also has wider interests in the digital heritage and could do more to influence UN member states. At a national level, deposit institutions can enter dialogue with rights holder groups and government, but it may be more effective to gather support through targeting specific stakeholder groups, such as authors and creators, rather than publishers and aggregators. These groups can, in some circumstances, exert pressure on publishers. Gathering public support could also be used to exert pressure on legislators to take a broader view of the issue.

Evidence gathering and more carefully planned lobbying efforts can also be applied to the issue of copyright. Prioritizing what is needed and which groups to lobby may be an effective approach. As far as rights holders are concerned, most discussions have been with publishers and representative groups. It is not clear the extent to which such groups are representative of rights holders. Rights holders are not a homogenous group. Much discussion in this area focuses on copyright as an economic right. It may be worth also focusing on authors, and particularly on academic authors who may have different priorities from other types of rights holders, such as photographers. The emphasis in such discussions could be on how to preserve while fully respecting authors' moral rights and not interfering with economic rights. There should also be a focus on the key roles deposit, digitization, and preservation play in opening up access to knowledge, and the cultural and societal benefits that ensue.

The focus should be on identifying benefits for stakeholders or "win-win" situations. Statements of benefits could be supported by case studies, but there is also a need for education on different traditions when talking about rights and how to manage them. There is also a need to engage the beneficiaries of preservation more generally. It is not clear if and how they are being engaged at the moment. As in the case of legal deposit, it is not clear whether the preservation community is talking to the public about the benefits of preservation and what it means to them. Again, illustrative and possible inspiring case studies could be of assistance here. An effective way forward could be to focus on specific initiatives, to achieve smaller wins, as a way of making progress. This could involve working with specific publishers, as is the case at the Royal Library of the Netherlands.

Compelling cases demonstrating the risks to vulnerable analogue material could be compiled and statistical data from rights clearance efforts could be collected and compared to provide documented evidence of the time and resources required to clear rights and show the extent to which rights holders consent to preservation activities. The judgments and outcomes of relevant court cases could be identified, if any exist, to show the impact of the law as interpreted by the courts on preservation of the cultural heritage. These sources of evidence could be used to make the case for changes to the law. It is interesting to note that academic lawyers are becoming interested in preservation of cultural heritage;[39] curators and academics in curatorial fields could work together on carrying out research.

Evidence from rights clearance activities, particularly in the case of Web archiving, could be used in developing risk management approaches to the legal issues in digital preservation. Preservation institutions tend to be legally compliant and take a conservative and responsible approach to their activities. It may be possible in the light of a full understanding of possible legal liabilities and evidence gathered to take an opt-out approach. In the context of Web archiving, this could mean that content is archived and made available until a rights holder objects. Related to this issue is finding efficient and effective ways to identify orphan works and to disseminate information on tools, models, or

---

[39] For example, see Derclaye, E, ed, *Copyright and cultural heritage: preservation and access to works in a digital world.* (Edward Elgar, 2010).

methodologies and to test whether they could be extended to or shared with other institutions.

Cooperative Agreements

Distributed preservation, infrastructure, and architectures are emerging as the predominant model. Such activities need to be governed and implemented in a more certain and supportive legal environment, not just in terms of the agreements, but also the laws governing how content can be managed for preservation purposes. Some central contract considerations that were useful in MetaArchive deliberations, and would likely be important in other digital preservation contract design processes are:

- Who are the parties? Do they have authority to enter into the agreement?

- Is the agreement neutral or slanted toward one party? Will the structure produce simple or complex negotiations and thus require more or less administration and resource allocation?

- Do the parties need to define specific terms that are either unique to the agreement or that need more precise meaning in order to manifest agreement?

- What is the duration of the agreement? How is the duration calculated?

- What happens if one party fails in satisfying its obligations? What is "breach" and how do the parties define it? Any second chances? Can a party "cure" a breach? How and under what timeframe? Should there be an opt-out clause for either party in certain circumstances—and if so, what circumstances would apply?

- What is the subject matter of the agreement? Service, goods, or a combination thereof?

- Is the subject matter intellectual property (copyright, trademark, patent) or the use of intellectual property? How do you define use and who is responsible for misuse? Who owns the intellectual property?

- Will the agreement result in the creation of intellectual property? If so, who owns it or how is ownership allocated? Are institutional or corporate policies involved in the academic or business realm?

- Does the agreement include any technological considerations or limitations? How are access and custodial issues handled if using protected or proprietary information? What about network intrusions and rogue programs or software routines? How will digital rights management (DRM) with technological protection measures (TPMs) be dealt with? Will these be able to be decoded or decrypted for purposes of preserving works? Provisions must be made for this.

- Are existing copyright exceptions protected in the Agreement so that contract law will not override them?

- Does the agreement take into account privacy considerations regarding compiled information or data or have other overarching contract or legal limits on dissemination, use, or access?

- How do the parties assure compliance with the terms? Mediation? Arbitration? Litigation?

- Who is responsible for violations of law that might occur in the contract context? Which jurisdiction will be chosen for litigation purposes, if necessary?

- Is indemnification or waiver of liabilities important? How do the parties shift liability appropriately or nefariously?

- What happens when the contract ends? What about the original subject matter? Are there defined or liquidated damages?

- How can the parties make changes to the terms of the agreement? Ideally changes should be made in writing. Are unilateral changes permitted? If so, under what circumstances? How much notice of changes is required?

- Does the agreement "incorporate by reference" any other documents? What do those documents include? Any specifications or technology requirements or limits?

- Does the agreement coexist with another concurrent agreement or "license" that might have conflicting terms? Which agreement ultimately controls the relationship? Does the license impose limits on the subject matter of the agreement in question?

- Does the agreement create a partnership? Cooperative agreement? Shared or separate ownership of infrastructure? Does the agreement address governance issues? Any conflicts of interest in the agreement?

- What law governs the interpretation and enforcement of the agreement? What, if any, are the international implications of the agreement?

- What if one party cannot meet its responsibilities because of circumstances beyond its control?

This broad spectrum of considerations may seem daunting. However, not all of these considerations arise in all situations. Equally important, under more careful analysis, the considerations themselves are often factual or may already reflect an ongoing set of conversations about informal understandings and practices. In that sense, much of the information for structuring the agreement has probably already been gathered or at least discussed among interested parties and communities. More importantly, the apparent complexity of the above list of considerations may also reveal the vast flexibility for crafting agreements to serve the inevitably unique facts and circumstances of complex relationships. These unique circumstances may occur in an infinite variety of digital preservation strategies and efforts.

One value of formalizing shared understandings is to clarify each participant's perspective on what ought to happen now and in the future. Another value is not surprisingly to identify points of agreement and disagreement. In some ways, disagreement encourages broader thinking and even innovation in approaches to difficult social challenges. A third value arises from the pragmatic recognition that even great relationships end from time to time and managing that separation in advance is often far simpler that managing it later. The fourth value is perhaps the simplest: developing a legal relationship gives interested parties the incentive to identify and describe what they want from the relationship and what it might help them accomplish. These are the rights and responsibilities of a contractual relationship.

Contract law is clearly a means to create and enforce agreements. However, given the scarcity of contract litigation in general, relative to the innumerable contracts in existence, contract law must have a value and purpose beyond the pure possibility of ensuring legal "compliance" by using judicial solutions. In fact, the greatest value of contract law in many situations may derive from applying proven principles to organizing complex undertakings and fostering discussion about principles, perspectives, and needs among those most interested in that undertaking.

Collective Licensing

Preserving and providing access to digital material does not just take place at a national level, but current approaches to managing copyright tend to operate at this level. Copyright laws are territorial by nature and do not provide for cross-border sharing of copied material. Cross-border licensing is an issue that is not only relevant to preservation, but to all aspects of dissemination and use of digital material. The cross-border work that is being done at the European level (as described above) needs to move forward. There is also a precedent for extended collective licensing in the Nordic countries that can provide a model. Extended collective licensing could help address issues of orphan works and cross-border access.

Conclusions

Legislative change—to copyright exceptions, to legal deposit laws and the interaction between copyright and contract law—is required. Alignment between national approaches could be facilitated by international organizations, such as IFLA, UNESCO and WIPO. National libraries and archives, through their international groupings and within their own countries could also lead on lobbying governments and engaging with other stakeholder groups. They could also act as catalysts for the development of shared positions and actions between other members of the preservation community. National groupings such as the Digital Preservation Coalition in the UK and NESTOR in Germany could facilitate dialogue between members of their national communities through dedicated events and also work together to organize international events.

National institutions could also take the take in providing case studies to illustrate the benefits of digitizing orphan works and digital preservation. This work may require funding from research or other bodies and cooperative working with researchers in the field. Existing sources of funding should be identified and funding bodies should also be lobbied to support this work.

In the meantime, preserving institutions may also need to accept more risk in their approaches to ensure that their collections are preserved and made accessible for future generations. It is up to institutions to identify and assess risks and decide for themselves how much risk they wish to accept. However, institutions already taking this approach could share their experience and provide some advice on avoiding pitfalls. This is a sensitive area as prominent institutions could suffer damage to their reputations if they are perceived to be anything other than scrupulous in their legal compliance. On the other hand, the current legal action against the HathiTrust might serve to clarify the applicability of fair use to digital preservation in the US.

The need for simple and practical agreements is crucial. Some general points to consider in agreements are identified in this essay. A further step should be an analysis of existing successful agreements to extract some basic standard terms that could be used, with or without adaptation in cooperative agreements.

Legal alignment in digital preservation is challenging, perhaps more challenging than any other aspect of alignment. It is clear that there are legal barriers to digital preservation, particularly copyright law. In the current legal environment, the work required to obtain the permission to preserve is intensive and cumbersome, creating a real risk that portions of the world's digital heritage will not be preserved.

References

17 USC Sec. 108

Arrangement for depositing electronic publications at the
Koninklijke Bibliotheek:
http://www.kb.nl/dnp/overeenkomst-nuv-kb-en.pdf (last accessed 4-10-2012).

Berne Convention for the Protection of Literary and Artistic Works, Article 9.

Besek, J. et al. "International study on the impact of copyright law in digital preservation: a joint report of the Library of Congress National Digital Information Infrastructure and Preservation Program, the Joint Information Systems Committee, the Open Access to Knowledge (OAK) Law Project and the SURFfoundation," 2008. See: http://www.digitalpreservation.gov/documents/digital_pre

servation_final_report2008.pdf (last accessed 4-16-2012).

Boyle, J. "A copyright black hole swallows our culture," *Financial Times,* September 6, 2009. http://www.ft.com/cms/s/0/6811a9d4-9b0f-11de-a3a1-00144feabdc0.html#axzz1LgCBWo5A (last accessed 4-10-2012).

"Code of practice for the voluntary deposit of non-print publications:" http://www.bl.uk/aboutus/stratpolprog/legaldep/voluntary deposit/ (last accessed 4-10-2012).

"Charter on the Preservation of Digital Heritage," http://portal.unesco.org/en/ev.php-URL_ID=17721&URL_DO=DO_TOPIC&URL_SECTI ON=201.html (last accessed 4-16-2012).

Comité des Sages, "The New Renaissance: Report of the 'Comité des Sages' Reflection Group on Bringing Europe's Cultural Heritage Online" (January 2011), at: http://ec.europa.eu/information_society/activities/digital_l ibraries/doc/refgroup/final_report_cds.pdf (last accessed 4-16-2012).

Commission Recommendation 2006/585/EC of 24 August 2006 on the digitization an online accessibility of cultural content and digital preservation: http://eur-lex.europa.eu/LexUriServ/LexUriServ.do?uri=OJ:L:2006: 236:0028:0030:EN:PDF (last accessed 04-16-2012).

Communication from the Commission to the European Parliament, the Council, the European Economic and Social Committee and the Committee of the Regions i2010: Digital Libraries, Brussels, 30.9.2005 COM (2005) 465 final.

Conference of European National Libraries & Federation of European Publishers. "International declaration on the deposit of electronic publications." CENL & FEP, 2001: http://www.ddb.de/news/epubstat.htm (last accessed 4-16-2012).

Copyright Act (R.S.C., 1985, c. C-42), s. 30.1(1).

Copyright, Patent and Design Act 1988, s. 42.

Derclaye, E, ed, *Copyright and cultural heritage: preservation and access to works in a digital world.* Edward Elgar, 2010.

Directive 2001/29/EC of the European Parliament and of the Council of 22 May 2011 on the harmonization of certain aspects of copyright and related rights in the information society.

Dutch Copyright Act, article 16.

Elferink, M., H. & A. Ringnalda."Digitale Ontsluiting van historische archieven en verweesde werken: een inventarisatie." Utrecht: Universiteit Utrecht, Centrum voor Intellectueel Eigendomsrecht (CIER), WODC July 2008.

European Commission, Proposal for a Directive of the European Parliament and of the Council on certain permitted uses of orphan works, Brussels 24.5.2011, COM (2011) 289 final: http://ec.europa.eu/internal_market/copyright/docs/orphan -works/proposal_en.pdf (last accessed 4-16-2012).

European Digital Libraries initiative, Sector-specific guidelines on Due Diligence Criteria for Orphan Works: Joint Report at: http://ec.europa.eu/information_society/activities/digital_l ibraries/doc/hleg/orphan/guidelines.pdf (last accessed 4-10-2012).

i2010 Digital Libraries Initiative High Level Expert Group on Digital Libraries. "Final report: digital libraries: recommendations and challenges for the future" December 2009: http://ec.europa.eu/information_society/activities/digital_l ibraries/doc/hleg/reports/hlg_final_report09.pdf (last accessed 4-16-2012).

i2010; Digital Libraries High Level Expert group—Copyright Subgroup, Final report on Digital preservation, Orphan Works and Out-of-Print Works at: http://ec.europa.eu/information_society/activities/digital_l ibraries/doc/hleg/reports/copyright/copyright_subgroup_fi nal_report_26508-clean171.pdf (last accessed 4-16-2012).

Kenney, A. et al. *E-Journal Archiving Metes and Bounds: A Survey of the Landscape.* (CLIR, 2006): http://www.clir.org/pubs/abstract/pub138abst.html (last accessed 4-10-2012).

Larivière, J. "Guidelines for legal deposit legislation". (Rev., enl. and updated ed.) Paris: Unesco, 2000: http://archive.ifla.org/VII/s1/gnl/legaldep1.htm (last accessed 4-16-2012).

Memorandum of Understanding on Diligent Search guidelines for Orphan Works at: http://ec.europa.eu/information_society/activities/digital_l ibraries/doc/hleg/orphan/memorandum.pdf (last accessed 4-10-2012).

"Regeling elektronisch depot KB" at: http://www.kb.nl/dnp/overeenkomst-nuv-kb.pdf (last accessed 4-16-2012).

The Section 108 Study Group report at: http://www.section108.gov/docs/Sec108StudyGroupRepo rt.pdf (last accessed 4-10-2012).

"Self-regulated code for offline publications" at: http://www.bl.uk/aboutus/stratpolprog/legaldep/offlinevol untary/offline.html (last accessed 4-10-2012).

Van Gompel, S, & P.B.Hugenholtz, The Copyright conundrum of digitizing large-scale audiovisual archives, and how to solve it, *Popular Communication: The International Journal of Media and Culture,* 8(1 2010), pp. 61-7.

Vetulani, Agnieszka, "The Problem of orphan works in the EU: an overview of legislative solutions and main actions in this field". European Commission, 2008: http://ec.europa.eu/information_society/activities/digital_l ibraries/doc/reports_orphan/report_orphan_v2.pdf (last accessed 4-16-2012).

U.S. Copyright Office. "Report on orphan works." Library of Congress, 2006: http://www.copyright.gov/orphan/orphan-report.pdf (last accessed 4-16-2012).

LEGAL DEPOSIT AND WEB ARCHIVING: ISSUES IN ACQUIRING DIGITAL PUBLICATIONS FOR LONG-TERM PRESERVATION

Adrienne Muir (Loughborough University)

Abstract

Legal deposit obliges publishers to deposit publications with designated stewardship institutions that preserve and to provide limited access to these publications. For the last 20 or so years, governments have been updating legal deposit provisions to take into account developments in digital publishing. UNESCO produced an updated version of its guidelines on legal deposit in 2000, which included a legal framework for national legal deposit schemes. Despite this, there are still differences between national approaches, with some countries adopting comprehensive and/or technology-neutral provisions, expanding regulation on a piecemeal basis or relying on a wholly voluntary approach to deposit. Other countries are currently taking a hybrid approach with formal regulations for some types of material and voluntary or no deposit arrangements for digital material. The crucial area for alignment is the scope of legal deposit as the current situation runs the risk of the development of gaps in coverage of the global digital published output in the long term. The challenges of adapting a mechanism designed for print publishing to the digital environment is discussed. The UNESCO guidelines are used as a framework for discussion of legal deposit provisions. Examples of national approaches to key elements of legal deposit framework are identified, including definitions of digital publications, territoriality issues in online publishing, and other requirements to allow legal deposit institutions to access and preserve material. The legal issues arising from non-statutory approaches to collecting digital publications for long-term preservation are identified.

Introduction

Legal deposit places an obligation on publishers or other relevant parties to deposit publications with specified institutions. While legal deposit may have had its origins in the control of intellectual output, there was also a notion that the intrinsic value of this output makes it worth collecting and keeping for the benefit of society. These days the primary purpose of legal deposit is usually to preserve the national published heritage. The underlying rationale for imposing mandatory obligations is that this is the most effective and efficient way of ensuring material is preserved. There is an assumption that without deposit, much of this heritage will be lost. As voluntary arrangements cannot be enforced, there is a risk of incomplete collections.

Legal deposit has been implemented through various instruments, including parliamentary acts or laws; cabinet decrees and orders; ministerial regulations and directives; government departmental orders; regulations, circulars, rules, and policy statements; library regulations and statutes; and municipal ordinances (Jasion, 1991, p. 7). Extending legal deposit to digital publications has presented many challenges for the framing of legislation. The issue of current access to legal deposit collections can be a source of concern to rights holders, which is magnified in the digital environment given the potential ease with which digital information can be replicated and disseminated.

International organizations have provided guidelines for countries planning to amend or introduce legal deposit legislation. The Conference of Directors of National Libraries (1996) issued a document on the legal deposit of electronic publications. Its target audience was countries thinking of preparing a case for introducing legislation. Later, the Council of Europe and EBLIDA (1999) produced guidelines on library legislation and policy in Europe that included legal deposit. These guidelines were based on the UNESCO legal deposit guidelines of 1981 (Lunn, 1981), which were superseded by a revised and updated edition (Larivière, 2000). The new guidelines include a separate chapter for electronic publications and a suggested legal framework for legal deposit.

This paper focuses on legal arrangements and not on how the arrangements are implemented in practice. However, the practicalities of dealing with digital material can have an impact on the framing of legal provisions. In some jurisdictions, legislation may be updated to take new developments into account as they emerge or are better understood. This has been the case for example in some European countries, where provisions for digital deposit have been extended over time from offline to online publications. Legislation may be drafted to be technology neutral so that activities in theory can be more easily extended over time, as has been the case in Norway and South Africa. The UK approach has been to introduce enabling legislation with the intention of expanding the scope of legal deposit to different categories of material over time through further regulation.

The deposit of digital publications raises other legal issues, including copyright and liability for unlawful content. This paper focuses on how copyright issues are dealt with in the legal deposit context where appropriate copyright exceptions for preservation do not already exist. The paper also touches on the copyright issues arising from acquisition and access provision in the legal deposit context.

Traditional publishing provides a degree of quality control that is not always present in Internet publishing. Whilst problems of, for example, copyright infringement, plagiarism, defamation, obscenity, and encouragement of terrorism may arise in traditionally published material, these issues are likely to be more acute on the Internet as publishing in this medium often takes place without professional editorial control. If legal deposit institutions (or any other collecting body) use a Web-harvesting approach to collecting material, they may well inadvertently sweep up and provide access to potentially unlawful material. Whilst legal deposit institutions may only provide access to material collected in this manner within their own premises, wider access provisions may expose institutions to liability in other legal jurisdictions with different rules. The conflicting obligations on publishers, for example the contractual obligations they have with third-party content or software providers and the obligation to deposit, also have to be resolved.

Hybrid deposit systems consist of a mix of legal deposit and contractual arrangements between parties. The intention can be to use voluntary schemes as a stop-gap measure until legislation can be passed, as a means of understanding the practical issues to inform the framing of legal issues and/or to gauge compliance levels to inform a decision on whether a more formal regulatory approach is required. Alternatively, voluntary arrangements may work better for certain types of material than others. In the Netherlands all deposit of print and non-print material is carried out on a voluntary contractual basis between the national depository and publishers and there does not appear to be a need for statutory enforcement. However, this is not the case in all jurisdictions. In the context of film and audiovisual content, the results of a 2010 survey carried out by IFLA suggested that there is a link between the lack of legal obligation (or more specifically penalty) and deposit.[1]

A Basic Framework for Legal Deposit of Digital Publications

Legal deposit laws differ from country to country, but they have some features in common.

- Nature of material to be deposited;
- Nature of the deposit mechanism, including rights and responsibilities of depositories and publishers, including any sanctions for non-compliance; and
- Designated depositories entitled to legal deposit copies.

Regulations do not always specify the purpose of legal deposit or specify access arrangements. Whilst a case could be made for the need for legal deposit arrangements in all countries, legal deposit exists within an existing legal framework, which differs between jurisdictions. Where such frameworks do not adequately support publishers and depositories, it may be necessary to provide special arrangements to allow publishers to deposit and deposit institutions to collect and preserve digital publications.

One of the requirements for legal deposit identified by Jasion is exhaustiveness (1991, p. 3). Exhaustiveness implies all material, regardless of quality or format, should be deposited. Jasion also included preservation and access in his requirements for legal deposit. While legal deposit material is accessible, this access is usually restricted in some way. Legal deposit libraries are often styled "last resort;" users usually must have a research need that cannot be fulfilled elsewhere and legal deposit collections should not have a negative impact on the economic interests of the publishing industry. The following discussion addresses the three key requirements of scope of legal deposit, whether material is deposited or collected through Web archiving, preservation, or access arrangements.

Scope and Coverage

Given the long-term mandate of legal depositories and the fact that national collections are also of interest to users in other

---

[1] See Howard Besser, "Why is legal deposit important" at:
http://besser.tsoa.nyu.edu/howard/Talks/legal-deposit.pdf (last accessed 05-16-2012).

countries, a lack of alignment between national frameworks would result in gaps in collections that, over time, would have an international impact. This issue is especially acute for countries with a sizeable digital publishing output. Printed publications are really the only common factor between national frameworks. Whilst analogue sound recordings and audiovisual material are included in some legal regimes, they are excluded from others, for example the UK legislation specifically excludes such material. Some frameworks include digital publications of all kinds, including software in the case of France, but others have only partial or no provisions for digital publications.

The UNESCO guidelines recommend that digital publications should be included in legal deposit, no matter what practical problems there are, anticipating that these problems will be resolved over time. If the rationale for legal deposit is that it is the most effective way of achieving the aim of preserving national published output, then digital publications of all kinds should be included in the framework. What depositories choose to collect is another matter and may be based on practical arrangements with publishers. The scope of deposit would be then be widened incrementally, with "easier" categories of material, such as offline publications or freely available Web material being prioritized. There is no clear rationale for excluding commercial online publications other than to reduce the burden of deposit on publishers as commercially available print publications are not excluded.[2] The UNESCO guidelines recommend that dynamic, or continuously updated, publications should be deposited, perhaps on a snapshot basis. For some types of dynamic material, thought would have to be given as to whether all real-time information services should be considered part of the published heritage. The UNESCO guidelines were drafted before the explosion in social networking services (SNS) and associated user-generated content. They do refer to material that, whilst publicly available, may not be considered "published" in the conventional sense, for example listservs and newsgroups. Taking a selective and subjective approach to the scope of deposit would go against the underlying rationale and increase the risk of material potentially useful for future scholars being lost. This is another area that may require

---

[2] See "Government response to the public consultation on the draft regulations and guidance for non-print legal deposit" at:
http://www.culture.gov.uk/publications/8029.aspx (last accessed 03-06-2012).

coordination between deposit institutions and other collecting institutions, such as national archives.

Legal deposit legislation may include technology neutral definitions of the material to be collected. For example Norwegian law refers to "mediums" (Act 1989, s. 3), which are a means of storing information, and "documents," which are copies of a medium. Documents made available to the public are to be deposited. South Africa's Legal Deposit Act 1997 takes a similar approach. In France "every sign, signal, writing, image, sound or messages of every kind communicated to the public by electronic channels" (Loi 2006, art. L131-1-L133-1) is included. A draft regulation for the legal deposit of non-print publications in the UK refers to off-line and online publications (Draft 2001, s. 2), which seems at first glance to be technology neutral. However, the definition of online publications specifies the Internet as the only publishing medium, whereas the definition of off-line publications only specifies CD or DVD technologies as examples. The potential advantage of not listing specific types of publications in the legislation is that depositories can adjust their collecting activities over time to accommodate changes in publishing and technology, rather than having to periodically add new types of digital publishing to those listed in the legislation.

The question of how to define the national digital published output and therefore the territorial scope of legal deposit is complex. The definition of "publication" often involves making available to the public. However, digital publications might potentially be available to anyone in any country. The publishing process may involve different entities located in different countries and it may be difficult to work out which country material originated from. The UNESCO guidelines acknowledge this issue (Larivière, p. 18) and refer to Mackenzie Owen and Van De Walle's (1996) recommendations that the following criteria can be used to identify the nationality of a digital publication:

> geographic location given in the publication or its accompanying metadata; the location of the publishing organization if it can be established; the domicile of the first author; the author's nationality; or the primary location of the publication on the network (Owen and van de Walle, p. 22).

These criteria were recommended in order of significance. References to the domicile or nationality of authors may not be relevant if their published output is not made available in the country. It may not be possible to legally enforce legal deposit for the nationality criterion if a national resides and publishes in another jurisdiction. Equally, the location of a publication on a network may not be relevant if the publication has no other obvious connection with a country. These issues suggest a need for some alignment between national selection criteria to ensure material is collected somewhere.

More recent approaches to addressing territoriality include the UK's Legal Deposit Advisory Panel (LDAP), which recommended two criteria relating to territoriality: publishers should be based in the UK or have a UK address (physical or electronic) *and* publications should be lawfully published or made available by or on behalf of that publisher from a UK address. However, the draft Legal Deposit Libraries (Non-print publications) Regulations 2011 that were produced did not reproduce this recommendation, referring instead to material published in the UK by a person that "publishes for an indefinite period using a fixed establishment in the United Kingdom" (s. 36). Given that country top-level domain codes do not represent the entire national output, there are challenges for implementing deposit of material published on the Internet. Definitions referring to addresses may be the only way to address territoriality through statutory means.

Implementation is more of a practical issue than a legal one. Depositors and depositories need to work out processes and procedures together. Depositories need to put appropriate technical architectures in place to receive, store, and provide access to deposited material.

Deposit or Collection Mechanisms

Legal deposit regulations usually specify how publications are to be deposited. Increasingly legal depositories are collecting digital content through automated bulk harvesting and/or more selected crawls. Unless this activity is specifically permitted through legal deposit arrangements, institutions wishing to make copies of material, preserve it, and make it accessible have to do so through agreements with rights holders. Obtaining permissions can be a time consuming process as, for example, the UK Web Archiving Consortium's experience has shown. In the absence of legal provision for such activity, there is the question of how cautious the approach should be. Strictly speaking, archiving the Web infringes copyright unless there are relevant exceptions, but if it is being done for archival purposes should more of a risk be taken for publicly available Web sites? Should it be a case of publishers opting out rather than opting in?

Deposit institutions involved in bulk harvesting of freely available material will inevitably collect material that is unlawful in some way. The UNESCO Guidelines addressed the issue of material that is "forbidden." The examples given in the guidelines include pornographic and hate material. The guidelines recommend that even though national laws prevent the creation and distribution of such material, where it exists, it should be subject to legal deposit (Larivière, 2000, p.15). The rationale for this is that the value of the historical record may be compromised if material is excluded under earlier, less tolerant standards. So the material should be deposited but access should comply with legal requirements. Unless provisions already exist to exempt legal deposit institutions from prohibitions on possessing illegal material, legal deposit laws would need to provide such protections. It may be that this can only be implemented for some categories of unlawful content. It may be impossible to justify preserving child pornography, for example.

It may also be necessary to deposit supporting materials to allow depositories to access and preserve publications. The UK Legal Deposit Libraries Act 2003 (s. 6(2)(b)) contains a provision that any future regulations for deposit of non-print publications may require deposit of computer programs, "information necessary in order to access the work," manuals and "other material that accompanies the work and is made available to the public."[3] The Canadian Legal Deposit of Publication Regulations[4] (s. 2) make similar provisions, but are more specific in some respects. For example, the Canadian regulations specify that depositors

> (i) provide a copy of software specifically created by the publisher that is necessary to access the publication,

---

[3] This paper cites several sections of the Legal Deposit Libraries Act 2003 enacted in the UK.
[4] The Legal Deposit of Publications Regulations enacted in Canada in 2006 are available here: http://laws.justice.gc.ca/eng/regulations/SOR-2006-337/page-1.html (last accessed 03-07-2012).

(ii) provide a copy of technical or other information necessary to access the publication, including a copy of manuals that accompany the publication, and

(iii) provide any available descriptive data about the publication including its title, creator, language, date of publication, format, subject and copyright information

If legal deposit institutions do provide access to harvested content, legal deposit regulations may need to include provisions on exemption from liability for publishers and depositories. For example the UK's Legal Deposit Libraries Act 2003, s. 9 provides that compliance with legal deposit does not breach any contracts or infringe various intellectual property rights. The legislation also exempts both publishers and libraries from liability for defamation in line with current UK libel law. These provisions do not address the full range of unlawful materials that are likely to be collected, but there is scope to extend these provisions.

Preservation

Legal deposit regulations should make it clear that depositories will have to take actions to preserve digital materials. As far as legal deposit is concerned, if national copyright law does not already include appropriate exceptions for preservation copying by prescribed libraries and archives, legal deposit legislation should contain such provisions. The UK Legal Deposit Libraries Act 2003 provides that future regulations could make provision for copying (s. 7(2)(b)) or adapting "relevant material comprising or containing a computer program or database" (s. 7(2)(c)) and such actions will not infringe copyright (s. 8(1)(2)) or database rights (s. 8(2)). Copying of Internet material would not infringe copyright as long as it was done according legal deposit provisions (s. 8(1)(1)).

Access to some digital publications is controlled through the use of technological protection measures (TPMs), for example IDs and passwords. Deposit institutions will require access to the publications in order to preserve them, and national copyright laws may forbid circumvention of TPMs. If this is the case, there will need to be an exemption for legal deposit institutions to allow them to store and preserve publications. The Canadian Legal Deposit of Publication Regulations (s. 2) require that depositors carry out certain actions on their content before depositing

(a) before providing a copy of the publication to the Librarian and Archivist,
> (i) decrypt encrypted data contained in the publication, and
> (ii) remove or disable security systems or devices that are designed to restrict or limit access to the publication

Legal depositories need to access digital material to store and preserve it. The provision of access to deposited publications to users is another issue.

Access Arrangements

Legal deposit regulations usually refer to restricted access arrangements. This is fair given the potential for interfering with the commercial exploitation of intellectual property rights. Whilst the aim of legal deposit is to preserve the national intellectual heritage, legal deposit collections are not only used by scholars residing in a particular country. In addition, legal deposit obligations might be less onerous for large international publishers to deposit their entire output one or two deposit institutions for preservation purposes. There are examples of this in practice in scholarly publishing, including the e-depot at the Koninklijke Bibliotheek (KB) in the Netherlands.[5] The combination of digital collections and information and communications technologies could facilitate improved access to legal deposit collections. There have been cooperative efforts to open up access to digital collections across national borders, including the Europeana initiative.[6] Whilst this aspect of international alignment is desirable in the long-term, it may be politically unacceptable to have single country deposit couple with multiple country access at least in the short term. International access to copyright deposited publications would also be a cause of concern to publishers and other rights holders.

Legal deposit is concerned with published material. Whilst there is always the possibility of inadvertent collection of information that could be considered personal data, bulk harvesting

---

[5] See the KB e-depot: http://www.kb.nl/dnp/e-depot/operational/suppliers/national_suppliers-en.html (last accessed 03-12-2012).
[6] See the Europeana Web site at: http://www.europeana.eu/portal/ (last accessed 03-07-2012).

will collect personal data that is already publicly available. However, legal deposit institutions should process such data in accordance with national data protection laws.

Voluntary Arrangements

The UNESCO guidelines advise against voluntary deposit arrangements, recommending that deposit should be a statutory obligation. In 2001, the Conference of European National Libraries (CENL) and the Federation of European Publishers (FEP) made a declaration advocating the immediate implementation of voluntary schemes (Conference of European National Libraries & Federation of European Publishers 2001). This was in recognition that it takes time to update legal deposit arrangements. The declaration included a model voluntary code for local adaptation. The model code was based on the then UK scheme[7] and included both offline and online digital publications. Voluntary agreements will be made within broader regulatory frameworks, but model codes are useful for identifying different elements that should be covered in agreements. Voluntary agreements can also be more flexible than statutory provisions, so issues such as access provision can potentially be tailored to different categories of material and the needs for different types of publishers if desired.

The current UK self-regulated code for offline publications has been endorsed by all the libraries benefitting from UK legal deposit.[8] The elements of the code include the scope of the arrangement, or the publications to be deposited; exclusions from deposit; the number of copies to be deposited; access and use arrangements; and copying for preservation purposes. The original 1999 agreement between the KB and the Dutch Publishers Association[9] covers both offline and online digital publications and addresses the same issues as the UK Code. The Dutch agreement provides more detail on how the KB will store and provide access

---

[7] See "Code of practice for the voluntary deposit of non-print publications" at:
http://www.bl.uk/aboutus/stratpolprog/legaldep/voluntarydeposit/ (last accessed 03-07-2012).

[8] See "Self-regulated code for the voluntary deposit of microform and offline (hand held) electronic publications" at:
http://www.bl.uk/aboutus/stratpolprog/legaldep/offlinevoluntary/offline.html (last accessed 03-07-2012).

[9] See "Arrangement for depositing electronic publications at the Deposit of Netherlands Publications in the Koninklijke Bibliotheek" at:
http://www.kb.nl/dnp/overeenkomst-nuv-kb-en.pdf (last accessed 03-07-2012).

to deposited publications and warranties against third-party claims against the publications.

Legal deposit or voluntary deposit arrangements have always functioned alongside the efforts of individual libraries to preserve and provide access to collections for the benefit of their own user communities. Much progress has been made in cooperative digital preservation in recent years. The legal issues of these, sometimes, international, voluntary arrangements between libraries and rights holders are discussed elsewhere in this volume. The existence of such arrangements does not remove the need for legal deposit but there is much scope for coordination between initiatives. This can be seen, for example in Web archiving initiatives where different organizations work together on coordinating selection of and responsibility for collecting material and developing technological infrastructure. There is also scope to learn from each other on developing appropriate voluntary legal agreements.

Conclusions

The scope of legal deposit provisions differs between different countries. This may have a negative impact on future generations' access to the world's intellectual heritage, as there will be gaps in global coverage. This issue is particularly important for countries with growing digital publishing outputs. Whilst voluntary schemes may work well in certain national contexts, there is no clear rationale from a long-term perspective for a selective approach to deposit. It does, however, seem reasonable to balance the interests of rights holders and society. There is a need to further explore the concerns of rights holders. This does not just mean the content industries, but also the creators and other rights-holder groups. It is not clear whether the public in general is aware of the potential gap in digital cultural output or what it thinks about this. Then there are the policy makers and the legislators in the middle.

This suggests a need to identify the potential impact of not collecting material under legal deposit and the benefits of doing so. Such use cases would provide a tool for informing stakeholders and allaying any concerns. Legal deposit regulation should allow stewardship organizations to carry out necessary activities to collect and preserve material for posterity, whilst avoiding placing an undue burden on rights holders or compromising their ability to exploit their rights. Legal deposit arrangements should incorporate or operate alongside other measures to protect fundamental rights such as privacy, freedom of expression, and reputation and address liability for depositors and depositories in these areas. In terms of alignment, there are examples of approaches to extending legal deposit to digital material that can be adapted for local jurisdictions. European countries, such as Norway, have comprehensive legislation. Other countries, such as France, Germany, or Canada have expanded provisions in stages over time. The more challenging aspect of alignment is in lobbying at national and international levels and changing attitudes of stakeholders. Gathering evidence demonstrating impact, whether positive or negative, is not an easy task. It is necessary if the case for digital legal deposit is to be made in an environment where policy makers are focused on supporting digital economies and the content industries.

References

Act No. 32 of 9 June 1989 relating to the legal deposit of generally available documents (Norway).

Code of practice for the voluntary deposit of non-print publications (2000). Retrieved March 12, 2012, from http://www.bl.uk/aboutus/stratpolprog/legaldep/voluntary deposit/

Conference of Directors of National Libraries (1996). *The legal deposit of electronic publications*. Retrieved March 31, 2011, from http://www.unesco.org/webworld/memory/legaldep.htm

Conference of European National Libraries & Federation of European Publishers (2001). *International declaration on the deposit of electronic publications*. Retrieved March 31, 2011, from http://www.ddb.de/news/epubstat.htm

Council of Europe & EBLIDA (1999). *Guidelines on library legislation and policy in Europe*. Retrieved March 31, 2011, from http://www.coe.int/T/E/Cultural_Co-operation/Culture/Resources/Texts/DECS_CULT_POL_BOOK(99)14_EN.pdf?L=EN

Europeana (2012). *Explore Europe's cultural colletions*. Retrieved March 12, 2012, from http://www.europeana.eu/portal/

Jasion, J.T. (1991). *The international guide to legal deposit*.

Aldershot: Ashgate.

Koninklijke Biliotheek (2012) *Information for international publishers*. Retrieved March 12, 2012, from http://www.kb.nl/dnp/e-depot/operational/suppliers/national_suppliers-en.html

Larivière, J. (2000). *Guidelines for legal deposit legislation.* (Rev., enl. and updated ed.) Paris: UNESCO.

Legal Deposit Libraries Act 2003 (UK).

Legal Deposit Libraries (Non-print Publications) Regulations 2011 [Draft] (UK).

Legal Deposit of Publication Regulations SOR-2006-337 (Canada).

Legal Deposit Act 1997 (South Africa).

Loi n°2006-961 du 1 août 2006 relative au droit d'auteur et aux droits voisins dans la société de l'information (1) NOR: MCCX0300082L. Titre IV. Le dépot légal. Arts L131-1-L133-1 (France).

Lunn, J. (1981). *Guidelines for legal deposit legislation.* Paris: UNESCO.

Mackenzie Owen, J.S. & J. van de Walle (1996). *Deposit collections of electronic publications.* EUR 16910 EN. Luxembourg: Office for Official Publications of the European Communities.

Nederlands Uitgeversverbond and Koninklijke Bibliotheek (1999). *Arrangement for depositing electronic publications at the Deposit of Netherlands Publications in the Koninklijke Bibliotheek*, Retrieved March 12, 2012, from http://www.kb.nl/dnp/overeenkomst-nuv-kb-en.pdf

Self-regulated code for the voluntary deposit of microform and offline (hand held) electronic publications (2010). Retrieved March 12, 2012, from http://www.bl.uk/aboutus/stratpolprog/legaldep/offlinevoluntary/offline.html

ORGANIZATIONAL ALIGNMENT

Inge Angevaare (Netherlands Coalition for Digital Preservation)
Michelle Gallinger (Library of Congress)
Martha Anderson (Library of Congress)
David Giaretta (Alliance for Permanent Access)
Martin Halbert (University of North Texas)

Abstract

Digital preservation is not just a technical issue: there are also many organizational implications that must be addressed. This essay first identifies requirements that distinguish successful from unsuccessful modes of organizing digital preservation and long-term access, then presents a series of case studies that examine examples of addressing those requirements. These case studies all represent cooperative or collaborative approaches, in keeping with current research that demonstrates that institutions must share the financial and organizational burden of digital preservation in order to make it cost-effective. The case studies are drawn both from Europe and the United States, and include both single repository solutions and distributed preservation networks. A special role is played by so-called "enabling institutions"—national or regional initiatives established to raise awareness of the issues and promote cooperation in research and development. The essay concludes by considering possible areas for community alignment and next steps.

Introduction

The challenge of preserving digital objects is as much an organizational issue as it is a technical one. Both the possibilities and the special requirements of digital objects have their impact not just on storage systems, but on entire organizations, as was clearly described in the Open Archival Information System (OAIS) model.[1] Moreover, the emergence and explosive growth of the

---

[1] (ISO) Reference Model for an Open Archival Information System (OAIS). "An OAIS is an archive, consisting of an organization of people and systems, that has accepted the responsibility to preserve information and make it available for a Designated Community. It meets a set of such responsibilities as defined in this document, and this allows an OAIS archive to be distinguished from other uses of the term 'archive.' ... The information being maintained has been deemed to need Long Term Preservation, even if the OAIS itself is not permanent. Long Term is long enough to be concerned with the impacts of changing technologies, including

Internet have fundamentally changed the environment in which memory institutions operate.

Laura Campbell of the US Library of Congress has summarized some of the major changes between the analog information space and the digital information space as follows:[2]

Then (Analog)	v.	Now (Digital)
Atoms	v.	Bits
High level of curation	v.	Bulk download
Ownership	v.	Shared access
Consumers	v.	Discoverers
Watching	v.	Creating
Institutional identity	v.	Loose collaboration
Push	v.	Pull
Systematic planning	v.	Fluid cooperation
Closed platforms	v.	Open platforms
Expert vetting	v.	Cognitive surplus

Figure 1. Differences between the analog information space and the digital information space (Laura Campbell, 2011).

This is to say, digital information is capable of flowing freely across boundaries between institutions, sectors, and countries. Today's users have come to expect to access the information they need 24/7 and wherever they find themselves, preferably on platforms that bring the content together from any number of institutions. Moreover, individuals have become co-creators of digital information at a large scale, thereby disrupting existing chains of custody and existing preservation regimes.

All of this means that to secure access to our digital heritage in the long term, new ways of organizing the work are needed at a scale never seen before and which, indeed, stretches the boundaries of imagination. Organizational alignment strategies are needed on two related levels—first, to organize our collections and our workflows according to common standards to facilitate long-term

---

support for new media and data formats, or with a changing user community. Long Term may extend indefinitely."
http://public.ccsds.org/publications/RefModel.aspx (last accessed 04-10-2012).

[2] Laura Campbell, "Exploring what we can do together: strategic alignments for international collaboration," Keynote at the ANADP Conference, May 2011. Slides at http://www.educopia.org/sites/default/files/keynote1_campbell.pdf (last accessed 04-10-2012).

curation and preservation, and second, to optimize our work for collaboration and provide organizational models for coordinating our efforts to ensure long-term access.

Some institutions and sectors are adapting more quickly to the new situation than others. Scientific communities with a strong dependency on longitudinal data (e.g., climate data, sociology) have been early adopters of the new technology and have numbered among the first to develop long-term preservation systems and work processes in tune with the digital reality. In other sectors, the uptake has been a lot slower and organizational principles based on the analog world still prevail.

This essay first identifies requirements that distinguish successful from unsuccessful modes of organizing digital preservation and long-term access, then presents a series of case studies that examine examples of addressing those requirements. It concludes by considering possible areas for community alignment and next steps. In keeping with the theme of the volume, this essay focuses on organizational cooperation and collaboration between institutions rather than on internal organizational issues.

Digital Preservation Requirements

The authors of this essay have identified the following six characteristics as requirements for successful digital preservation endeavors:

1. Digital preservation requires long-term commitment;

2. Digital preservation is most cost-efficient at scale;

3. Digital preservation requires effective interaction between producers, digital archives, and users;

4. Digital preservation benefits from the exploitation of commonalities rather than a focus on uniqueness;

5. Digital preservation initiatives must make a large enough impact right now to make the case to funders and society at large for sustaining these efforts;

6. Digital preservation requires a division of labor from a digital perspective.

Each of these characteristics is defined and reviewed below to determine the role it plays in successful digital preservation activities. These characteristics are then applied to evaluate a series of organizational case studies.

1. Digital preservation requires long-term commitment

This is a key factor in organizing digital preservation that sets it firmly apart from other digital developments such as Wikipedia, crowdsourcing, etc., which are largely based on spontaneous groupings of people and organizations. As valuable as these movements are in *producing* content and/or metadata, they do not have the robustness to secure the type of continuous lifecycle management that digital objects require.[3] Any disruptions of such lifecycle management can lead to irreparable loss of data and must be avoided. In principle, long-standing institutions such as national libraries, national archives, and institutional repositories with an express mandate for long-term preservation are better positioned to provide long-term preservation—but even those institutions are not risk-free. It is therefore important that one think and act in terms of a *chain of preservation* (also known as *a chain of custody*) in which each custodial organization plans for its own demise and succession planning is a key effort.

2. Digital preservation is most cost-efficient at scale

Preserving and providing access to digital objects in the long term is an activity that involves a robust infrastructure that is run by knowledgeable staff members who are continually educated in response to technological progress. Few organizations have the means to support such an infrastructure by themselves. Especially smaller, underfunded institutions are vulnerable in this sense. Forging alliances with other institutions is a means to reach the economies of scale that make digital preservation more cost-efficient.[4]

3. Digital preservation requires effective interaction between producers, archives, and users

As noted above, digital objects require active management throughout their lifecycle and that lifecycle starts at the production stage, where many decisions are made that affect a digital object's long-term prospects. The Dutch national digital preservation

---

[3] See, e.g., the DCC lifecycle model at http://www.dcc.ac.uk/resources/curation-lifecycle-model (last accessed 04-24-2012).

[4] For an inventory of the economic issues surrounding digital preservation and a summary of recent research, see *Sustaining Economics for a Digital Planet: Ensuring Long-term Access to Digital Information*, Final Report of the Blue Ribbon Task Force on Sustainable Digital Preservation and Access, February 2010, http://brtf.sdsc.edu/ (last accessed 04-24-2012).

survey,[5] among others, concluded that lack of alignment between producers of digital information and the archives that might preserve them is one of the major reasons for digital information being lost. Once the so-called *chain of preservation* is broken, it either cannot be repaired or repair can only occur at great expense. Therefore, digital preservation initiatives must seek to bridge the gap between producers and archives. The OAIS model itself has described the need for interaction between the digital archive and users, the *designated community*.[6]

It must be noted here that effective interaction between producers and archives cannot always be achieved. Large quantities of information that are created and uploaded to the Internet by private individuals still elude a structured work flow between creator and archive.

4. Digital preservation requires exploitation of commonalities rather than a focus on uniqueness

This requirement is related to the one about scale, but it goes a level deeper than issues of economy. The digital information space is an interconnected information space where smooth interaction between collections is instrumental in securing access for many users all over the world. Some examples include the standardization of file formats and interaction protocols and the level of detail in required metadata schemas. Each domain that joins the digital community has a tendency to believe that its requirements are special, more challenging, or even unique, making it difficult to see digital content commonalties that cut across digital content wherever it occurs.

5. Digital preservation initiatives must make a large enough impact in the present to make the case for digital preservation vis-à-vis funders and society at large

The report of the Blue Ribbon Task Force (2010) describes in detail how difficult it is to attract funding for digital preservation, chiefly because the benefits are long-term and the direct relationship between investment and benefit is not clear (the so-

---

[5] NCDD (Netherlands Coalition for Digital Preservation), *A Future for our Digital Memory: Permanent access to information in the Netherlands*, English summary, http://www.ncdd.nl/en/documents/Englishsummary_000.pdf (last accessed 04-24-2012).

[6] For more in-depth analysis of the role of the designated community in the OAIS model, see, a.o., David Giaretta, *Advanced Digital Preservation*, Springer 2011, chapters 1-3.

called *free rider problem*). Yet, it is evident that in order to secure funding, the digital preservation community must develop convincing arguments and find the words to make the case for digital preservation. As long-term benefits hardly ever convince politicians and other power-holders, more direct benefits must be shown and the argument must be made by a large enough group of stakeholders to make their voices heard.

6. Digital preservation requires a division of labor from a digital perspective

Practices developed for the long-term management of analog content need to be adjusted to adapt to digital content. In the analog era, information was managed and often owned locally. The digital era has opened up new possibilities to provide access to objects stored and/or preserved elsewhere. In addition, dividing lines between domains and sectors are blurring and born-digital categories of information have emerged that have not yet been incorporated into memory institutions' collection profiles. Roles and responsibilities with regard to these types of content have yet to be defined.

Reviewing all the requirements listed above, it is reasonable to conclude that there are strong reasons for seeking cooperation and collaboration in digital preservation, but collaboration between whom, at what level, and under what conditions?

Types of Cooperation and Collaboration in Digital Preservation

Cooperative efforts in digital preservation come in many shapes and sizes. As described in *Beyond the Silos of the LAMs* (Zorich, Waibel, and Erway, 2008) actual collaboration does not come about easily, and in quite a few countries *enabling* organizations have been established to do advocacy work, promote sharing of knowledge, and, more generally, bring different parties around one table to discuss possibilities for cooperation. Typically, these enabling organizations represent a gradual approach to cooperation and collaboration. They include the National Digital Information Infrastructure and Preservation Program (NDIIPP, US), the Digital Preservation Coalition (DPC, UK and Ireland), the Netherlands Coalition for Digital Preservation (NCDD, Netherlands), nestor (Germany), the Alliance for Permanent Access (APA, Europe), the International Internet Preservation Consortium (IIPC, worldwide), the Open Planets Foundation

(OPF, Europe), and PrestoCentre (Europe, audiovisual). All of these organizations will be described in more detail below.

Enabling organizations cannot themselves embody all of the requirements listed above, as they are not legal entities that are responsible for preserving digital collections. However, they can and do encourage the projects and partnerships they facilitate to address these requirements as grounded in community standards and practice.

Cooperation in projects or within enabling organizations evolves into *collaboration* when partners actually start sharing the burden of digital preservation by taking custody of third parties' digital collections.

Case Studies

This section takes a closer look at a few of the organizations mentioned in the previous section. The case studies include two enabling organizations, NDIIPP and APA, as well as several national and international preservation organizations that include OPF, PrestoCentre, LOCKSS, MetaArchive, Chronopolis, and DuraCloud. The coverage is not intended to be exhaustive but illustrative.

NDIIPP

Since 2000, the US National Digital Information Infrastructure and Preservation Program (NDIIPP) has established, strengthened and expanded a network of digital preservation partners. The charter for NDIIPP called for collaboration between private and public organizations.[7] The results include practical experience in defining roles and responsibilities and building trust across a distributed preservation network. By successfully leveraging the strengths of a variety of partners, the network has proven flexible in the face of technological unpredictability, economic downturn, and the exponential growth of digital material. More than sixty sponsored projects demonstrated the value of collaboration around common work and values. The 2010 founding of a more structured network, the National Digital Stewardship Alliance (NDSA), grew out of this collective experience and out of the desire for program-based, long-term collaboration.

The NDIIPP Program's strategy of collaboration led to significant outcomes for the six requirements for digital

---

[7] Public Law 106-554 2001, Consolidated Appropriations Act.

preservation stated in this chapter. To sustain commitment to digital preservation, the NDIPP program moved from sponsoring special projects to founding and supporting an ongoing national alliance of partners to collect, preserve, and make available significant digital content for current and future generations. The shift from special project to ongoing program has also been evident in many of the institutions within the collaborative network. The NDIIPP-sponsored projects fostered partners' long-term commitment to digital preservation by demonstrating concrete examples of the value of preserving digital materials to stakeholders. In addition to catalyzing a national commitment to digital preservation, NDIIPP leverages lessons learned through the partners to support preservation activities within the Library of Congress's traditional preservation units via development of guidelines, policy, software, tools, assistance with content acquisition, and educational activities.

A major tenet of NDIIPP is that collaboration is needed to achieve digital preservation results at scale. This approach leverages the wide variety of experience and resources that institutions have to offer. Sharing knowledge and services, such as storage and data management tools, amongst institutions allows the partners to maximize local resources while contributing to the digital preservation community. NDIIPP has sponsored innovation projects, investing in tools, research, standards, and other developments for the benefit of the partner network.

The heterogeneity of the collaborative network is experienced as an asset; it provides resilience in the face of changing technical, policy, and economic environments. The Program has served to catalyze interactions between producers, consumers, archivists, and curators of diverse digital information. In some cases, working directly with the Library of Congress, communities have been able to tackle issues that have challenged the individual institutions. One example is the Preserving Creative America initiative to support the preservation of a wide range of works created by photographers, and music and motion picture producers.[8] Diverse business enterprises were able to find common ground on metadata, tools, and outreach to creators.

The Program has also been able to encourage stakeholders across diverse domains to work together, even though they are confronted by unique content, business, and technology challenges. Early in the Program, common concerns and issues were identified

---

[8] See the press release from the Library of Congress for additional information: http://www.loc.gov/today/pr/2007/07-156.html (last accessed 07-12-2012).

including rights management, technical environments, and economic sustainability. To this day, storage has been an area of common interest. The annual Designing Storage Architectures for Digital Preservation meeting[9] provides opportunities for the commercial storage community and the preservation community to discuss their needs and activities. Together they address key data storage issues, including: data integrity, compression, de-duplication practices, processing and analytics of large data sets, format and technical migration, and more. Across time each community has worked on appropriate standards and improved practices. This exchange exemplifies the importance of consistent communication between different groups over time.

A major result of the NDIIPP Program has been to clarify roles in order to successfully distribute digital preservation tasks throughout the network.[10] The collaborative approach recognizes that each institution brings special abilities and expertise to the network.

There are four categories of roles in the network: *Committed Content Custodians* are institutions with a stewardship mission; *Communities of Practice* include standards, policy, and guidelines working groups; *Services* include tools developers, infrastructure, legal, or other business service providers; *Capacity Building* includes educational and funding institutions. A single institution can serve in one or more of these roles depending upon resources and expertise. Not every institution is going to be good at every stage of the digital preservation lifecycle, but by collaborating, we ensure that all stages can be adequately handled

The NDIIPP partner network has demonstrated the value of digital preservation for a number of years. Evidence of the impact can be seen in the dissemination of US public policies on digital data and records management and in the growing adoption of digital preservation practices across stewardship institutions. There is also growing public awareness of digital preservation. The most popular section of digitalpreservation.gov[11] highlights the importance of personal digital preservation by providing the general public with information on how to manage their digital photos, music, videos, and other personal data.

---

[9] See http://www.digitalpreservation.gov/meetings/storage11.html (last accessed 04-24-2012).
[10] Martha Anderson, "Evolving a Network of Networks," *The International Journal of Digital Curation*, Issue 1, vol 3, 2008.
www.ijdc.net/index.php/ijdc/article/download/59/38 (last accessed 04-24-2012).
[11] See http://www.digitalpreservation.gov/personalarchiving/ (last accessed 04-24-2012).

The NDIIPP Program, working with over 245 organizations from 48 states and 26 countries, continues to bring together diverse stakeholders to share expertise and build common understanding. By approaching digital preservation collaboratively, the Program, through the National Digital Stewardship Alliance, is able "to avoid duplicate work, build a community of practice, develop new preservation strategies, flexibly respond to a changing economic landscape, and build relationships to increase capacity to manage content beyond institutional boundaries."[12]

The Alliance for Permanent Access (APA)[13]

In 2005, a group of mostly European institutions involved in scholarly communications and scientific research came together in order to pool their resources and work together on digital preservation by creating the Alliance for Permanent Access (APA). The APA is a not-for-profit membership organization that includes large international and national science institutions, national libraries, funders, publishers, and national coalitions, and is now open to all interested in digital preservation including public and commercial organizations and individuals from across the world. A key sentence in the APA's strategic plan was: "The creation of a *sustainable infrastructure* to support permanent access to the digital scientific record raises many technical, organizational, economic, legal, and social issues."[14] The establishment of the APA was welcomed by the European Commission, which since 2001, had taken an active interest in developing a digital agenda for Europe, and which has funded a considerable number of Europe-wide research and development projects in the area of digital preservation.

One of the key activities for the Alliance is to act as an umbrella institution putting together consortia to bid to the EU for digital preservation projects. These projects take their lead from a project that preceded the APA: Cultural, Artistic, and Scientific knowledge for Preservation, Access, and Retrieval (CASPAR),

---

[12] See National Digital Stewardship Alliance Value Statement, www.digitalpreservation.gov/ndsa (last accessed 04-24-2012).
[13] Further details are available at the APA website http://www.alliancepermanentaccess.org (last accessed 04-24-2012). Details of the projects CASPAR, PARSE.Insight, APARSEN, ODE, SCIDIP-ES are available at http://www.alliancepermanentaccess.org/index.php/community/current-projects/ (last accessed 07-12-2012).
[14] See APA: http://www.alliancepermanentaccess.org. (last accessed 04-24-2012).

part funded by the EU.[15] CASPAR was based on the realization that the "migrate or emulate" mantra that is often heard, while perhaps adequate for documents and images, was not adequate for digitally encoded information in general, especially more complicated objects, and those that cannot be, for example, simply rendered on a screen; the mantra must be extended at least to "migrate, emulate or *describe*". Amongst other things CASPAR produced prototypes for discipline-independent infrastructure components which could help preserve any type of data, as shown by the many examples used in the testbeds;[16] the preservation effectiveness was checked by what might be termed "accelerated lifetime" scenarios, with simulated changes in hardware, software, environment, and tacit knowledge, verified by the "designated community" from the OAIS model.

The first of the projects under the APA umbrella was PARSE.Insight.[17] This initiative gathered fundamental information about what people actually think and do about digital preservation through a set of surveys and case studies of researchers, data managers, and publishers. There were thousands of responses from around the world and from a great variety of disciplines. Given this substantial number of respondents, there was surprising agreement about key threats to digital preservation. Based on these results, the PARSE.Insight roadmap identified the need for a relatively modest and overarching operational infrastructure.

The results also recognized the need to combine all types of digitally encoded information in future, e.g., as described in *Riding the Wave* report by the European High Level Expert Group on Scientific Data.[18] That report draws attention to the future value and benefits arising from keeping our digitally encoded intellectual capital. The same arguments apply right now and must be deployed to justify resources used for preservation.

APARSEN is another EU project that started in 2011.[19] The project envisions a large Network of Excellence that aims to

---

[15] The project website is available at www.casparpreserves.eu (last accessed 04-24-2012).

[16] CASPAR Validation/Evaluation Report, available at http://www.alliancepermanentaccess.org/filestore/CASPAR-deliverables/CASPAR-4104-RP-0101-1_0.pdf (last accessed 04-24-2012).

[17] The project website is available at http://www.parse-insight.eu/ (last accessed 04-24-2012).

[18] Available at http://cordis.europa.eu/fp7/ict/e-infrastructure/docs/hlg-sdi-report.pdf with press release http://ec.europa.eu/information_society/newsroom/cf/itemlongdetail.cfm?item_id=6204 (last accessed 04-24-2012).

[19] The project website is available at www.aparsen.eu (last accessed 04-24-2012).

reduce fragmentation in digital preservation efforts by bringing together research in digital preservation across Europe—academia, industry, vendors, and large science laboratories, as well as libraries—to reach a common vision for research in digital preservation. This is not to say that some tools or techniques will be labeled as wrong. Instead the project expects to provide an overall view that will allow practitioners to be clear where each tool/technique applies. It will also identify gaps. Equally importantly, the project will enable the community to create coherent training courses and formal qualifications that will equip those dealing with digital objects of all kinds to preserve them in whatever way is appropriate and effective.

Complementing APARSEN and also founded in 2011 is SCIDIP-ES, SCIence Data Infrastructure for Preservation with its focus on Earth Science.[20] This project will develop e-infrastructure services that will make it easier for institutions to maintain the understandability and usability of digital objects in the long term. The services address the threats identified by PARSE.Insight, using the techniques developed and proven by CASPAR.

Cumulatively, these outcomes provide a starting point for the infrastructure and tools the community needs. However, there is no guarantee that simply providing a set of services will be sufficient. Therefore, SCIDIP-ES is working with user communities to build up interest and a critical mass of users.

Summing up, the APA community provides a means for sharing the responsibility for digital preservation between institutions as well as a means to control the costs of digital preservation. These efforts are built upon community standards, OAIS in particular, as well as the new standards for audit and certification of digital repositories.[21] The audit and certification process that will be based on these will allow funders to be assured that the repositories they fund are able to demonstrate good practice.

The APA illustrates the value of organizing digital preservation on an international scale, with a European beginning and the potential for global relevance, following a strategic roadmap supported by evidence.

National Digital Preservation Coalitions

Unlike the United States, where the Library of Congress took a clear lead, Europe saw the development of a number of bottom-

---

[20] The project website is available at www.scidip-es.eu (last accessed 04-24-2012).
[21] See http://www.trusteddigitalrepository.eu (last accessed 06-05-2012).

up national digital preservation coalitions, established by libraries, archives, and research institutions that became aware of a joint interest in dealing with digital collections. The first national enabling organization was the Digital Preservation Coalition (DPC, UK and Ireland, established 2001), which broke new ground with its *Mind the Gap* report (2006), a first attempt at putting the special requirements of digital objects in a national organizational context. In 2003, the creation of the DPC was followed by the founding of nestor in Germany. Both coalitions have a broad aim to foster awareness of the issues, promote collaboration in digital preservation and, especially, develop and share knowledge. nestor's *Handbuch—Eine kleine Enzyklopädie der digitalen Langzeitarchivierung* has proven to be a valuable instrument.[22] The DPC has evolved into an active advocate for digital preservation issues.

The Netherlands Digital Preservation Coalition (NCDD) was established in 2008. The NCDD took its starting point from earlier research (e.g., by the UK DPC) indicating that digital preservation is an issue that cannot successfully be addressed by any one organization, sector or even country. The NCDD drafted a rather ambitious mission "to establish a national infrastructure for providing long-term access to digital objects in the public domain."[23] This infrastructure is broadly understood to include hardware, software, requirements, policy, manpower, knowledge, and money. To lay the groundwork for such an infrastructure, the NCDD carried out its own digital preservation survey in 2009.[24] As of 2011, two working groups were actively researching possibilities for sharing storage space and for providing preservation services for the entire public domain. The working group reports are expected in 2012 and may signal a move to more intensive collaboration.

Meanwhile, a number of notable initiatives have been taken within sub-sections of the Coalition[25] to facilitate the fulfillment of the requirements of this essay. In an attempt to bring about alignment with record producers, the National Archives have established a voluntary shared e-Depot service where non-current records that are still in the custody of government agencies are managed and preserved by the National Archives long before the

---

[22] See nestor's *Handbuch*: http://nestor.sub.uni-goettingen.de/handbuch/ (last accessed 04-24-2012).
[23] See NCDD: http://www.ncdd.nl/en/index.php (last accessed 04-24-2012).
[24] NCDD, A future for our digital memory,.
[25] For more information about the different alliances within the NCDD network, see http://www.ncdd.nl/en/over-organisatie.php (last accessed 04-24-2012).

Archives take legal custody. In order to make the plan work, the National Archives had to lower its rather high metadata standards, thereby fulfilling the requirement to maximize commonality.[26]

Choices made at an early stage by the Dutch National Library, Koninklijke Bibliotheek, also reflect clear digital thinking: a digital repository that was developed for the national deposit collection was opened up to international publishers, because international publications really have no national base and the KB considered it highly unlikely that they would deposit their digital publications in every single country where they are sold. In this way, the KB maximized one of digital objects' key benefits: that ownership is no longer a precondition for access. Long-term preservation in just a few places can serve the world.

Nevertheless, as elsewhere, the Dutch landscape still has a lot of features of the analog age that need to be addressed. Examples are social media and other born-digital content, which still elude collection patterns, and new composite objects such as enhanced publications and websites.

The International Internet Preservation Consortium (IIPC)

The Internet is a truly global information space where much is published that eludes or exceeds traditional collection profiles and preservation regimes. It is mostly national and university libraries that have taken on the task of preserving web content, and in 2003, eleven national libraries joined forces with the Internet Archive (US) to establish the International Internet Preservation Consortium (IIPC).[27] The IIPC's aim is "to enable the collection, preservation and long-term access of a rich body of Internet content from around the world."

The IIPC is a lightly-governed network organization that requires little more of its members than active engagement in the mission of the organization. The IIPC is increasingly referred to as one of the most successful collaborative initiatives in the digital preservation field. The IIPC has developed tools for web archiving, and, more importantly, the network has brokered joint initiatives to harvest online information about major (international) events, e.g., the 2008 Olympic Games and the 2011 Arab Spring.[28]

---

[26] Presentation by Ruud Yap to the Tallinn Digital Deposit Conference, 15 November 2011, see http://www.ncdd.nl/blog/?p=549 (last accessed 04-24-2012).
[27] See IIPC: http://netpreserve.org/about/index.php (last accessed 04-24-2012).
[28] See, e.g., presentations at the 2011 General Assembly at http://netpreserve.org/events/2011GA.php (last accessed 04-24-2012).

Open Planets Foundation (OPF) and PrestoCentre

As mentioned above, the European Union has been actively funding digital preservation research projects that bring together heritage communities from across Europe. As in the case of NDIIPP, however, the need for a more sustainable effort was felt in due course.

The Planets project[29] developed digital preservation tools for the library and archives community, whereas PrestoPrime[30] addressed similar issues in the audiovisual domain. When the projects ended, a number of project participants took the initiative to establish ongoing organizations to ensure maintenance and further development of the tools and expertise, resulting in the Open Planets Foundation (OPF)[31] and PrestoCentre.[32] These initiatives are funded by the members. The ultimate success of these initiatives will inform the future of organizational alignment.

MetaArchive and LOCKSS

This case study shifts the focus from *enabling organizations* to *collaborative initiatives* in which the burden of preserving collections of digital content is shared by a number of organizations. The MetaArchive Cooperative[33] and the LOCKSS Alliance[34] have each implemented digital preservation networks that adhere to the above requirements using *distributed* approaches.

The LOCKSS Alliance, MetaArchive Cooperative, and other similar distributed digital preservation (DDP) organizations have arisen in recent years as collaborative efforts between existing cultural memory institutions (libraries, archives, etc.). They intentionally establish affordable means for digital content to survive over the long periods of time in which such cultural memory institutions are accustomed to operating.[35]

The LOCKSS Alliance was established near the end of the 20th century to preserve electronic journal content. LOCKSS was

---

[29] See Planets: http://sourceforge.net/projects/planets-suite/ (last accessed 07-12-2012).

[30] See PrestoPrime: http://www.prestoprime.org/ (last accessed 04-24-2012).

[31] See OPF: http://www.openplanetsfoundation.org/ (last accessed 04-24-2012).

[32] See PrestoCentre: http://www.prestocentre.org/ (last accessed 04-24-2012).

[33] See MetaArchive: http://metaarchive.org (last accessed 04-24-2012).

[34] See LOCKSS: http://lockss.org (last accessed 04-24-2012).

[35] For more information about the distributed approach to digital preservation, see *A Guide to Distributed Digital Preservation*. K. Skinner and M. Schultz, Eds. (Atlanta, GA: Educopia Institute, 2010), http://www.metaarchive.org/GDDP (last accessed 04-24-2012).

established specifically to recreate in the digital realm the capability that libraries had historically possessed to preserve serial publications through distributed collecting strategies. This capability was difficult or impossible to implement in the digital realm because electronic serial publishers have increasingly tended to provide libraries with access to online serial content rather than actually transmitting the content to the libraries.

The LOCKSS software was developed at Stanford University in order to enable libraries to once again affordably maintain and manage journal content within their own infrastructures without ceding control of this important category of scholarly content to large publishing conglomerates. The software operates as a peer-to-peer (P2P) network for preservation purposes, and provides a variety of internal authenticity and integrity checking mechanisms for subscribed electronic journal content stored in the network.

The LOCKSS Alliance is an organizational framework created to coordinate usage of the LOCKSS software by libraries for these purposes. Today the LOCKSS Alliance includes hundreds of libraries around the world, acting together to preserve electronic journal content to which they subscribe.

The MetaArchive Cooperative was established in 2004 to preserve digital archives developed at local cultural memory institutions. MetaArchive was one of the first National Digital Information Infrastructure and Preservation Program (NDIIPP) projects, and was one of the founding members of the National Digital Stewardship Alliance (NDSA) in 2010. The organization is structured as a cooperative of libraries and archives operated jointly for mutual benefit through distributed digital preservation of member collections. MetaArchive used the LOCKSS software to create a separate peer-to-peer network for digital archives. Much like the LOCKSS network, MetaArchive has internal automated mechanisms for content integrity checks and monitoring. The MetaArchive Cooperative has layered a variety of additional digital curation tools onto the underlying LOCKSS software to provide additional curation and reporting capabilities for collections reposited in the network. As of this writing, the cooperative encompasses more than fifty institutions in four countries on two continents.

Variations in the basic DDP P2P model provided by LOCKSS have been implemented by several organizations. Thus far, apart from the MetaArchive Cooperative, two groups, Data-

PASS and LuKII,[36] have designed their private preservation networks in a similar manner. Like MetaArchive, each of these networks runs as an independent entity, organizationally distinct from the LOCKSS Alliance. A number of other DDP networks for digital archives have been created which depend upon the LOCKSS team at the Stanford University Libraries to run their core technical infrastructure (examples include the Alabama Digital Preservation Network (ADPN), the Canadian COPPUL project, and the PeDALS project in Arizona.)[37] All of these projects have collectively been referred to as "Private LOCKSS Networks" (or PLNs), meaning networks that use the LOCKSS software to enable particular groups of institutions to preserve targeted bodies of content. To date, there are almost a dozen PLNs successfully preserving content on behalf of their constituent members.

The three common functions of all DDP networks, LOCKSS-based or otherwise (as this phrase is understood here) that distinguish them from other preservation approaches are as follows:

- *Replication* of content;

- *Distribution* of these replicated copies to distinct geographical locations; and

- *Network organization* to connect these replicated copies through routine operations, including checksum comparisons and repair activities.

In the DDP approach, long-term commitment is achieved by the collective actions of the entire consortium of collaborating institutions. In the case of MetaArchive, individual institutions may come and go, but the network survives. This attribute intentionally emulates the sustainability of the Internet itself, in which no single node or group of nodes is required to continue functioning for the network as a whole to continue functioning. It is important to note that, while participating in the network, institutions are bound by a Cooperative Charter[38] and a

---

[36] See DataPASS: http://www.data-pass.org/ and LuKII: http://www.lukii.hu-berlin.de/ (both last accessed 07-12-2012).
[37] See ADPNet: http://adpn.org; COPPUL: http://www.coppul.ca/pln.html; PeDALS: http://www.pedalspreservation.org/ (all last accessed 04-24-2012).
[38] See the MetaArchive Cooperative Charter: http://www.metaarchive.org/public/resources/charter_member/2011_MetaArchive _Charter.pdf (last accessed 04-24-2012).

Membership   Agreement[39]   outlining   their   rights   and responsibilities.

By structuring the organization as a collaborative effort, PLNs are able to achieve scale in technical expertise and infrastructure for digital preservation. Whereas any single cultural memory organization will typically lack the resources for deep investments in such expertise and infrastructure, a cooperative of many individual institutions can share the burden of such investments and thereby make it affordable.

DDP networks such as MetaArchive possess another powerful element of sustainability in that all members of such networks simultaneously act as producers, archives and consumers. Each institutional member of the network acts as a producer when creating digital content locally, often through digitization programs. Each institutional node in the network functions as an archive for such content, with groups of institutional nodes acting in concert to preserve content in multiple locations that are securely maintained.

By providing a functioning DDP network that is affordable and practical today, MetaArchive has enabled more than 50 institutions to begin digital preservation activities now, not in some distant hypothetical future.

There are relatively slight but nevertheless significant differences between the original LOCKSS e-journal preservation network and PLNs. First, the genre distinction is significant. While PLNs are typically aimed at preservation of content produced in and owned by the institutional member sites (especially locally digitized archives), LOCKSS is aimed at preservation of commercially purchased electronic journal content. This distinction means that institutional members do not function in the role of content producers. Second, the nature of inter-organizational agreements in the LOCKSS Alliance is different from the contractual agreements that link the PLN's members. For example, LOCKSS Alliance members are more loosely coupled than MetaArchive members, with no contractual obligations to continue maintaining their respective DDP nodes. This slightly changes the circumstances of the first requirement above, in that there is a less specific set of commitments in place to ensure the long-term preservation of content. The LOCKSS Alliance counts on the inborn motivation of libraries and other members to

---

[39] See the MetaArchive Membership Agreement:
http://www.metaarchive.org/public/resources/charter_member/2011_Membership_Agreement.pdf (last accessed 04-24-2012).

preserve the content that they have purchased at great institutional expense. This motivation means that members have a vested interest (albeit not a contractual one) in preserving one others' content.

Chronopolis: A Federated Grid Solution

In the US, the Chronopolis network[40] has been developed by the San Diego Supercomputer Center (SCSC), the UC San Diego Libraries (UCSDL), the National Center for Atmospheric Research (NCAR) and the University of Maryland's Institute for Advanced Computer Studies (UMIACS). Integrating digital library, data grid, and persistent archive technologies, Chronopolis has created a trusted environment that spans academic institutions and research projects, with the goal of long-term digital preservation.

Chronopolis provides replication (three copies), however, format obsolescence is considered to be the responsibility of the data provider.

Other Types of Solutions

A National Facility

In Scandinavia, both Denmark and Finland have adopted national approaches to digital preservation. Finland is planning the establishment of a national digital preservation facility in the context of the Finnish National Digital Library.[41] An in-depth report quantifying the benefits of such a centralized approach was published in September 2010.[42] It must be noted, however, that this central facility is intended to serve only museums, archives and libraries within the purview of the Ministry of Education and Culture. Notably scientific digital data are not included in the plans. As of early 2012, implementation of the plans has not yet begun.

---

[40] See Chronopolis: https://chronopolis.sdsc.edu/about/index.html; for an overview, see David Minor, Don Sutton, Ardys Kozbial, Brad Westbrook, Michael Burek and Michael Smorul, "Chronopolis Digital Preservation Network," *International Journal of Curation*, Vol. 5, Issue 1 (2010), http://www.ijdc.net/index.php/ijdc/article/view/150 (both last accessed 04-24-2012).

[41] See Finish National Digital Library: http://www.kdk.fi/en (last accessed 04-24-2012).

[42] See the National Digital Library Initiative Long-term Preservation Project, Final Report, v. 1.0, http://www.kdk.fi/images/stories/LTP_Final_Report_v_1_1.pdf (last accessed 04-24-2012).

In Denmark three national institutions (the Royal Library, the State Archives and the State and University Library at Aarhus) are presently implementing a National Danish Bit Repository (*Bitmagasin*)[43] where multiple copies of digital objects can be kept with the express aim of facilitating long-term preservation. Interestingly, the three "pillars" of the repository have different digital preservation hardware, allowing for the content to be replicated and stored truly independently. In time, it is expected that more institutions will start making use of the repository, whereby they can choose between the different "pillars."

In the Netherlands, major archives have joined forces to propose a plan for a joint shared services center for the archives at all three tiers of government: national, provincial, and municipal.[44] The plan was presented in June 2010, but as of early 2012, implementation is still awaiting government approval and funding.

Single-Repository Solutions

Libraries' concerns that licensed digital content might at some point in time no longer be accessible to them led not only to solutions with distributed governance such as LOCKSS and MetaArchive, but also to more centralized solutions whereby one institution acts as a steward for third-party content.

Centralized solutions include Portico[45] (US) and the Dutch KB's e-Depot,[46] both of which include archiving agreements with major international publishers to ensure continued access for libraries in case the publishers' service breaks down.

The HathiTrust Digital Library,[47] which archives digitized collections from libraries, is perhaps an intermediate solution between a distributed network and a centralized approach: it works with a single repository, but its governance is shared by the participating institutions.[48]

---

[43] See Bitmagasia: http://digitalbevaring.dk/det-nationale-bitmagasin/ (Danish; but Google translate will help);
https://sbforge.org/display/BITMAG/The+Bit+Repository+project;jsessionid=CD5EDF2756B2505530D5564E5E1D93E4 includes information in English, especially of a more technical nature (last accessed 04-24-2012).
[44] See http://www.ncdd.nl/en/artikel.php?id=83 (last accessed 16-05-2012)
[45] See PORTICO: http://www.portico.org/digital-preservation/ (last accessed 04-24-2012).
[46] See e-Depot: http://www.kb.nl/hrd/dd/index-en.html (last accessed 04-24-2012).
[47] See HathiTrust: http://www.hathitrust.org/about (last accessed 04-24-2012).
[48] Originally, governance was restricted to the founding partners; as of 2012, the Board of Governors also includes other participating institutions.

DuraCloud

DuraSpace is a not-for-profit organization that has recently launched a cloud-based storage service, DuraCloud,[49] with some digital preservation services, such as "health check-ups." Cloud storage is flexible and scalable, and the subscription models can be attractive. However, institutions do lose some control over their collections which raises privacy and copyright issues. DuraCloud addresses some of these issues by allowing customers to choose where their content is stored.

Progress to Date

Reviewing the case studies in this essay, it is clear that in the past ten years, memory institutions have made substantial progress in meeting the challenge of their digital collections.

The requirements listed at the beginning of this essay, as well as the experiences of the institutions described above, clearly show that initiatives to promote digital preservation and long-term access benefit greatly from a cooperative approach. Very often, the reasons to seek cooperation will be economic. Many new challenges of the digital world can only be faced by the community as a whole: a new division of labor, agreements about succession planning, technical interoperability.

But collaboration does not come easy. The stakeholders in the digital preservation chain have different backgrounds, different technical systems, and often speak different languages. *Enabling organizations,* such as those described in this essay: NDIIPP, APA, OPF, PrestoCentre, and the national coalitions (DPC, nestor, NCDD), play a mediating role. All of them raise awareness of the digital preservation issues, make the case with funders, bring together stakeholders with different backgrounds and facilitate constructive discussions between them to leverage their commonalities. This is vital work, but it is also challenging and time-consuming. The availability of funding, as in the case of NDIIPP, can help bring stakeholders together. In other cases (APA, OPF), active participation in research and development helps avoid the possible pitfalls of voluntary membership organizations: that stakeholders may be reticent to commit and years go by discussing good intentions without any real practical results. Whereas in the European context international alliances have been instrumental in procuring project money from the European Union, national coalitions may be better positioned to

---

[49] See DuraCloud: http://www.duracloud.org/tour (last accessed 04-24-2012).

influence the legal agendas of lower tiers of governments and procure *structural funding* for long-term repositories.

It can be argued that enabling organizations are temporary phenomena to facilitate the transition from an analog to a digital world. Indeed, William Kilbride, Director of the UK DPC, has been known to tell conferences that the DPC's mission must be to make itself redundant—when digital preservation will have become "business as usual" and the requirements are fulfilled.[50]

A look at the alliances that share responsibility for digital preservation finds considerable progress, especially in Western countries. The United States has spawned quite a number of distributed preservation networks, such as LOCKSS, MetaArchive, HathiTrust, Chronopolis, and others. These initiatives have been particularly useful in enabling institutions to replicate their content and form communities.

File format obsolescence is one of the core challenges of digital preservation and differing approaches and perspectives have emerged. For example, LOCKSS Director David Rosenthal has argued that format obsolescence is much less of a problem than Jeff Rothenberg assumed in 1995.[51] Rosenthal asserts that preservation actions such as migration are unnecessary for widely accepted file formats from 1995 until the present, as the IT industry is expected to guarantee backwards compatibility.[52] Should accessibility problems arise anyway, Rosenthal argues, we should deal with them at the access end, not at ingest. Portico and the KB do not put their trust in this philosophy, and the Danish National Archives take what they see as a more active approach to preservation planning: they migrate every object they receive to standardized formats (PDF/A) for reasons of cost reduction and manageability of the collections (while preserving the original as a back-up).[53] Results over time will demonstrate the effectiveness of

---

[50] A.o. his presentation before 2010 IS&T conference in The Hague, "Digital Preservation in Byte-Sized Chunks: Good Practice, Best Practice and Why We Should Be Careful What We Wish For" in *Archiving 2010*, available from http://www.imaging.org/IST/store/physpub.cfm?seriesid=28&pubid=941 (last accessed 04-24-2012).

[51] Jeff Rothenberg, "Ensuring the longevity of digital documents," 1999 update of 1995 article, http://www.clir.org/pubs/archives/ensuring.pdf (last accessed 04-24-2012).

[52] David S. Rosenthal, "How are we ensuring the longevity of digital documents?," Presentation to CNI Plenary Session, 7-9 April 2009, http://vimeo.com/5407401 (last accessed 04-24-2012).

[53] See Alex Thirifays, Anders Bo Nielsen and Barbara Dokkedal, "Evaluation of a Large Migration Project," *iPRES2011 Proceedings*, pp. 24ff. The proceedings

these approaches. It is the case that collaborative (distributed) initiatives are rarer in Europe than they are in the US, possibly leaving smaller institutions more vulnerable than those that have joined distributed networks.

Opportunities for Alignment

Looking ahead at where the community might be in five years, there are two main areas where alignment provides beneficial results: furthering the geographic spread of the lessons learned from case studies as just described and as documented in emerging good practice, and working together to extend the scope of content preserved by sustainable digital preservation programs.

Geographically, community efforts to date have largely covered only portions of the world (mainly Europe, North America, Australia, and New Zealand). This is partly because other parts of the world are at a different stage of development. On the other hand, the digital environment offers new possibilities to reach across borders and collaborate to save content. Issues like these will be addressed at the 2012 UNESCO Conference (September 26-28, Vancouver, Canada[54]), but as they are closely intertwined with general issues of development, it is difficult to estimate where we should or could be in five years.

As the case studies show, the type of content currently preserved in collaborative (central or distributed) preservation facilities is generally of the more "manageable" kind, in the sense that a) the producers are known, within reach of archiving institutions, and generally well organized (libraries, publishers), and b) the types of objects preserved are often relatively simple and certainly renderable (PDF, jpeg, tiff, etc.).[55] However, vast amounts of data on the Internet are, at present, not being collected and never become part of any type of chain of preservation, because they do not fit into traditional collection profiles. The transformation from analog to digital practice is in progress (Requirement 6); effective interaction between producers, stewards, and users is often lacking (Requirement 3), and a long-

---

were published in 2012 at http://ipres2011.sg/conference-procedings (last accessed 07-12-2012).

[54] See the UNESCO calendar for the event listing:
http://www.unesco.org/new/en/communication-and-information/events/calendar-of-events/events-websites/the-memory-of-the-world-in-the-digital-age-digitization-and-preservation/ (last accessed 04-24-2012).

[55] Admittedly, scientific e-journals increasingly include research data of a much more complicated kind. It is unclear how well the present arrangements are suited to deal with these.

term commitment to preservation is also lacking (Requirement 1). Categories of data that are particularly threatened in this way include (but are not limited to):

- Scientific data held by individual researchers or research groups;

- Social media (blogs, Facebook, etc.);

- Audiovisual objects produced by individuals then published on the internet; and

- Websites (international websites and countries lacking domain harvesting).[56]

In five years' time, the community may have made progress on addressing these issues. Alignment will require international and cross-domain action at a global scale.

The shift from the analog paradigm to the digital paradigm includes the shift from local/regional information spaces to a global information space and the shift from separate library, archive, and scientific information spaces to a globally linked information space. This paradigm shift is not yet sufficiently reflected in our institutions or our infrastructures. Parts of the e-infrastructure are in place or being developed, as demonstrated by the case studies in this essay, but too much information continues to elude existing frameworks and it is urgent that we find ways to select, collect, and preserve it before it is lost.

Next Steps

While local and regional collaborative initiatives are helping individual institutions cope with the digital challenge, the issues of global inclusion and of born-digital content that is presently eluding collection frameworks are indeed so global in nature that national and regional efforts cannot deal with them. These issues should be elevated to an international level.

Laura Campbell (Library of Congress) has encouraged the establishment of an international preservation body with a focus on policy, perhaps assisted by an advisory expert group to identify what categories of digital objects are most at risk.[57] The body

---

[56] In addition scientific and commercial data with specialised syntax and semantics are in danger of becoming unusable after quite a short time. In particular re-use in new contexts would become increasingly impossible without capturing sufficient Representation Information, as outlined in Giaretta, However, as this is more of a technical issue, it is not discussed further in this essay.

[57] Laura Campbell, see note 2 above.

could promote an international notion of collection, work on standards and tools, and perhaps maintain a common index of preserved materials. This idea merits further exploration. One opportunity will be the UNESCO Conference "The Memory of the World in the Digital Age: Digitization and Preservation" (26-28 September 2012). In addition, the iPres Conference offers an annual opportunity to address digital preservation challenges and opportunities. The enabling organizations described in this essay should continue to contribute to international organizational alignment.[58]

References

Anderson, Martha, "Evolving a Network of Networks," *The International Journal of Digital Curation*, Issue 1, vol 3, 2008. www.ijdc.net/index.php/ijdc/article/download/59/38 (last accessed 04-24-2012).

A Guide to Distributed Digital Preservation. K. Skinner and M. Schultz, Eds. (Atlanta, GA: Educopia Institute, 2010), http://www.metaarchive.org/GDDP (last accessed 04-24-2012).

Mind the Gap: Assessing Digital Preservation Needs in the UK, DPC, 2006, http://www.dpconline.org/advocacy/mind-the-gap (last accessed 04-24-2012).

NCDD (Netherlands Coalition for Digital Preservation), *A Future for our Digital Memory: permanent access to information in the Netherlands*, English summary, http://www.ncdd.nl/en/documents/Englishsummary_000.pdf (last accessed 04-24-2012).

New Roles for New Times: Digital Curation for Preservation, by Tyler Walters and Katherine Skinner, Report prepared for the Association of Research Libraries, March 2011, http://www.arl.org/bm~doc/nrnt_digital_curation17mar11.pdf (last accessed 06-05-2012).

Preserving Our Digital Heritage: The National Digital Information Infrastructure and Preservation Program

---

[58] http://www.unesco.org/new/en/communication-and-information/events/calendar-of-events/events-websites/the-memory-of-the-world-in-the-digital-age-digitization-and-preservation/

2012 Report.
http://www.digitalpreservation.gov/documents/NDIIPP20
10Report_Post.pdf (last accessed 05-17-2012).

Rothenberg, Jeff, "Ensuring the longevity of digital documents,"
1999 update of 1995 article,
http://www.clir.org/pubs/archives/ensuring.pdf (last
accessed 04-24-2012).

Rosenthal, David S., "How are we ensuring the longevity of digital
documents?," Presentation to CNI Plenary Session, 7-9
April 2009, http://vimeo.com/5407401 (last accessed 04-
24-2012).

*Sustaining Economics for a Digital Planet: Ensuring Long-term
Access to Digital Information*, Final Report of the Blue
Ribbon Task Force on Sustainable Digital Preservation
and Access, February 2010, http://brtf.sdsc.edu/ (last
accessed 04-24-2012).

Zorich, Diane; Gunter Waibel, Ricky Erway: *Beyond the Silos of
the LAMs: Collaboration among Libraries, Archives and
Museums*, OCLC, 2008;
http://www.oclc.org/research/publications/library/2008/20
08-05.pdf (last accessed 07-12-2012).

Standards Alignment

Raivo Ruusalepp (Tallinn University)
Christopher A. Lee (University of North Carolina at Chapel Hill)
Bram van der Werf (Open Planets Foundation)
Matthew Woollard (UK Data Archive, Economic and Social Data Service)

Abstract

A standard is a specification of precise criteria designed to be used consistently and appropriately. This essay discusses standards that are relevant to digital preservation. We start by presenting an overview of what has been achieved in terms of standards and standards alignment and follow this with a discussion of what we perceive to be the main challenges in aligning standards for preservation requirements. We then propose an agenda for action for the coming five years.

Introduction

Standards cover a variety of topics and issues; they may be *normative*—setting requirements for quality and actions, or *informative*—describing and guiding the use of methods. In all cases they represent agreements that are generally, but not always, considered to be best practice.

A standard of any form or type represents a statement by its authors, who believe that their work will be understood, accepted, and implemented by the market. This belief is tempered by the understanding that the market will work in its own best interests, even if those best interests do not coincide with the standard. A standard is also one of the agents used by the standardization process to bring about market change (Cargill, 2011).

Standards "embody the outcomes of negotiations that are simultaneously technical, social, and political in character" (Edwards, 2004, p.827). Standards usually are designed by institutions and individuals who have aligned their interests and have been able to reach a consensus on these negotiating factors. Standards are often categorized along one dimension as being either *de jure* (what the law states) or *de facto* (what actually happens in practice), and along another dimension as being either open or closed (proprietary). The concept of openness itself addresses several different factors; for example, a proprietary standard may be public, but not open (Tiemann, 2005). Some technical texts that are widely used as standards are publically available specifications (PAS) or requests for comments (RFC), while other standards are established by institutions and intended only for their own internal use, but can have a wider applicability.

An important distinction is between anticipatory and *ex poste* standards (Byrne and Golderb, 2002; Schumny, 2002). The former are introduced before products are developed, while the latter are codifications of characteristics reflected in existing products. Anticipatory standards development is a "future oriented and self-creating process of defining standards: writing for the future now" (Bonino and Spring, 1999, p.101).

Other sources of guidance are not official standards, but since they are a form of agreement for controlling activities that may lead to repeatable ways of carrying out activities, they should be mentioned briefly here. Legislation is not usually seen as a standard, but it can impinge on some institutions' digital curation activities. National differences in copyright and data protection legislation can produce different processes being applied across boundaries.

A major trend since the mid-1980s, has been that parts of the information and communication technology (ICT) industry, sometimes combined with university researchers, have moved away from well-established formal standards development organizations (SDO) such as the International Organization for Standardization (ISO) and have instead formed more *ad hoc* consortia in order to establish specific standards or classes of standards (Weiss and Cargill, 1992; Updegrove, 1995; Cargill, 1999). While industry consortia can often act much more quickly than SDOs in the development of standards, consortia are likely to have much less incentive than publicly funded SDOs to develop standards that require significant time and energy, have little immediate financial payoff (Spring and Weiss, 1994), or are designed to have very wide applicability.

Carl Cargill (1997) describes a chain of standards at increasing levels of specificity. The highest level of standard is a *reference model*, which characterizes a problem space, providing fundamental concepts and terminology. At the next level down, an *industry consensus* standard describes a subset of the functions or capabilities identified in the reference model. At the third level, a *functional profile* describes a set of functions from the industry standard for a specific, but large, class of users. Next down, the fourth category of standard is the *systems profile*, which describes the system requirements of a smaller group of users than that addressed by the functional profile. Finally, a specific organization that has its own needs and requirements can often be addressed by a *document* or set of documents that specifies the implementation in its particular organizational and technical context.

Standardization can help to set the direction of product development within an industry, but it can also help to shape and reinforce particular approaches to professional work. For example, the development of formal management hierarchies and the systematic management movement in the 19th century were based on an intersection between standardized metrics, tools and resources; and the differentiated professional status of managers and engineers who had the expertise to control and coordinate the use of such metrics, tools and resources (Cargill, 1989; Yates, 1989; Zuboff, 1988; Chandler, 1980).

Digital preservation relies on interoperability between computer systems and is thus dependent on standards. Standards are essential for the ability of software and hardware to exchange and use information. They can be seen as tools that can help to make digital collections accessible, sustainable and interoperable. The difficulty usually lies in the selection of the appropriate combination of standards and, if necessary, their customization to suit the specific needs of the organization using them. Navigating at least 200 standards[1] that are related to preservation and digital curation can be a daunting task. Attempts to maintain a community-based standards watch have faced issues of sustainability.[2]

The literature on the preservation and management of digital objects includes many references to the important role of standards (Walch, 1990). Several authors have identified standards and

---

[1] There is no register of standards relating to digital curation. This number is based on those (current) standards known to the authors.

[2] For example, updates to the DIFFUSE project ended in 2009, and updates to the Preserving Access to Digital Information (PADI) page on standards likewise ended when the National Library of Australia ceased to support it in 2010. See DCC DIFFUSE Standards Frameworks: http://www.dcc.ac.uk/resources/standards/diffuse/ and PADI Standards http://www.nla.gov.au/padi/topics/43.html (both last accessed 03-21-2012).

standardization as important components of professional education of those responsible for managing and preserving digital resources (Gilliland-Swetland, 1993; Hedstrom, 1993; Walch, 1993). In 1992, Charles Dollar recommended that archivists "identify archival functional requirements" and then participate in standards development organizations in order "to ensure that these functional requirements are incorporated into" relevant standards (Dollar, 1992, p.81). Soon after, David Bearman (1994) presented standards as one of the four "tactics" for achieving the functional requirements for evidence in record-keeping.

In addition to developing standards, many sources have also suggested the value of adopting standards in order to facilitate long-term access to digital objects. According to one early report on electronic records in the US federal government, "Machine incompatibility…will undoubtedly be solved both by standardization and by development of universal conversion machines" (Jacobs, 1961, p. 11). Although this prediction seems overly optimistic in retrospect, there is still considerable hope for the role of standards within the digital preservation literature. A federal report in the US entitled "Taking a Byte out of History" (1990), indicated, "Sometimes, files can be readily converted to a format that uses generic software and standard hardware. When this is possible, specific software and hardware are not needed to ensure long-term access" (p. 3). Dollar and Weir (1991) argued that open standards help to address problems of interoperability over time, much as they support interoperability across systems at a given point in time. Stielow (1992) argued, "Electronic preservation has a chance of success only at the place where standards exist and where we can reasonably project some constancy over time" (p. 334). In 1996, the Task Force on Archiving of Digital Information argued for the potential value of incorporating "data standards" into digital preservation strategies. Dollar (1999) presented standards and open systems as vital components of a digital preservation strategy, though he also raised warnings about the danger of adopting standards that do not ultimately win out in the market. The most outspoken critic of reliance on standards is Jeff Rothenberg, Senior Computer Scientist at the RAND Corporation. He has warned that standards, like proprietary formats, will become obsolete over time and has suggested that "standards may play a minor role in a long-term solution by providing a way to keep metadata and annotations readable" (1999, p. 12).

Digital Preservation Standards

The development of standards within a particular domain is often regarded as a sign of maturity of that domain. Preservation in general and digital preservation more specifically are quite established in this regard with families of standards that are interlinked and that stem from common antecedents. As an example, the Task Force on Archiving of Digital Information's report *Preserving Digital Information* (1996) is notable for its influence on standards currently in use.

Preservation Standards from the Analog Era

Description standards traditionally used in libraries, museums, archives, research data centers, or heritage institutions have often been extended to accommodate their use for accessing digital objects. Significance of metadata standards in ensuring interoperability in the digital environment has grown rapidly and a new brand of standards for metadata exchange has emerged (see below) that did not exist in the analog era.

Standards have also emerged to guide the conversion of analog materials into digital objects (e.g., ISO/TR 13028, 2010). A whole series of standards and technical reports on scanning of microfilms and paper documents has been published by the ISO technical committee on document management applications.[3]

Reference Models for Digital Repositories

The first international standard to describe a digital archive system was the Reference Model for an Open Archival Information System (OAIS) (ISO 14721, 2003) that has become the "ur-standard" for many other standards that have emerged to address digital repositories and digital preservation.[4] The OAIS Reference Model defines the processes required for effective long-term preservation and access to information objects and establishes a common language to describe them. It does not specify an

---

[3] These are currently shown at the links available at:
http://www.iso.org/iso/iso_catalogue/catalogue_tc/catalogue_tc_browse.htm?com mid=53650 (last accessed 03-21-2012). Details of the committee are available at: http://www.iso.org/iso/iso_technical_committee.html?commid=53650 (last accessed 03-21-2012).

[4] For example, PAIMAS (Producer-Archive Interface Methodology Abstract Standard), the PREMIS (Preservation Metadata Implementation Strategies) metadata data dictionary and TRAC (Trustworthy Repositories Audit and Certification) are all influenced by the OAIS Reference Model.

implementation, but instead provides the framework to make a successful implementation possible, through describing the basic functionality and types of information required for a preservation environment. OAIS identifies mandatory responsibilities and interactions of producers, consumers, and managers of both paper and digital records. It provides a standardized method to describe repository functionality by providing detailed models of archival information and archival functions. Although the OAIS grew out of a standards body—the Consultative Committee for Space Data Systems (CCSDS)—that is focused on terrestrial and space data, its development took on a much wider scope, involving and gaining visibility among a much broader set of stakeholders than simply members of the CCSDS (Lee, 2009). The parties involved in the creation of the OAIS attempted to make it applicable to a wide variety of repository types. In this way, OAIS became a *lingua franca* for archival information systems that has since become widely adopted because it enables effective communication among projects on a national and international scale (Klump, 2011).

The OAIS reference model represents a rare case in the history of use of ICT methods—a model that found broad acceptance across a diversity of audiences and professional communities; from around 1999 to the present, it has appeared in numerous presentations on digital preservation. The exploratory, catalytic, and standard-setting model has contributed to the discussions and the exchange of conceptual and practically realizable ideas within the community of preservation specialists (Oßwald, 2010). The OAIS reference model has been revised by CCSDS and at the time of writing is available as a draft revised standard (CCSDS, 2009).

The OAIS reference model is supplemented by another standard—Producer-Archive Interface Methodology Abstract Standard (PAIMAS) (ISO 20652, 2006)—that describes the workflow of negotiating and coordinating the submission and transfer of objects to an archive. Standards for transfer and ingest of electronic records are also beginning to emerge at a national level (e.g. DIN 31645, 2011).

Other digital repository models have been developed and, although they have not been issued as formal standards, their *de facto* impact on the preservation community and other interest groups is significant. The InterPARES project Chain of Preservation Model (InterPARES, 2007) covers all stages in the life of digital records, from their creation, through their maintenance by their creator, and during their appraisal, disposition, and long-term preservation as authentic memorials of the actions and matters of which they are a part. The model places the function of preserving records into the context of other business functions of an organization.

The Digital Library Reference Model originally created by the EU-funded DELOS project (DELOS, 2007) and developed further by the DL.org project (DL.org, 2011) provides a formal and conceptual framework describing the characteristics of a digital library management system. The model seeks to overcome the heterogeneity of existing digital library systems and provides a conformance checklist.

The UK-based Digital Curation Centre has published its Curation Lifecycle Model (DCC, 2009) that provides a graphical, high-level overview of the stages required for successful curation and preservation of data from initial conceptualization or receipt. The model can be used to plan activities within organizations to ensure that all of the necessary steps in the curation lifecycle are covered. It is important to note that the model is an ideal and focuses on interrelationships between stages of curation work.

Digital preservation standards have also influenced communication among those outside of the digital preservation domain. For example, a report of the National Academy of Sciences' on ensuring the integrity, accessibility, and stewardship of research data (Committee on Ensuring the Utility and Integrity of Research Data in a Digital Age, 2009) makes use of terms including ingest, data producer, and other phrases which may once have been considered exclusive to those working in digital repositories. Standards can help to provide a common language to work across domains.

Digital Repository Audit Methods

One of the first uptakes of the OAIS reference model was for establishing conventions for determining the trustworthiness of repositories. To determine whether an archive or repository is following practices that will ensure long-term digital preservation required a community consensus. As stated some years earlier by the Task Force on Archiving of Digital Information:

A critical component of the digital archiving infrastructure is the existence of a sufficient number of

> trusted organizations capable of storing, migrating, and providing access to digital collections. [...] A process for certification of digital archives is needed to create an overall climate of trust about the prospects of preserving digital information (Task Force, 1996).

The models that emerged, especially OAIS (because it is a reference model and not a process model) lacked the granularity required for an auditable certification process. Individual, emerging standards lacked a framework for what constituted a trustworthy repository, and the community remained incapable of coming to a collective agreement on an exact definition of "trusted archives" as called for by the task force (Dale, Gore, 2010).

In 2003, the Research Libraries Group (RLG) and US National Archives and Records Administration (NARA) established a joint Digital Repository Certification Task Force with membership from the US, UK, France, and the Netherlands, representing multiple domains including archives, libraries, research laboratories, and data centers from government, academic, non-profit, e-science, and professional organizations (Ambacher, 2007). The task force developed an audit checklist for digital repositories that was published in 2007 as the Trustworthy Repositories Audit and Certification (TRAC) checklist (RLG/NARA, 2007). It presents almost 90 organizational, technological and digital object management criteria for digital repositories. Many are based heavily on the principles, terminology and functional characteristics outlined in the OAIS reference model. The Center for Research Libraries received a grant from the Andrew W. Mellon Foundation to investigate the means for audit and certification of digital archives and to complete a series of test audits to inform the investigation. As a result of these tests, two digital repositories were "certified" by CRL on behalf of its membership as trustworthy digital repositories in 2010 and 2011.[5]

---

[5] The CRL's advice on certification and assessment can be found at: http://crl.edu/archiving-preservation/digital-archives/certification-and-assessment-digital-repositories (last accessed 03-21-2012). This certification process predated the formal issuance of the Trustworthy Repository Audit and Certification (TRAC) ISO standard in 2011 (ISO 16363: *Audit and certification of trustworthy digital repositories*, described below), but was based upon the 2007 TRAC checklist.

In 2004 the German Network of Expertise in Long-term Storage of Digital Resources (nestor) established a working group[6] on the certification of trustworthy archives. Building on the RLG/NARA draft version of TRAC checklist, the nestor group focused on identifying features and values that are relevant for evaluating both existing and planned digital object repositories. The first version of the nestor criteria for auditing digital preservation repositories was released in 2006 (nestor, 2006) with an update in 2008 (nestor, 2008). This checklist covers the technical, organizational, and financial characteristics of a digital repository. It is structured similarly to the TRAC checklist, but additionally provides examples and perspectives that are of particular relevance to the legal and economic contexts and operational situation in Germany. On the conclusion of the nestor project, work on the trustworthiness criteria was transferred to the German national standards body[7] and a new version of the criteria was published as a national standard DIN 31644 (2010).

In February 2007 the DigitalPreservationEurope project (DPE) and the UK Digital Curation Centre (DCC) published their joint work on digital repository assessment methods as the Digital Repository Audit Method Based on Risk Assessment (DRAMBORA) (Hofman et al., 2007). This tool presents a methodology for repository self-assessment and characterizes digital curation as a risk management activity; the job of a digital curator is to rationalize the uncertainties and threats that inhibit efforts to maintain digital object authenticity and understandability, transforming them into manageable risks. An online assessment tool was released in 2008 to guide and document the repository assessment.[8]

The Data Archiving and Networked Services (DANS) in the Netherlands published 17 guidelines in 2008 to help data archiving institutions to establish trustworthy digital repositories for research data. An international editorial board modified these guidelines to deal more broadly with the different needs of a wider audience.

---

[6] See information regarding the nestor working group on the certification of trustworthy archives (an English-language version is at the bottom of the page): http://www.langzeitarchivierung.de/Subsites/nestor/DE/Arbeitsgruppen/AGZertifi zierung.html (last accessed 05-21-2012).

[7] The nestor "Trusted digital long-term repositories" working group of the DIN standardization committee "Records management and long-term preservation of digital information objects" (NABD 15).

[8] DRAMBORA Interactive can be accessed at: http://www.repositoryaudit.eu/ (last accessed 03-21-2012).

The Data Seal of Approval (DSA) method (DANS, 2009) characterizes the repository audit as a three-stage process in which a repository carries out its own assessment and is then peer-reviewed by a member of the international DSA assessment group. The reviewer recommends to the board whether the guidelines have been complied with and whether the DSA logo can be awarded to the data repository (Harmsen, 2008, p. 1). A number of organizations have already been through this process.[9]

An international joint effort[10] undertaken to develop a set of criteria on which full audit and certification of digital repositories can be based resulted in a 2011 ISO standard in support of the OAIS reference mode. The OAIS reference model standard included a roadmap for follow-on standards which included "standard(s) for accreditation of archives." The ISO 16363 (2011) *Audit and certification of trustworthy digital repositories* is based on the previously mentioned 2007 TRAC checklist, but with more detailed specification of criteria by which digital repositories are to be audited. The scope of the checklist is explicitly the entire range of digital repositories; its criteria are empirically derived and consistent measures of effectiveness have been ascertained. TRAC's evaluative metrics should be used to judge the overall suitability of a repository as being trustworthy to provide a preservation environment that is consistent with the goals of the OAIS. Separately, individual metrics or measures from TRAC can be used to identify possible weaknesses or pending declines in repository functionality.

The same working group has also developed another standard, *Requirements for Bodies Providing Audit and Certification of Candidate Trustworthy Digital Repositories* (ISO 16919, 2011). This standard is meant primarily for those setting up and managing organizations that perform the auditing and certification of digital repositories. The standard provides normative rules against which an organization providing audit and certification of digital repositories may be judged, and it describes the auditing process. A team of experts conducted a series of pilot

---

[9] A list of repositories which have achieved the DSA is at:
http://assessment.datasealofapproval.org/seals/ (last accessed 03-21-2012).
[10] The Digital Repository Audit and Certification Wiki is at:
http://wiki.digitalrepositoryauditandcertification.org/bin/view (last accessed 03-21-2012).

audits in spring and summer of 2011, to test the methodology promoted by the ISO 16363 standard.[11]

In 2010 a memorandum of understanding (MoU) was signed between three groups working on standards for trusted digital repositories. The CCSDS, the Data Seal of Approval Board, and the DIN "Trustworthy Archives—Certification" Working Group together defined a framework consisting of a sequence of three levels. These levels, in increasing trustworthiness, are documented as follows:

- "Basic Certification" should be granted to repositories that obtain DSA certification through a process of self-audit and the public release of a peer-reviewed statement from another organization which has previously received the DSA;

- "Extended Certification" is granted to Basic Certification repositories that also perform a structured, externally reviewed and publicly available self-audit based on ISO 16363 or DIN 31644; and

- "Formal Certification" is granted to repositories that in addition to Basic Certification obtain full external audit and certification based on ISO 16363 or equivalent DIN 31644.

This MoU was witnessed by the European Commission, but not explicitly endorsed by it.

With the increasing maturity of these two draft international standards, the standardization process for trustworthy digital repositories will have completed its first cycle. Much like the DCC's Curation Lifecycle Model, this cycle of understanding and standardization will continue as an iterative process. With a stable base that includes a process model, relevant standards, and best practices for individual parts of the process, measures of "trustworthiness" will continue to develop as the community's experience with and expertise in digital preservation grows (Dale, Gore, 2010).

Preservation Metadata

Among the many classes of metadata and description standards, preservation metadata has emerged as a separate category. Digital curation requires a provenance mechanism to

---

[11] These audits were undertaken as part of the EU-funded APARSEN project. Full details of the outcomes will be published later in 2012.

record preservation actions that have been applied to digital objects over time. Early conceptualizations of preservation metadata saw it as "all of the various types of data that allows the re-creation and interpretation of the structure and content of digital data over time" (Ludäsher, Marciano, and Moore, 2001). Thus, preservation metadata spans the popular division of metadata into descriptive, structural, and administrative categories. Understood in this way, it is clear that such metadata must support an extremely wide range of functions, including: discovery, the technical rendering of objects, the recording of contexts and provenance, and documenting the relevant repository policies in place at any given time and the repository actions taken to ensure data integrity. The wide range of functions that preservation metadata is expected to support means that the definition (or recommendation) of standards is not a simple task. The situation is complicated further by the knowledge that different kinds of metadata will be required to support different digital preservation strategies and that metadata standards themselves need to evolve over time (Day, 2005). The OAIS reference model has also become an influential source for preservation metadata standards—Preservation Metadata Implementation Strategies (PREMIS) being the most widely adopted of them.

National and research libraries began to develop preservation metadata standards in the late 1990s with the publication of a number of draft element sets. The National Library of Australia produced the first of these (NLA, 1999), quickly followed by the Cedars and NEDLIB projects (Russell, et al., 2000; Lupovici, Masanès, 2000). An international working group sponsored by RLG and the Online Computer Library Center (OCLC) then built upon these (and other) proposals to produce a unified *Metadata Framework to Support the Preservation of Digital Objects* (OCLC/RLG Working Group on Preservation Metadata, 2002). The National Library of New Zealand, finding past work too theoretical, developed its own preservation metadata element set in 2003 (NLNZ, 2003). While the earlier initiatives had all been informed by the (then) evolving OAIS reference model, the OCLC/RLG Metadata Framework was explicitly structured around the OAIS information model (Day, 2005).

The OAIS reference model provides a functional and information model for a digital archive but it does not define what specific metadata should be collected or how it should be implemented in order to support preservation goals. The

OCLC/RLG Working Group on Preservation Metadata: Implementation Strategies (PREMIS) published its first proposal for core preservation metadata elements in 2005 as the *PREMIS Data Dictionary for Preservation Metadata* (PREMIS Working Group, 2005). The *Data Dictionary* defined preservation metadata as "the information a repository uses to support the digital preservation process," specifically that "metadata supporting the functions of maintaining viability, renderability, understandability, authenticity, and identity in a preservation context" (PREMIS Working Group, 2005). PREMIS defines a common data model to encourage a shared way of thinking about and organizing preservation metadata. The PREMIS data model contains five types of entities: Intellectual Entities, Objects, Rights, Agents and Events. The semantic units that describe the entities in this data model are rigorously defined. PREMIS supports specific implementations through guidelines for metadata management and use, and it puts an emphasis on enabling automated workflows. It makes, however, no assumptions about specific technology, architecture, content type, or preservation strategies. As a result, it is "technically neutral" and supports a wide range of implementation architectures (Dappert, Enders, 2010). PREMIS (2011) is currently maintained by the US Library of Congress and has been translated into multiple languages, including French, German, Italian, and Spanish.

While PREMIS is in use internationally, in Germany a national standard Long Term Preservation Metadata for Electronic Resources (LMER) is more commonly used for preservation metadata. LMER is a standard of the German National Library and is based on a data model originally developed by the National Library of New Zealand. As with PREMIS, each metadata element is associated with a particular type of entity, which in LMER are objects, processes, files, and metadata modification.

Metadata Encoding and Transmission Standard (METS) is a standard for encoding in Extensible Markup Language (XML) the metadata describing or characterizing digital objects. It provides a flexible means of associating all the metadata about a digital object with the object—it is a "container format" specifying how different kinds of metadata can be packaged together (Caplan, 2008). One extension of METS—METSRights provides for the documentation of the intellectual rights associated with a digital object or its parts.[12]

Currently, few metadata specifications contributing to digital assets' long-term preservation are sanctioned by national or international standards bodies. Some, like PREMIS or METS, have the status of *de facto* standards with well-defined community processes for maintaining and updating them. While communities have a strong desire for long-lasting, stable metadata standards, practices continue to evolve as the number of repository implementations and applications grows. Experience remains too limited to set a preservation metadata standard in stone (Dappert, Enders, 2010).

The OAIS information model continues to influence metadata initiatives, especially in its detailed requirements for comprehensive representation information. It also provides the theoretical basis for projects that aim to capture representation information in terms of file formats.

File Format Description

Format is a fundamental characteristic of a digital object that governs its ability to be used effectively. A number of phases of digital curation—appraisal, selection, acquisition, ingest, preservation, and access—include file format considerations. While preservation planning is a much broader activity that involves many other factors, monitoring for incipient obsolescence is a key activity, especially given that numerous preservation projects have reported difficulties with obtaining complete and reliable file format specifications and documentation (Lawrence, et al., 2000; Representation and Rendering Project, 2003). This has led to calls for the creation of sustainable format repositories to manage representation information about formats so that information will be available for future curation and preservation practitioners (Representation and Rendering Project, 2003; Christensen, 2004b). Such file format registries have emerged to serve the whole preservation community and codify the information that is required about formats for digital curation (cf. Planets, 2008a). However, the present lack of test corpora of digital objects for evaluating file format identification tools

---

[12] See METS schema: http://www.loc.gov/standards/rights/METSRights.xsd (last accessed 03-21-2012).

demonstrates suggests that the benchmarking of these tools has not yet been treated as a high priority.

The National Archives (TNA) of the UK has developed the PRONOM format registry[13] to provide a service for both human and machine clients. The PRONOM information model manages the relationships between the technical properties of formats, including classification; signatures; software, hardware, and media dependencies; and external entities such as actors, documentation, intellectual property rights, and identifiers which relate to these properties (Brown, 2005).

The development of a similar service, the Global Digital Format Registry (GDFR[14]), was initiated at the Harvard University Library with participation from OCLC. Its goal was to provide sustainable distributed services to store, discover, and deliver representation information about digital formats.

In 2009, the PRONOM and GDFR joined forces under a new name—the Unified Digital Format Registry (UDFR).[15] The UDFR aims to support the requirements and use cases compiled for GDFR and is seeded with PRONOM's software and formats database.

Information on file formats and their use for preservation has also been collected and published by the US Library of Congress as part of the National Digital Information Infrastructure and Preservation Program (NDIIPP).[16] A Registry/Repository of Representation Information has been created by the UK Digital Curation Centre, and focuses upon the representation information listed in the OAIS reference model.[17] The Open Planets Foundation (OPF) has proposed a new concept for representation information registries in digital preservation called "registry

---

[13] See the PRONOM registry:
http://www.nationalarchives.gov.uk/PRONOM/Default.aspx (last accessed 03-21-2012).

[14] See Global Digital Format Registry: http://www.gdfr.info/index.html (last accessed 03-21-2012).

[15] See Unified Digital Format Registry: http://www.udfr.org/ (last accessed 03-21-2012).

[16] See the Library of Congress' Sustainability of Digital Formats:
http://www.digitalpreservation.gov/formats/fdd/descriptions.shtml (last accessed 03-21-2012).

[17] See the Registry Web GUI, allowing browsing of the CASPAR/DCC Representation Information Repository: http://registry.dcc.ac.uk/ (last accessed 03-21-2012).

ecosystem." It is based on interlinking various sources of information to create interconnected "registry collections" using Linked Data, rather than creating and maintaining a single registry (OPF, 2011).

The data model of these file format registries has developed over the years to include new aspects of representation information that are required in preservation planning processes. The continuing work on significant properties of digital objects (e.g. the Investigating the Significant Properties of Electronic Content Over Time (InSPECT) project[18]), characterization languages (e.g. the Planets (2008b) project's Extensible Characterization Description language), and development of preservation planning tools (e.g., the Planets project's Plato[19] tool) have further advanced the standardization of information about file formats.

Other Pertinent Standardization

Digital preservation professionals must address numerous dependencies upon systems and processes that were developed by entities not specifically focused on preservation. Successful digital preservation thus relies heavily on standards developed for a variety of purposes.

Many of the existing standards that pertain to archival collections and digital preservation have served primarily to advance work within specific streams of activities, rather than spanning multiple professions. For example, before the recent "recognition that digital preservation poses issues and challenges shared by organizations of all descriptions" and the emerging prominence of the OAIS as a common framework, work on preservation metadata by several organizations was "conducted largely in isolation, lacking any substantial degree of cross-organizational coordination" (OCLC/RLG Working Group on Preservation Metadata, 2002, p.1).

Storage Media

One core set of issues in digital preservation involves the physical medium. The bits stored on an optical or magnetic medium degrade over time and are subject to damage from

---

[18] See Investigating the Significant Properties of Electronic Content Over Time (InSPECT): http://www.significantproperties.org.uk/ (last accessed 03-21-2012).
[19] See the Plato preservation planning tool:
http://www.ifs.tuwien.ac.at/dp/plato/intro.html (last accessed 03-21-2012).

environmental factors. One area in need of standardization was thus the physical storage media and storage conditions (Carneal, 1977). This is the area of digital preservation that has seen the most active standardization and consensus. Standards have been developed and adopted by the Preservation Committee of the Audio Engineering Society (AES), United Nations Educational, Scientific, and Cultural Organization (UNESCO), National Institute of Standards and Technology (NIST) (formerly the National Bureau of Standards), Institute of Electrical and Electronics Engineers (IEEE), American National Standards Institute (ANSI), and the International Organization for Standardization (ISO).

Memory institutions have a long tradition of using their own domain-specific standards for storage, some of which continue to be relevant for handling digital storage media. For example, ISO 11799 *Document storage requirements for archive and library materials* (ISO 11799, 2003) with its national predecessor BS 5454 *Recommendations for storage and exhibition of archival documents* (BS 5454, 2000), set general requirements for storage rooms. Similarly, ISO 18925 (2008), ISO 18938 (2008), ISO/TR 10255 (2009) or BS 4783-8 (1994) all discuss storage requirements of specific storage media types, including magnetic tapes and optical discs.

Data Description, Data Management and Recordkeeping

Standards for descriptive metadata of archival materials have also developed along several distinct paths, based on the boundaries between different types of institution or document. For example, the archival profession developed MAchine Readable Cataloging, Archives and Manuscript Collections (MARC-AMC) (Smiraglia, 1990); Archives, Personal Papers and Manuscripts (APPM) (Hensen, 1989); Encoded Archival Description (EAD) (EAD Working Group, 1998); Rules for Archival Description (RAD) (Duff, 1999); and Describing Archives: A Content Standard (DACS) (2007) in order to develop access systems particular to its collections.

Several standards developed in the last two decades are intended to facilitate the design and management of "recordkeeping systems," which ensure the authenticity of electronic records as evidence. One of the most prominent standardization efforts in this area was a metadata schema for the Commonwealth of Australia (McKemmish et al, 1999). Design

Criteria Standard for Electronic Records Management Software Applications (DOD 5015.02 – STD) provides a set of requirements for the design and certification of applications used to manage electronic records (Assistant Secretary of Defense, 2007). A high-level international standard for records management was adopted in 2001 (ISO 15489, 2001). The body that was responsible for ISO 15489 (TC46/SC11) has subsequently worked on a variety of more specific standards. The Model Requirements for the Management of Electronic Records (MoReq) were released in 2001, updated and substantially revised as MoReq2 in 2008 (MoReq2, 2008) and MoReq2010 in 2011 (MoReq2010, 2011).

Social Science data archivists have also developed metadata standards that cater to the specific types of data residing in their collections, often for the purpose of exchanging data among collections of the same type. The American Council of Social Science Data Archives began discussing options for "study description schemes" at its annual meeting in 1967, and this conversation eventually resulted in a recommended unified scheme (Scheuch, 2003, p. 393). Several generations of proposed conventions for data exchange (De Vries, Van der Meer, 1992; Leighton, 2002; Rasmussen, 1978) and development of codebooks have followed. One important effort to this end is the Data Documentation Initiative (DDI).[20] The first public version of the DDI document type definition (DTD) was published in 2000 (DDI, 2000). Virtually every scientific domain has metadata standards for the description of its data, but not always created within a domain-specific archival context.

Other scientific communities have also followed relatively autonomous paths toward standardization related to their data. For example, the Consultative Committee for Space Data Systems (CCSDS) was formed in 1982, and it then served as an active forum for the development and promulgation of numerous standards for use by space agencies. As described previously, the CCSDS was the body responsible for development of the OAIS Reference Model, which took place between 1994 and 2002; its development involved a level of interaction with other disciplines that had not been the case for any of the CCSDS's previous activities. Space agencies have also developed and adopted several influential standards that have emerged outside of the CCSDS

---

[20] See Data Documentation Initiative (DDI): http://www.ddialliance.org/ (last accessed 03-21-2012).

process. For example, several separate efforts have attempted to address the need for device-independent data models and software for multidimensional data sets. Common Data Format (CDF) was developed in 1985 by the National Space Science Data Center (NSSDC); Network Common Data Form (NetCDF) was then developed at the Unidata Program Center managed by the University Corporation for Atmospheric Research in Boulder, Colorado; and the Hierarchical Data Format (HDF) was developed at National Center for Supercomputing Applications (NCSA) in 1988. Each initiative boasts a long list of private and public sector adopters. In 1993, NASA chose to adopt HDF for data in its Earth Observing System (EOS), resulting in its own flavor, known as HDF-EOS. Even with this customization of HDF, several actors within the EOS did not perceive it be appropriate to their needs and failed to adopt HDF-EOS (Duerr, et al., 2004).

Standards for File Formats

Using standard file formats that will remain accessible over time is a common digital preservation strategy. Formats that are stable and have been widely adopted are much more likely to be supported over a long period. File format standards that are open often are less likely to become obsolete in a short period, because there is a large user base willing to participate in ensuring that the standards are maintained (Harvey, 2010).

A number of file formats have been explicitly developed through a formal standardization process, such as PNG (ISO/IEC 15948, 2004), JPEG 2000 (ISO/IEC 15444), MPEG-4 (ISO/IEC 14496) and MPEG-7 (ISO/IEC 15938). Others, such as PDF/A (ISO 19005), TIFF/EP (ISO 12234-2, 2001), TIFF/IT (ISO 12639, 2004), Open Document Format (ODF) (ISO/IEC 26300, 2006), and Office Open XML (ISO/IEC 29500) were existing formats, or newly developed variants, that were subsequently promulgated through an accredited standards process.

In contrast to these *de jure* standards, many popular file formats fall into the category of *de facto* standardization on the basis of ubiquity. Although of potentially broad applicability, these standards are generally the result of parochial community interest (Abrams, 2007). For example Scalable Vector Graphics (SVG) (W3C, 2009) is an open file format standard which has not been formalized by a standards organization, and the Broadcast WAVE Format (BWF) was developed by the European Broadcasting

Union to simplify the interchange of broadcast media (EBU, 2011).

While standardization is obviously better than non-standardization, the mere existence of standards does not necessarily mean that they will be widely implemented. For example, the JPEG 2000 image format is an ISO standard, but it is not widely supported by the current generation of Web browsers, although less preservation-friendly formats such as GIF (Graphics Interchange Format), Joint Photographic Experts Group (JPEG), and Portable Network Graphics (PNG) are well supported (Abrams, 2007).

Regardless of their formal status, all of the formats discussed in this section share one important type of openness—whether proprietary or not, their specification documents are published. For most memory institutions, it will be nearly impossible to ensure that all acquired digital objects use file formats that are based on open standards, or indeed even that the formats a curator selects for archiving are all standard formats. The diversity of formats available in the digital domain is so vast and growing at such a rapid pace that the comparatively slow process of standardization does not cover the whole variety of content types and their *en vogue* formats. Thus far the impact of the preservation community on the development of format standards has been quite limited, although rare cases exist in which preservation specialists have been invited to contribute to the standards (e.g., PDF/A, MPEG-7). For practical reasons, many memory institutions have updated their policies by replacing lists of (limited) supported formats and standards, with more detailed criteria for the selection of preservation-friendly formats (e.g., Christensen, 2004b; Brown, 2008; The National Archives, 2011; Arms, et al., n.d.).

Tools for converting from one file format to another or exchanging information between systems remain pertinent for digital preservation.

Representation of Contextual Information

Preservation is a set of activities devoted to ensuring the conveyance of meaning over time. In the case of digital preservation, this involves ensuring that important characteristics and values of digital objects can be consistently reproduced over time within an acceptable range of variability. For a given target digital object, there are contextual information entities that play a role in conveying meaning. Consequently, digital preservation metadata must convey information about whether or not these contextual information entities exist, and whether they have been altered. There are several types of contextual entities that can be important to describe in order to ensure meaningful use of digital objects over time, including objects, agents, occurrences, purposes, times, places, forms of expression, concepts/abstractions, and relationships (Lee, 2011). It would be neither feasible nor appropriate for digital preservation professionals to attempt to invent their own standards for representing information about such a rich diversity of contextual entities. Fortunately, no such effort is necessary. There are existing and emerging standards that can be applied to information about all of the contextual entity types. The International Standard Archival Authority Record for Corporate Bodies, Persons and Families (ISAAR/CPF) (ICA Committee on Descriptive Standards, 2004) and Encoded Archival Context – Corporate bodies, Persons, and Families (EAC-CPF) (EAC Working Group, 2010) are two recent efforts specifically to formalize contextual information related to archival materials.

There are also numerous standards and conventions for representation of information about each of the nine types of contextual entities (Lee, 2011; for further detail, see the appendix to that paper). A few specific examples include:

- **Objects** - There is extensive guidance for generating information about physical objects, including the Global Trade Item (GTIN) for commercial products (GS1 US, 2006), the Categories for the Description of Works of Art (CDWA) (Baca and Harpring, 2009) for art and material culture, and the relatively institution-specific conventions for representing archaeological artifacts (Snow et al., 2006). There are also numerous standards for packing and representation of digital objects already discussed in this essay.

- **Agents** - Librarians and archivists have been working for some time on the elusive goal of uniquely identifying and describing agents over time. An Agents Working Group was formed in 1998, in order to address the agent information that was potentially embedded in (or missing from) the Dublin Core elements (Wilson and Clayphan, 2004). A project within the International Organization for Standardization (ISO) is developing the International Standard Name Identifier (ISNI) (ISO/CD 27729) to uniquely identify "public identities" across multiple areas of creative activity. The International Standard Archival Authority Record for Corporate Bodies, Persons and

Families (ISAAR(CPF)) and Encoded Archival Context: Corporate Bodies, Persons and Families (EAC-CPF) are two rich sources of guidance on the types of information one might hope to provide about agents. Resource Description and Access (RDA) (2011) provides detailed guidance for recording attributes of persons, families, and corporate bodies. In 2006, the Text Encoding Initiative also initiated the Personography Task Force, one product of which has been a report that describes and compares many existing schemes for marking up information about individuals (Wedervang-Jensen and Driscoll, 2006). METS and PREservation Metadata: Implementation Strategies (PREMIS) also provide simple taxonomies for identifying types of agents.

- **Occurrence** - There is a growing body of building blocks for the identification and encoding of occurrence information. Guidance for the detailed representation of processes includes the Process Specification Language (Bock and Gruninger, 2005); extension and application of the Unified Modeling Language (Penker and Eriksson, 2000); XML Process Definition Language (Workflow Management Coalition, 2008); and the Business Process Modeling Notation Specification (White, 2008). TimeML (Pustejovsky et al., 2003) and the Historical Event Mark-up and Linking (HEML) Project (Robertson, 2009) provide conventions for encoding and storage of event information.

- **Purpose** - Two sources of guidance for representing functional entities and their relationships from Australia are the Australian Governments' Interactive Functions Thesaurus (2007) and Keyword AAA (Robinson, 1997), and one from Canada is the Business Activity Structure Classification System (BASCS) Guidance (Library and Archives Canada, n.d.). The International Standard for Describing Functions (ICA Committee on Best Practices and Standards, 2008) has been designed to describe functions within archival information systems.

- **Time** - The most straightforward case of representing time is a precise time and date, as specified in ISO 8601 (2004). However, there is a myriad of other possible temporal units and expressions, which TIMEX2 attempts to accommodate (Ferro, et al., 2005). ISO 19108 (2002) provides detailed guidance for representing "temporal feature attributes, feature operations, and feature associations, and for defining the temporal aspects of metadata about geographic information," though it is potentially applicable for describing other types of information. The Time Period Directory initiative aims to support translations between common language labels, such as the Civil War, and specific time spans (Petras et al., 2006). There are many other relevant specifications and research activities that fall within the arena of "temporal modeling," which attempt to address the deep connections between events (see above) and time (e.g. Grandi et al., 2005).

- **Place** - There are a number of detailed standards and guidance documents for encoding place information. The Alexandria Digital Library (ADL) project offers a "Guide to the ADL Gazetteer Content Standard" (2004). A well-established set of conventions for encoding locations as coordinates is available in the Department of Defense World Geodetic System 1984 (2000), which is supported by vCard and the geo microformat (Çelik, 2007). vCard also allows for specifying location based on time zone. The X.500 and Lightweight Directory Access Protocol (LDAP) families of standards identify ways to encode geographic and postal addresses. There are several detailed elaborations of places and types of places, including the Alexandria Digital Library Feature Type Thesaurus (2002), Geographic Names Information System, and the Getty Thesaurus of Geographic Names (TGN).

- **Form of Expression** - Many sources of guidance are available for encoding information related to form of expression or genre, with several of the most prominent ones listed in the Library of Congress "Genre/Form Code and Term Source Codes." MARC 21 (2010) also uses fixed-length fields for designating forms of material, has a field for Index Term— Genre/Form, and recently added several fields in the 300 range related to form of expression.

- **Concept or Abstraction** - For several centuries, librarians and other information professionals have been developing and refining systems to represent the concepts and abstractions associated with target information objects. The representation systems have often taken the form of nomenclatures, controlled subject headings, thesauri and, more recently, ontologies. The depth and diversity of standards—ranging from general subject headings for library cataloging to extremely specialized conventions for naming scientific entities—is far too extensive to address here.

- **Relationship** - Thesauri have traditionally expressed three primary types of relationships: equivalence, hierarchical and associative (ISO 2788, 1986). There are innumerable other types of relationships that can hold between entities (e.g. ancestral, emotional, logistical, causal, temporal, and polyhierarchical). Entity-relationship models have long been used to represent relationships of many types, which have generally been implemented using relational databases. Within computer science, the term "ontology" is used to describe data models that accommodate and define an arbitrarily complex set of relationships between entities, concepts, classes or elements. RDA (2008) provides detailed guidance on assigning various types of "relationship designators." In order to make effective use and sense of a digital object, it can be important to differentiate and provide separate information about: 1) the function (purpose), organization (high-level agent) or role responsible for its creation and use, and 2) "personal provenance," i.e., particular individuals involved (Hurley, 1995). Several detailed taxonomies are available for job roles and occupations, including the ERIC Thesaurus, North American Industry Classification System (2007), O*NET Content Model, O*NET-SOC Taxonomy (2009), and Standard Occupational Classification System (2000). METS, Interoperability of Data in E-commerce Systems (INDECS) (Rust & Bide, 2000), OAIS (ISO 14721, 2003), and InterPARES (Long-Term Preservation of Authentic Electronic Records, 2002) all elaborate roles of agents. MARC 21 (2010) includes numerous fields that can be used to identify relationships between the items being catalogued and other resources, as well as allowing for a relator term, which "describes the relationship between a name and a work;" the Library of Congress provides a detailed Relator and Role Code and Term Source Codes. In his investigation of collection relationships, Heaney (2000) also provides a list of "Types of Agent-Object Relationship." The Union List of Artist Names (ULAN) (Harpring et al, 2006) elaborates several dozen roles for use in a Person/Corporate Body record.

Information Security Standards

An emerging area in which memory institutions are subjected to external standards is information security. The international series of information standards (ISO 27000) started off as a British Standard (BS 7799) in the mid 1990's. The ISO 27000 has now developed into a management system standard with a whole family of standards that support an industry of its own. There are also national versions of benchmarks and standards with which memory institutions may need to comply in their roles as public sector agencies, e.g., information security standards may be compulsory.

Information security standards are for preserving confidentiality, integrity, and the availability of information. However, in general there is a lack of provision for the long-term view in all information security measures that are being enforced on memory institutions except in terms of business continuity plans. The main aim of information security is to ensure protection of existing services and, hence, these standards do not replace preservation standards that the digital preservation community has produced, rather they augment existing standards. Awareness of information security requirements and standards is rising in memory institutions, but competence to apply them and to conceptualize the digital collection management tools in the same framework as other information systems and databases is not yet widespread. A number of procedures required for compliance with the ISO 16363 are closely related to ISO 27001 and could engender greater understanding and conformance to broad information security measures.

Security standards, like many other externally developed standards, suffer from the problem that many memory institutions, because of their lack of awareness of the complex information security requirements, can often take them at face value without consideration of the various contexts in which they can be implemented. Security standards often need significant contextualization to implement them for the needs and requirements of different organizations.

Summary

In summary, the range of standards available for use by and for the digital preservation community is huge and highly diverse in terms of subject and detail. The most significant standard, OAIS, while highly influential, is an informative standard that can be implemented in countless different ways and thus does not ensure interoperability. Standards and guidelines for the audit of organizations carrying out digital preservation have flourished in the environment post-OAIS, but have been hampered by the informative models on which they have been based. At the time of writing, there is increasing convergence on the application of these standards. In terms of normative standards including those surrounding preservation metadata, the representation of contextual information, file format descriptions, and data and records management are in advanced stages of development, if not implementation.

Currently, there is no easily navigable map of all these standards. The digital preservation community should be in a position now to codify standards that relate to its activities. Digital preservation professionals should also be able to determine which standards are applicable and implement those which are beneficial to their individual organizations: every organization that carries out any digital curation activities should have a list of the appropriate standards which inform its practices, and be able at the least to report on its required level of conformity. We should also understand that standard adherence is more about continuous improvement than getting it right the first time, and it is important to keep a very good watch on what is happening in the future.

Challenges, Gaps, and Opportunities

As a community we often feel that on the one hand, we have too many standards and on the other, too few (of our own standards). The very large number of pertinent standards can fall into agreed categories, but sometimes the exact nature of these categories or classes is confusing. For example, should we treat legislation as a standard? Compliance to standards is voluntary, while legal acts must be adhered to, and in some jurisdictions legislation makes following a standard mandatory, even while not always defining that standard (EC, 2007). Often, what are considered the *de jure* standards are really just standards approved by standards organizations, which are often commercial organizations. How reliable are the *de facto* standards that are endorsed by popular acclaim? When is a standard an open standard? Proprietary standards can be public (e.g., PDF file format specification) but are not considered to be open. Which controlled vocabularies exist within a particular domain? Which standards for the representation of commonly used descriptive information (e.g., country code) is most appropriate for information interchange? What happens when present-day standards no longer address historical information? (For example, the ISO 3166-1 code of YU for Yugoslavia may still be relevant for historical material.) Navigating the standards' library requires more than basic know-how and even a map, to help decide what is best for our organizations.

Many existing standards seem impractical, with unnecessary detail (e.g., the 16 page explanation of the representation of human sexes in ISO 5218 (2004)), or too technical to be applicable in everyday work of a memory institution (e.g., standards describing how files are written onto optical storage media (ISO/IEC 13490)), but there will be domains in which they are important, and may have applicability for both the preservation and the longer-term interpretation of the items curated. Other standards appear to be directly relevant to digital preservation yet are intended for a very specific purpose or domain (e.g., ISO/TR 15801 (2009) that discusses issues specific to document imaging). We firmly believe that standards should not be hoops to be jumped through—they must be useful and applicable and organizations should know when they are applicable and how to implement them in a pragmatic and consistent form.

In the following paragraphs we present some key issues and challenges facing the digital preservation community relating to standards and standardization.

Establishing Trust

Defining attributes of a trustworthy digital repository has been a discussion topic for more than a decade; several approaches to establishing trustworthiness exist and we are about to have *de jure* standards for measuring it. The European Commission has endorsed a three-tier system of assessment through which organizations can receive a basic certification of trust based on the Data Seal of Approval, an extended certification through adherence to the Data Seal of Approval principles and completion of a self-audit against one of the standards for trusted digital repository auditing (ISO 16363 or DIN 31644), or a formal certification through a formal external audit against one of these two standards.

What these approaches have in common is the underlying thinking that trust is something to be achieved by a standards-based approach to preservation planning. The standards that establish auditing criteria are generic in their nature and do not themselves address the needs of specific domains, cultures or nations (McHugh et al., 2008). This will require interpretation and conceptualization from the different types of digital repositories. The immediate challenge with these standards is how to embed them within contractual requirements and to get support for implementing them.

Memory institutions satisfy the needs of society by safekeeping and providing access to information. Over time it has become clear that preservation practices—and in particular those practices relating to digital data—have proven more challenging than expected. Is society losing trust in the ability of memory institutions to fulfill their mission? Is this loss of trust factually based? Is there any proof that organizations have really "lost" digital collections? There is an increasing awareness that best practice requires a reliable process that can be verified by an independent body. The independence of verification, auditing, and certification requires a further level of trust in itself. Can one trust the auditing and certifying bodies?

It is important that the emerging audit and certification efforts do not simply create a business model for consultants, auditors, and certification bodies, and pile extraneous and unnecessary requirements onto a repository. Standardization with compliance and certification will hopefully satisfy large groups of stakeholders, but obtaining and retaining certification will require significant resources. Is formal certification the appropriate method of inculcating this trust? Similar to other standards, with their compliance and certification schemes, a trusted repository standard with a mandatory certification could increase operational overhead which might in turn increase the risk of losing digital objects and thus the long-term access to these objects. A proven best practice that evolves into a standard with certification will partially mitigate this risk. Simply implementing external standards that are not wholly relevant can be counter-productive.

One threat to trustworthy digital preservation relates to the continuous availability of highly trained and highly skilled human resources.

Conformity to Preservation Metadata Standards

While a great deal of progress has been made in defining preservation metadata requirements over the last several years, there are several important concerns about preservation metadata. First, there has been limited experience in the application of preservation strategies. This makes it difficult to know whether today's preservation metadata schemes will actually support the process of long-term preservation. Second, neither PREMIS nor LMER define format-specific technical metadata, which is crucial.

Only technical metadata for digital still images is formally standardized (NISO MIX, 2008); specifications for audio, video, text, vector graphics, and other formats are in various stages of development (or not). Third, it is important that the values of preservation metadata elements can be supplied and processed automatically, as many preservation projects will be very large in scale. Hand-entered, natural-language descriptions do not scale. However, there are few standard code lists or controlled vocabularies for the values of even the most important preservation metadata elements (Caplan, 2008).

Applying and Implementing Standards

The digital preservation community is not homogenous—memory institutions sit alongside research and government institutions, businesses, and service providers. Many of the standards that have been developed within this community deal with workflow control, but it is impossible (and undesirable) to completely homogenize preservation workflows across the whole community. This lack of homogeneity presents a paradoxical situation—if the success of a standard is dependent upon its community uptake, and a successful standard is one which gets the widest uptake, the most successful standards are ones which do not address the necessary differences within the community.

The type of standards that the digital preservation community has agreed upon—what could be called voluntary compliance standards—are mainly suitable for improving work processes (in their broadest sense). However, the uniform use of voluntary standards is difficult to coerce. More enforceable standards do exist but usually in areas such as quality control, security, safety, and environment controls, and are mostly implemented in sectors in which something has gone seriously wrong or there are serious threats. Digital preservation as an activity in its own right is, so far, not universally perceived as facing serious threats and, thus, it is, and will be in the future difficult to enforce uniform practices through standards. While we believe in the importance of the establishment of trust within (and between) repositories (see above) we do not believe that "enforceable" but highly homogenized standards will provide a panacea. Conformity in all matters is not necessarily desirable, especially if the primary purpose of the activity of digital preservation is to ensure that the materials being preserved can be used at some defined point in the future for some particular purpose, and that the defined point in the future and the particular purpose will differ across organizations.

Perhaps the biggest technology challenges for the digital preservation community are the *de facto* standards that the IT industry generates with every new format or device. To date it has been very difficult for anyone outside the computer industry and a few large government agencies to have any real impact on these standards. Hence, memory institutions are more "trend followers" than "trend setters" in technical standards, since they form a relatively small part of the market for computer systems and their influence is, correspondingly, relatively small. The digital preservation community can take action in one specific area: playing a more substantial role with standards bodies and working groups organized around formats. Digital preservation professionals could also attempt to detect relevant trends and actions sooner by undertaking active monitoring of technical developments in other domains.

Furthermore, as discussed above, successful digital preservation must be attentive to and draw from standards that were developed for other purposes. Any time a given community or industry has attempted to systematically share data or support interoperability across systems, there is the potential for digital preservation professionals to build upon those efforts rather than trying to invent entirely new or independent standards. This should also be understood as an opportunity for digital preservation specialists to continue to develop specific standards for the community.

Determining the Appropriate Scope for Digital Preservation Standards

A question frequently asked in standards-making is: "What is so special about this that it requires a standard?" The same can be asked about digital preservation—what about it necessitates standardization? Despite cutting across different domains and carrying out digital preservation for somewhat different purposes and in different organizational settings, there are some activities that are requirements for the whole community. However, as a community we do not yet have much experience with identifying situations in which standards are essential. Defining the appropriate level of granularity and detail required in standards remains a challenge—overly prescriptive or overly domain-specific standards will not be applicable across the numerous domains that must preserve digital objects.

Currently, the mainstream thinking on digital preservation is repository-centric—digital preservation is thought of as something that should happen within the digital repository environment. Consequently, most of the existing standards both from within and outside of the community are focused on repositories and how digital objects are managed within them. This is a clear demonstration of the maturity of preservation as the core business of the memory institutions that have successfully been doing it for at least two centuries.

At the moment, digital preservation standards are most successful in addressing issues that are not temporally dynamic. There are separate standards for compatibility, safety, commoditization, etc. However, digital preservation is not a static challenge and the future dependencies on present-day activities should not be underestimated. Will standardization, compliance testing, auditing, and certification provide the ability to address the issue of acting against a moving target? *De facto* technical standards appear and disappear at a rapid rate, and change is their only permanent characteristic. Digital preservation practitioners need to address this and learn to cope with continually changing external standards that represent a considerable organizational and management challenge, not least because withdrawn and obsolete standards are not always retained within any national standards organization registry.

The maturity curve of applying standards starts from testing and benchmarking then moves through risk management towards quality management, eventually reaching an apogee in an organization capable of learning. Standardization in digital preservation is still at the beginning of this curve, focusing primarily on benchmarking the performance of curation tasks and beginning to look at risk management of preservation. The existing "best practice" activities that have been formalized as standards can be tested through self-assessment and essentially peer-reviewing until formal certification bodies have been set up based on ISO 16363 and ISO 16919 auditing standards. An organization that is mature and able to adapt to changes is, however, looking more at efficiency of processes than controls over products (systems) and their interoperability. When moving from quality control to quality assurance to quality management, the management of people and skills becomes the biggest challenge, instead of technology and workflow. Reshaping an organization is more connected to its employees than the technologies it uses.

Demonstrating the benefits of using digital preservation standards remains a challenge. Positive use cases will help to improve user uptake of standards but it is also possible to bring benefits to users by including the concepts and requirements of digital preservation into other standards. The case of records management standards is a good example—aligning digital preservation standards with record-keeping standards can ensure that digital materials are created and maintained in such a way that allows memory institutions to preserve them for the long term. There is a lot of potential in stating the long-term retention requirements and including them in standards of other domains to achieve the aim of making sure that digital content remains accessible.

Next Steps: A Five-Year Forecast

We present four significant areas where we believe the digital preservation community will focus attention over the next five years.[21]

Interoperability Standards

Digital curation will increasingly be seen as an interoperability exercise along the whole chain of steps that form the lifecycle of an object—from its conception to its re-use through the process of preservation. Interoperability in turn requires adherence to standards. Interchange between software systems is currently known (and will increasingly be seen) as the main "at risk" point in the digital object lifecycle, since export-import functionality is generally not supported at a level that is required for legal or scientific requirements in commercial systems. Quality criteria for what must (or at least should) be transferred (i.e., digital objects with their metadata), how the transfer process should be documented, and how the success of this process can be validated, are all becoming urgent issues as larger volumes of content than ever before will be migrated between systems in the coming years. Part of this process is likely to include the education of content creators to help them understand the issues surrounding digital preservation (Van den Eynden et al., 2011).

---

[21] These recommendations were first outlined in a different form at the standards alignment panel at the ANADP 2011 conference. This discussion benefited greatly from the open discussion that followed the panel session.

Digital Preservation Requirements

Digital preservation standards will move away from a repository-centric world-view and become sets of requirements, that is, functional requirements that can be implemented in other information systems that manage digital assets for the short to medium term. Developing and setting technical and quality criteria/benchmarks for the successful management of digital information in systems that do not behave like collection management tools would be one way to demonstrate the value and feasibility of digital preservation.

Standards for Skill-Sets

Technical quality and success criteria should be accompanied by codes of practice that rely on clear requirements for skills and know-how. This will mean setting standards for education and training courses in digital preservation. Accreditation of digital preservation teaching programs and training courses based on quality criteria or competence standards are beginning to emerge, but should be pursued as an international alignment effort.

Engaging the Users of Standards

In order to better demonstrate the value of standards in digital preservation, the appropriate user communities should be engaged in the discussion of which standards are relevant in practice, which ones are still missing, and who should participate in creating new standards. It is likely that for many practitioners, the broad range of existing standards is fit for purpose, but remaining up to date is a non-trivial task. A standards-watch service providing up-to-date information would prove hugely useful.

Along with guidance and showcase examples, it will also be increasingly important for digital preservation practitioners to know how different sub-communities apply and use existing standards. Standards not only ensure standardization of processes, but also help the "customer" in the broadest sense make most use or take greatest value in the end products of processes.

It is likely that some digital preservation standards will need updating or re-standardization in the near future, because they tend to represent current best practices or current best thinking, rather than being extensively tested and generalized to apply in multiple domains.

Standards' Development

The development of standards is a time-consuming and often tediously bureaucratic process. The procedure followed by ISO is an eye-opener even to the most assiduous onlooker.[22] Tighter international collaboration between groups of experts and practitioners could possibly mitigate some of the delay. Other methods of streamlining or even circumventing the process may actually improve the implementation of standards in a pragmatic and organizationally specific manner.

Conclusions

Success in the arena of digital preservation standards requires identification of common priorities—across professional groups, (digital) heritage institutions, and all the end users, including what may eventually become the most "fickle" and changing group of all—the designated community. The development and implementation of standards should be guided by common priorities. Various parties can benefit from sharing schemas, tools, and methods, while acknowledging the importance and inevitability of different institutional limitations and strengths.

Standards bring about alignment or at least some commonality in thinking, but only if used appropriately and for the purposes that led to their creation. The digital preservation community has succeeded in developing a number of its own standards and often applies them quite successfully. The ease of use and universal applicability of these standards remains a challenge, as does the application of a multitude of external, mostly technical standards that characterize the materials to be preserved.

Just as memory institutions preserve materials that other organizations have created, they also apply many standards that have been created by other communities. Digital preservation is an inclusive domain and as far as standards are concerned cannot (and should not) rely on its own standards alone. Learning to piece together the jigsaw puzzle of standards from different domains is a skill that every digital curation specialist needs to have, alongside the skill of discriminating between what is or is not locally

---

[22] ISO's International harmonized stage codes are shown visually at:
http://www.iso.org/iso/standards_development/processes_and_procedures/stages_description/stages_table.htm (last accessed 03-21-2012).

appropriate. These are the key areas in which the international alignment of efforts can be beneficial, but cannot provide a complete solution.

References

Abrams, Stephen. (2007). *File Formats*. DCC Digital Curation Manual Installment.
http://www.dcc.ac.uk/sites/default/files/documents/resour ce/curation-manual/chapters/file-formats/file-formats.pdf (last accessed 08-03-2011).

Alexandria Digital Library Feature Type Thesaurus. (2002). University of California, Santa Barbara.
http://www.alexandria.ucsb.edu/gazetteer/FeatureTypes/v er070302/ (last accessed 10-03-2011)

Ambacher, Bruce. (2007). "Government Archives and the Digital Repository Audit Checklist." *Journal of Digital Information* 8, no. 2.
http://journals.tdl.org/jodi/article/view/190/171 (last accessed 08-04-2011).

Arms, C.R., Fleischhauer, C., Jones, J. *Sustainability of Digital Formats Planning for Library of Congress Collections*. NDIIPP.
http://www.digitalpreservation.gov/formats/index.shtml (last accessed 08-05-2011).

Assistant Secretary of Defense for Networks and Information Integration. (2007). Electronic Records Management Software Applications Design Criteria Standard, DOD 5015.02 – STD. U.S. Department of Defense.

Australian Governments' Interactive Functions Thesaurus – AGIFT. (2007). 2nd ed., National Archives of Australia, Canberra.

Baca, M., Harpring, P. (eds.). (2009). *Categories for the description of works of art*. J. Paul Getty Trust, Los Angeles, CA.
http://www.getty.edu/research/publications/electronic_pu blications/cdwa/index.html (last accessed 10-03-2011).

Bearman, David. (1994). Electronic Evidence: Strategies for Managing Records in Contemporary Organizations. Pittsburgh: Archives and Museum Informatics.

Bock, C., Gruninger, M. (2005). "PSL: a semantic domain for flow models." *Software and Systems Modeling* 4, (2): 209-31.

Bonino, Michal J., Michael B. Spring. (1999). "Standards as Change Agents in the Information Technology Market." *Computer Standards and Interfaces* 20, no. 4-5: 279-89.

Brown, Adrian. (2005). PRONOM 4 Information Model. TNA. http://www.nationalarchives.gov.uk/aboutapps/fileformat/pdf/pronom_4_info_model.pdf (last accessed 08-05-2011).

Brown, Adrian. (2008). *Digital Preservation Guidance Note 1: Selecting file formats for long-term preservation.* The National Archives. http://www.nationalarchives.gov.uk/documents/information-management/selecting-file-formats.pdf (last accessed 08-05-2011).

BS 4783-8 (1994). Storage, transportation and maintenance of media for use in data processing and information storage. Recommendations for 4 mm and 8 mm helical scan tape cartridges.

BS 5454 (2000). Recommendations for storage and exhibition of archival documents.

BS 7799-1 (1995). Information security management. Code of practice for information security management systems.

Byrne, Bernadette M., and Paul A. Golderb. (2002). "The Diffusion of Anticipatory Standards with Particular Reference to the ISO/IEC Information Resource Dictionary System Framework Standard." *Computer Standards and Interfaces* 24, no. 5: 369-79.

Caplan, Priscilla. (2006). *Preservation Metadata.* DCC Digital Curation Manual Installment. http://www.dcc.ac.uk/sites/default/files/documents/resource/curation-manual/chapters/preservation-metadata/preservation-metadata.pdf (last accessed 08-03-2011).

Caplan, Priscilla. (2008). *The Preservation of Digital Materials.*

Library Technology Reports 44, no. 2. Chicago: ALA TechSource

Cargill, Carl F. (1989). *Information Technology Standardization: Theory, Process, and Organizations*. Bedford, MA: Digital Press.

Cargill, Carl F. (1997). *Open Systems Standardization: A Business Approach*. Upper Saddle River, NJ: Prentice Hall.

Cargill, Carl F. (1999). "Consortia and the Evolution of Information Technology Standardization." *IEEE Conference on Standardisation and Innovation in Information Technology*, Aachen, Germany, September 15-17, 1999.

Cargill, Carl F. (2011). "Why Standardization Efforts Fail." *Journal of Electronic Publishing* 14, (1).

Carneal, Robert B. (1977). "Controlling Magnetic Tape for Archival Storage." *Phonographic Bulletin* 18: 11-14.

CCSDS. (2009) *Reference Model for an Archival Information System (OAIS). Draft Recommended Standard*. CCSDS 650.0-P-1.1. http://public.ccsds.org/sites/cwe/rids/Lists/CCSDS%2065 00P11/Attachments/650x0p11.pdf (last accessed 08-01-2011).

Çelik, T. *Geo – Microformats*. http://microformats.org/wiki/geo (last accessed 08-01-2011).

Chandler, Alfred D., Jr. (1980). "The United States: Seedbed of Managerial Capitalism." In *Managerial Hierarchies: Comparative Perspectives on the Rise of the Modern Industrial Enterprise*, edited by Alfred Dupont Chandler and Herman Daems, 9-40. Cambridge, Mass.: Harvard University Press.

Christensen, Niels H. (2004a). *Towards format repositories for web archives*. 4th International Web Archiving Workshop. http://netarchive.dk/publikationer/FormatRepositories-2004.pdf (last accessed 08-05-2011).

Christensen, Steen S. (2004b). *Archival Data Format Requirements*. The Royal Library, Copenhagen; The State and University Library, Århus, Denmark.

http://netarkivet.dk/publikationer/Archival_format_requir
ements-2004.pdf (last accessed 08-05-2011).

Committee on Ensuring the Utility and Integrity of Research Data
in a Digital Age, National Academy of Sciences. (2009).
*Ensuring the Integrity, Accessibility, and Stewardship of
Research Data in the Digital Age.* Washington: National
Academies Press.

Dale, Robin L., Gore, Emily B. (2010). "Process Models and the
Development of Trustworthy Digital Repositories."
Information Standards Quarterly 22, (2).

DANS. (2009). Data Seal of Approval.
http://www.datasealofapproval.org/ (last accessed 08-05-
2011).

Dappert, Angela, Enders, Markus. (2010). "Digital Preservation
Metadata Standards." *Information Standards Quarterly*
22, (2).

Data Documentation Initiative. DTD. Version 1. (2000). http://ddi-
alliance.cvs.sourceforge.net/viewvc/ddi-
alliance/ddi/dtd/Version1.dtd?view=log (last accessed 08-
05-2011).

Day, Michael. (2005). *Metadata.* DCC Digital Curation Manual.
http://www.dcc.ac.uk/sites/default/files/documents/resour
ce/curation-manual/chapters/metadata/metadata.pdf (last
accessed 08-03-2011).

DCC. (2009). *The DCC Curation Lifecycle Model.*
http://www.dcc.ac.uk/sites/default/files/documents/public
ations/DCCLifecycle.pdf (last accessed 06-03-2011).

DELOS. (2007). *A Reference Model for Digital Library
Management Systems.*
http://delos.info/index.php?option=com_content&task=vi
ew&id=345&Itemid (last accessed 06-03-2011).

Describing Archives: A Content Standard. (2007). Chicago, IL:
Society of American Archivists.

Department of Defense World Geodetic System 1984: Its
Definition and Relationships with Local Geodetic
Systems, Third Edition, Amendment 1. (2000). NIMA
Technical Report TR8350.2. National Imagery and
Mapping Agency, St. Louis, MO.

de Vries, Repke, and Cor van der Meer. (1992). "Exchange of Scanned Documentation between Social Scientists and Data Archives: Establishing an Image File Format and Method of Transfer." *IASSIST Quarterly* 16, no. 1-2: 18-22.

DIN 31645. (2011). Information und Dokumentation - Leitfaden zur Informationsübernahme in digitale Langzeitarchive. [*Information and documentation - Guide to the transfer of information objects into digital long-term archives*]

DIN 31644. (2010). Information und Dokumentation - Kriterien für vertrauenswürdige digitale Langzeitarchive. [*Information and documentation - Criteria for trustworthy digital archives*]

DL.org. (2011). *DL.org Reference Model.* http://www.dlorg.eu/index.php/outcomes/reference-modeloutcomes/reference-model (last accessed 06-03-2011).

Dollar, Charles M. (1992). *Archival Theory and Information Technologies: The Impact of Information Technologies on Archival Principles and Methods*. Edited by Oddo Bucci. Vol. 1, Informatics and Documentation Series. Macerata, Italy: Università degli studi di Macerata.

Dollar, Charles M. (1999). *Authentic Electronic Records: Strategies for Long-Term Access*. Chicago, IL: Cohasset Associates.

Dollar, Charles M., and Thomas E. Weir, Jr. (1991). "Archival Administration, Records Management, and Computer Data Exchange Standards: An Intersection of Practice." In *A Sourcebook of Standards Information - Education, Access and Development*, edited by Steven M. Spivak and Keith A. Winsell, 191-211. Boston, MA: G. K. Hall & Co.

Duerr, R., Parsons, M.A., Marquis, M., Dichtl, R., Mullins, T. (2004). "Challenges in long-term data stewardship." In: *Proceedings of 21st IEEE Conference on Mass Storage Systems and Technologies*. NASA/CP-2004-212750.

Duff, Wendy. (1999). "The Acceptance and Implementation of the Rules for Archival Description by Canadian Archives: A Survey." *Archivaria* 47: 27-45.

EBU. (2011). Specification of the Broadcast Wave Format (BWF). A format for audio data files in broadcasting. Version 2.0. EBU-TECH 3285.

EC. (2007). Directive 2007/2/EC of the European Parliament and of the Council of 14 March 2007 establishing an Infrastructure for Spatial Information in the European Community (INSPIRE). http://eur-lex.europa.eu/LexUriServ/LexUriServ.do?uri=OJ:L:2007:108:0001:0014:EN:PDF (last accessed 10-01-2011).

Edwards, Paul N. (2004). 'A Vast Machine': Standards as Social Technology. *Science* 304, no. 5672: 827-28.

Encoded Archival Context Working Group. (2010). *Encoded Archival Context—Corporate Bodies, Persons, and Families (EAC-CPF) Tag Library*. Encoded Archival Context Working Group of the Society of American Archivists and the Staatsbibliothek zu Berlin. http://www3.iath.virginia.edu/eac/cpf/tagLibrary/cpfTagLibrary.html (last accessed 08-03-2011).

Encoded Archival Description Working Group. (1998). EAD Tag Library for Version 1.0. Chicago, IL: Society of American Archivists and Library of Congress.

ERIC Thesaurus. U.S. Department of Education, Institute of Education Sciences. http://www.eric.ed.gov/ERICWebPortal/thesaurus/thesaurus.jsp (last accessed 08-03-2011).

Ferro, L., Gerber, L., Mani, I., Sundheim, B. and Wilson, G. (2005). *TIDES 2005 Standard for the Annotation of Temporal Expressions*. MITRE Corporation. http://timex2.mitre.org/annotation_guidelines/2005_timex2_standard_v1.1.pdf (last accessed 08-03-2011).

Genre/Form Code and Term Source Codes. Library of Congress, Washington, DC. http://www.loc.gov/standards/sourcelist/genre-form.html (last accessed 08-03-2011).

Geographic Names Information System. U.S. Board on Geographic Names. http://geonames.usgs.gov/ (last accessed 08-03-2011).

Getty Thesaurus of Geographic Names. J. Paul Getty Trust, Los Angeles, CA.

http://www.getty.edu/research/tools/vocabularies/tgn/
(last accessed 08-03-2011).

Gilliland-Swetland, Anne J. (1993). "From Education to
Application and Back: Archival Literature and an
Electronic Records Curriculum." *American Archivist* 56:
532-44.

Grandi, F., Mandreoli, F. and Tiberio, P. (2005). "Temporal
modelling and management of normative documents in
XML format." *Data & Knowledge Engineering* 54, (3):
327-354.

GS1 US. (2006). *An introduction to the global trade item number
(GTIN)*. Lawrenceville, NJ.
http://www.gs1us.org/library?EntryId=31&Command=Co
re_Download (last accessed 08-03-2011).

Guide to the ADL Gazetteer Content Standard. Version 3.2.
(2004). Alexandria Digital Library Project, Santa Barbara,
CA.
http://www.alexandria.ucsb.edu/gazetteer/ContentStandar
d/version3.2/GCS3.2-guide.htm (last accessed 08-03-
2011).

Harmsen, Henk. (2008). "Data seal of approval - assessment and
review of the quality of operations for research data
repositories." In: *Proceedings of the iPRES 2008
Conference*, British Library

Harpring, P., Beecroft, A., Johnson, R. and Ward, J. (Eds.). (2006).
Union List of Artist Names: Editorial Guidelines. J.Paul
Getty Trust, Los Angeles, CA.

Harvey, Ross. (2010). *Digital Curation: A How-to-do-it Manual*.
Neal-Schuman Publishers.

Heaney, M. (2000). *An Analytical Model of Collections and their
Catalogues*. Third Issue. UK Office for Library and
Information Networking.
http://www.ukoln.ac.uk/metadata/rslp/model/amcc-
v31.pdf (last accessed 08-03-2011).

Hedstrom, Margaret L. (1993). "Teaching Archivists About
Electronic Records and Automated Techniques: A Needs
Assessment." *American Archivist* 56: 424-33.

Hensen, Steven L. (1989). Archives, Personal Papers, and

Manuscripts: A Cataloging Manual for Archival Repositories, Historical Societies, and Manuscript Libraries. 2nd ed. Chicago: Society of American Archivists.

Hofman, Hans; McHugh, Andrew; Ross, Seamus; Ruusalepp, Raivo. (2007). *Digital Repository Audit Method Based on Risk Assessment (DRAMBORA).* DigitalPreservationEurope and the UK Digital Curation Centre

Hurley, C. (1995). Problems with Provenance. *Archives and Manuscripts* 23, (2): 234-259.

ICA Committee on Descriptive Standards. (2004). International Standard Archival Authority Record for Corporate Bodies, Persons and Families (ISAAR/CPF). 2nd ed. International Council on Archives, Paris.

ICA Committee on Best Practices and Standards. (2008). *ISDF: International Standard for Describing Functions.* 1st ed. International Council on Archives, Paris.

InterPARES. (2007). *Chain of Preservation (COP) Model.* http://www.interpares.org/ip2/ip2_models.cfm# (last accessed 06-03-2011).

ISO 2788. (1986), Documentation – Guidelines for the establishment and development of monolingual thesauri.

ISO/IEC 5218. (2004). Information technology – Codes for the representation of human sexes.

ISO 8601. (2004). Data elements and interchange formats – Information interchange – Representation of dates and times.

ISO/TR 10255. (2009). Document management applications – Optical disk storage technology, management and standards.

ISO 11799. (2003). Information and documentation – Document storage requirements for archive and library materials.

ISO 12234-2. (2001). Electronic still-picture imaging – Removable memory – Part 2: TIFF/EP image data format.

ISO 12639. (2004). Graphic technology – Prepress digital data exchange – Tag image file format for image technology

(TIFF/IT).

ISO/TR 13028. (2010). Information and documentation – Implementation guidelines for digitization of records.

ISO/IEC 13490. Information technology – Volume and file structure of read-only and write-once compact disk media for information interchange. Parts 1-2.

ISO/IEC 14496. Information technology – Coding of audio-visual objects. Parts 1-27.

ISO 14721. (2003). Space data and information transfer systems – Open archival information system – Reference model.

ISO/IEC 15444. Information technology – JPEG 2000 image coding system. Parts 1-13.

ISO 15489. (2001). Information and Documentation – Records Management. Parts 1 and 2.

ISO/IEC 15938. Information technology – Multimedia content description interface. Parts 1-12.

ISO/IEC 15948. (2004). Information technology – Computer graphics and image processing – Portable Network Graphics (PNG): Functional specification.

ISO/TR 15801. (2009). Document management – Information stored electronically – Recommendations for trustworthiness and reliability.

ISO 16363. (2011). Space data and information transfer systems - Audit and certification of trustworthy digital repositories.

ISO 16919. (2011). Space data and information transfer systems - Requirements for bodies providing audit and certification of candidate trustworthy digital repositories.

ISO 18925. (2008). Imaging materials – Optical disc media – Storage practices.

ISO 18938. (2008). Imaging materials – Optical discs – Care and handling for extended storage.

ISO 19005. Document management – Electronic document file format for long-term preservation. Parts 1-2.

ISO 19108. (2002). Geographic information – Temporal schema.

ISO 20652. (2006). Space data and information transfer systems –

Producer-archive interface – Methodology abstract standard.

ISO/IEC 26300. (2006). Information technology – Open Document Format for Office Applications (OpenDocument) v1.0.

ISO/IEC 27000. (2009). Information technology – Security techniques – Information security management systems.

ISO/CD 27729. (2008). Information and Documentation – International Standard Name Identifier (ISNI).

ISO/IEC 29500. Information technology – Document description and processing languages – Office Open XML File Formats. Parts 1-4.

Jacobs, Richard. (1961). *On Records Preparation and Magnetic Tape*. Washington, DC: National Archives and Records Service.

Klump, J. (2011, January/February). "Criteria for the Trustworthiness of Data Centres." *D-Lib Magazine*. 17,(1/2). http://www.dlib.org/dlib/january11/klump/01klump.print. html (last accessed 08-02-2011).

Lawrence, G., Kehoe, W., Rieger, O., Walters, W., Kenney, A. (2000). *Risk Management of Digital Information: A File Format Investigation*. Council on Library and Information Resources. http://www.clir.org/pubs/reports/pub93/pub93.pdf (last accessed 08-02-2011).

Lee, Christopher A. (2009). "Open Archival Information System (OAIS) Reference Model." In *Encyclopedia of Library and Information Sciences, Third Edition*, edited by Marcia J. Bates and Mary Niles Maack, 4020-4030. Boca Raton, FL: CRC Press.

Lee, Christopher A. (2011). "A Framework for Contextual Information in Digital Collections." *Journal of Documentation* 67, no. 1: 95-143.

Leighton, Vernon. (2002). "Developing a New Data Archive in a Time of Maturing Standards." *IASSIST Quarterly* 26: 5-9.

Library and Archives Canada. (n.d.). *Business activity structure classification system (BASCS) guidance*. Retrieved October 3, 2011, from http://www.collectionscanada.gc.ca/government/products-services/007002-2089-e.html

LMER:http://www.dnb.de/EN/Standardisierung/LMER/lmer_node.html (last accessed 03-21-2012).

Long-term Preservation of Authentic Electronic Records: Findings of the InterPARES Project. (2002), Vancouver, Canada. http://www.interpares.org/book/index.cfm (last accessed 08-02-2011).

Ludäsher, B., Marciano, R., Moore, R. (2001). "Preservation of digital data with self-validating, self-instantiating knowledge-based archives." *SIGMOD Record* 30, (3): 54-63.

Lupovici, C., Masanès, J. (2000). *Metadata for the long term preservation of electronic publications.* NEDLIB Report series 2. The Hague: Koninklijke Bibliotheek. http://www.kb.nl/hrd/dd/dd_links_en_publicaties/nedlib/NEDLIBmetadata.pdf (last accessed 08-02-2011).

MARC 21 Format for Bibliographic Data. (2010). U.S. Library of Congress, Washington, DC. http://www.loc.gov/marc/bibliographic/ecbdhome.html (last accessed 08-03-2011).

McHugh, A., Ross, S., Innocenti, P., Ruusalepp, R., Hofman, H. (2008). "Bringing Self-assessment Home: Repository Profiling and Key Lines of Enquiry within DRAMBORA." *International Journal of Digital Curation.* 2, (3). http://www.ijdc.net/index.php/ijdc/article/view/93 (last accessed 08-06-2011).

McKemmish, Sue, Acland, Glenda, Ward, Nigel, Reed, Barbara. (1999). "Describing Records in Context in the Continuum: The Australian Recordkeeping Metadata Schema." *Archivaria* 48: 3-43.

nestor:http://www.langzeitarchivierung.de/Subsites/nestor/EN/Home/home_node.html (last accessed 03-21-2012).

NISO Metadata for Images in XML (2008). http://www.loc.gov/standards/mix/ (last accessed 01-12-2012).

Model Requirements for the Management of Electronic Records:

Update and Extension (Moreq2 Specification). (2008).
Hampshire, United Kingdom: Serco Consulting.

*MoReq2010. Modular Requirements for Records Systems. Volume
1. Core Services and Plug-in Modules.* (2011). DLM
Forum Foundation. http://moreq2010.eu/pdf/MoReq2010-
Core+Plugin(v1-0).pdf (last accessed 08-11-2011).

The National Archives. (2011). *Evaluating Your File Formats.*
Version 1.2.
http://www.nationalarchives.gov.uk/documents/informati
on-management/evaluating-file-formats.pdf (last
accessed 08-05-2011).

National Library of Australia. (1999). *Preservation Metadata for
Digital Collections. Exposure Draft.* Retrieved August 4,
2011, from http://www.nla.gov.au/preserve/pmeta.html

National Library of New Zealand. (2003). *Metadata Standards
Framework - Preservation Metadata (Revised).* Retrieved
August 4, 2011, from
http://www.natlib.govt.nz/downloads/metaschema-
revised.pdf

nestor. (2006). *Criteria for Trusted Digital Long-Term
Preservation Repositories - Version 1* (Request for Public
Comment), edited by nestor - Network of Expertise in
Long-Term Storage of Digital Resources and nestor
Working Group on Trusted Repositories Certification,
nestor materials 8. Retrieved on August 5, 2011, from
http://nbn-resolving.de/urn:nbn:de:0008-2006060703

nestor. (2008). Kompetenznetzwerk Langzeitarchivierung /
Arbeitsgruppe Vertrauenswürdige Archive –
Zertifizierung: nestor-Kriterien, Kriterienkatalog
vertrauenswürdige digitale Langzeitarchive. Version 2.
Retrieved on August 5, 2011, from http://www.nbn-
resolving.de?urn:nbn:de:0008-2008021802

North American Industry Classification System. (2007). U.S.
Census Bureau. Washington, DC.
http://www.census.gov/eos/www/naics/ (last accessed 10-
02-2011).

OCLC/RLG Working Group on Preservation Metadata. (2002).
"Preservation Metadata and the OAIS Information Model,
A Metadata Framework to Support the Preservation of

Digital Objects."
http://www.oclc.org/research/projects/pmwg/pm_framew
ork.pdf   (last accessed 09-29-2011).

O*NET Content Model. National O*NET Consortium.
http://www.onetcenter.org/content.html (last accessed 10-
03-2011).

O*NET-SOC Taxonomy. (2009). National O*NET Consortium.
http://www.onetcenter.org/taxonomy.html (last accessed
10-03-2011).

Open Planets Foundation. (2011). A New Registry for Digital
Preservation: Conceptual Overview.
http://openplanetsfoundation.org/sites/default/files/OPF_
A_New_Registry_Conceptual_Overview_v1%201.pdf
(last accessed 08-05-2011).

Oßwald, A., Das Referenzmodell. "OAIS – Open Archival
Information System." In: Neuroth, H., Oßwald, A.,
Scheffel, R., Strathmann, S., Huth, K. (2010) *nestor
Handbuch: Eine kleine Enzyklopädie der digitalen
Langzeitarchivierung. Version 2.3.* nestor. http://nbn-
resolving.de/urn/resolver.pl?urn:nbn:de:0008-
2010071949 (last accessed 08-02-2011).

Penker, M., Eriksson, H.-E. (2000). *Business Modeling with UML:
Business Patterns at Work.* John Wiley & Sons, New
York, NY.

Petras, V., Larson, R.R., Buckland, M. (2006). "Time period
directories: a metadata infrastructure for placing events in
temporal and geographic context." In: *Opening
Information Horizons*: 6th ACM/IEEE-CS Joint
Conference on Digital Libraries: June 11-15, 2006,
Chapel Hill, NC, USA: JCDL 2006, ACM Press, New
York, NY, pp. 151-60.

Planets project. (2008a). *White Paper: Representation Information
Registries.* http://www.planets-
project.eu/docs/reports/Planets_PC3-
D7_RepInformationRegistries.pdf (last accessed 08-05-
2011).

Planets project. (2008b). *Final XCDL Specification.*
http://www.planets-project.eu/docs/reports/Planets_PC2-
D7_FinalXCDLSpec_Ext.pdf (last accessed 08-02-2011).

PREMIS Working Group. (2005). *Data Dictionary for Preservation Metadata*. Version 1.0. http://www.oclc.org/research/activities/past/orprojects/pmwg/premis-final.pdf (last accessed 08-02-2011).

PREMIS Editorial Committee. (2011). *PREMIS Data Dictionary for Preservation Metadata*. Version 2.1. http://www.loc.gov/standards/premis/v2/premis-2-1.pdf (last accessed 08-02-2011).

Pustejovsky, James, Castaño, José, Ingria, Robert, Saurí, Roser, Gaizauskas, Robert, Setzer, Andrea, Katz, Graham. "TimeML: robust specification of event and temporal expressions in text." In: Bunt, H., van der Sluis, I. and Morante, R. (Eds), *Proceedings of the IWCS-5 5th International Workshop on Computational Semantics*, Tilburg University, Computational Linguistics and AI Group, Tilburg, The Netherlands.

Rasmussen, Karsten Boye. (1978). "Technical Standards for Magnetic Tape Exchange between Data Organizations." *IASSIST Quarterly* 2, no. 3: 76-77.

RDA: Resource Description and Access. (2011). Chicago: American Library Association.

Relator and Role Code and Term Source Codes. U.S. Library of Congress. http://www.loc.gov/standards/sourcelist/relator-role.html (last accessed 10-03-2011).

Representation and Rendering Project. (2003). *Survey and assessment of sources of information on file formats and software documentation*. University of Leeds. http://www.jisc.ac.uk/media/documents/programmes/preservation/fileformatsreport.pdf (last accessed 08-05-2011).

Research Libraries Group and National Archives and Records Administration Digital Repository Certification Task Force. (2007). *Trustworthy Repository Audit and Certification (TRAC): Criteria and Checklist*. http://www.crl.edu/sites/default/files/attachments/pages/trac_0.pdf (last accessed 08-05-2011).

Robertson, B. (2009). "Exploring historical RDF with HEML." *Digital Humanities Quarterly*. 3, (1)

Robinson, C. (1997). "Records control and disposal using functional analysis." *Archives and Manuscripts*. 25, (2):

288-303.

Rothenberg, Jeff. (1999). "Avoiding Technological Quicksand: Finding a Viable Technical Foundation for Digital Preservation." Washington, DC: Council on Library and Information Resources.

Russell, K., Sergeant, D., Stone, A., Weinberger, E., Day, M. (2000). *Metadata for digital preservation: the Cedars project outline specification.* CEDARS, University of Leeds

Rust, G., Bide, M. (2000). *The <indecs> Metadata Framework: Principles, Model and Data Dictionary.* WP1a-006-2.0. http://www.doi.org/topics/indecs/indecs_framework_2000 .pdf (last accessed 10-03-2011).

Scheuch, Erwin K. (2003). History and Visions in the Development of Data Services for the Social Sciences. *International Social Science Journal* 55, no. 3: 385-99.

Schumny, Harald. (2002). "Standards Developed Ahead of Technology." *Computer Standards and Interfaces* 24, no. 5: 363-67.

Smiraglia, Richard P., ed. (1990). *Describing Archival Materials: The Use of the MARC AMC Format.* New York: Haworth Press.

Snow, D.R., Gahegan, M., Giles, C.L., Hirth, K.G., Milner, G.R., Mitra, P., Wang, J.Z. (2006). Cybertools and archaeology. *Science.* 311, (5763): 958-9.

Spring, Michael B., Weiss, Martin B.H. (1994). Financing the Standards Development Process. In: *Standards Policy for Information Infrastructure*, edited by Brian Kahin and Janet Abbate, 289-320. Cambridge, MA: MIT Press.

Standard Occupational Classification System. (2000). U.S. Department of Labor, Bureau of Labor Statistics. Washington, DC. http://stats.bls.gov/soc/ (last accessed 10-03-2011).

Stielow, Frederick J. (1992). Archival Theory and the Preservation of Electronic Media: Opportunities and Standards Below the Cutting Edge. *American Archivist* 55: 332-43.

"Taking a Byte out of History: the Archival Preservation of Federal Computer Records." House Report No.101-978,

101st Cong., 2nd Sess., Washington, D.C.: U.S.
Government Printing Office, 1990.

Task Force on Archiving of Digital Information. (1996).
Preserving Digital Information. Report of the Task Force
on Archiving of Digital Information commissioned by
The Commission on Preservation and Access and The
Research Libraries Group. Retrieved August 2, 2011,
from
http://www.clir.org/pubs/reports/pub63watersgarrett.pdf

Tiemann, Michael (2005). "An Objective Definition of Open
Standards." *Computer Standards and Interfaces* 28, no. 5:
495-507.

Tolk, Andreas, Muguira, James A. (2003). *The Levels of
Conceptual Interoperability Model*. Simulation
Interoperability Workshop, Orlando, Florida.

Updegrove, Andrew. (1995). "Consortia and the Role of the
Government in Standard Setting." In *Standards Policy for
Information Infrastructure*, edited by Brian Kahin and
Janet Abbate, 321-48. Cambridge, MA: MIT Press.

Van den Eynden, Veerle, Corti, Louise, Woollard, Matthew,
Bishop, Libby, Horton, Laurence. (2011). *Managing and
Sharing Data. Best Practice for Researchers*. Colchester,
Essex: UK Data Archive.

W3C. (2011). *Scalable Vector Graphics (SVG) 1.1* (Second
Edition). Retrieved October 1, 2011, from
http://www.w3.org/TR/SVG11/ (last accessed 10-01-
2011).

Walch, Victoria Irons. (1990). The Role of Standards in the
Archival Management of Electronic Records. *American
Archivist* 53: 30-43.

Walch, Victoria Irons. (1993). Automated Records and Techniques
Curriculum Development Project: Committee on
Automated Records and Techniques. *American Archivist*
56, no. 3: 468-505.

Wedervang-Jensen, E., Driscoll, M. (2006). *Report on XML mark-
up of biographical and prosopographical data*. Text
Encoding Initiative. http://www.tei-
c.org/Activities/Workgroups/PERS/persw02.xml (last
accessed 10-03-2011).

Weiss, Martin B.H., and Carl Cargill. (1992). "Consortia in the Standards Development Process." *Journal of the American Society for Information Science* 43, no. 8: 559-65.

White, S.A. (2008). *Business Process Modeling Notation.* version1.1. Object Management Group. Needham, MA.

Wilson, A., Clayphan, R. (2004). *Functional requirements for describing agents.* Draft 2. Dublin Core Metadata Initiative – Agents Working Group. http://dublincore.org/groups/agents/agentFRdraft2-2.html (last accessed 10-03-2011).

Workflow Management Coalition. (2008). *XML Process Definition Language.* Version 2.1. Workflow Management Coalition, Hingham, MA.

Yates, JoAnne. (1989). *Control through Communication.* Baltimore: Johns Hopkins University Press.

Zuboff, Shoshana. (1988). *In the Age of the Smart Machine: The Future of Work and Power.* New York: Basic Books.

TECHNICAL ALIGNMENT

Michael Seadle (Humboldt-Universität zu Berlin)
Andreas Rauber (Vienna University of Technology)
Adam Rusbridge (University of Edinburgh)
Sabine Schrimpf (Deutsche Nationalbibliothek)
Matt Schultz (MetaArchive Cooperative)

Abstract

This essay discusses the importance of the areas of infrastructure *and* testing *to help digital preservation services demonstrate reliability, transparency, and accountability. It encourages practitioners to build a strong culture in which transparency and collaborations between technical frameworks are valued highly. It also argues for devising and applying agreed-upon metrics that will enable the systematic analysis of preservation infrastructure. The essay begins by defining technical infrastructure and testing in the digital preservation context, provides case studies that exemplify both progress and challenges for technical alignment in both areas, and concludes with suggestions for achieving greater degrees of technical alignment going forward.*

Introduction

This essay considers two critical areas in which the maturing digital preservation field should seek to advance technical alignment both within and across national boundaries: infrastructure and testing.[1] Aligning work in these areas will help practitioners more effectively meet stakeholders' demands for high-levels of reliability, transparency, and accountability. The infrastructure for digital preservation has reached a stage of development that enables interoperability and benchmarking. To accomplish the former, we must continue to encourage transparency and collaboration between technical frameworks, and

---

[1] Infrastructure in the context of this essay refers to the technological components of an organization's infrastructure that are required for digital preservation. Other essays in this volume address additional components of infrastructure for digital preservation, e.g., organizational, economic, and education.

it is important to demonstrate and document the ways that the field benefits from digital archiving framework interoperability efforts.

To enable benchmarking and to establish a culture of infrastructure testing, we must first convince the community of the need for quantitative analysis, arrive at agreed upon metrics, and then gather and publish empirical results. Coordinated action across the community (particularly if it is combined with future requirements from funding agencies to incorporate testing into government funded projects) could lead to an evolving public test-bed in which we can fairly and accurately evaluate various archiving systems and preservation solutions. This essay discusses the importance of such developments: 1) by defining technical infrastructure and testing in the digital preservation context, 2) by providing case studies that exemplify both progress and challenges for technical alignment in both areas, and 3) by concluding with suggestions for achieving greater degrees of technical alignment going forward.

Infrastructure

For technical alignment, the term *infrastructure* can encompass far more than the hardware and software necessary for managing digital archiving systems and the communication protocols for sharing resources across a network or system. It can also extend to the ways in which digital information is structured: both separate data objects and the linkages within applications and environments that make them function as a visible and usable whole. In that sense, infrastructure also relates to the metadata used to describe digital information or the systems used to generate descriptive information on an as-needed basis. Using this broad definition, *infrastructure* may also include the software used for migration and emulation processes (although these depend heavily on assumptions about how archived information will be used in the future and thus require a strong user-behavior assessment component). Standards, organizational elements, and economic factors also play a role in infrastructure as well, since they influence the design process for infrastructure development. Each of these elements is addressed in regards to their own alignment issues in separate essays within this volume. The following discussion seeks to account for facets of these broader influences on the digital preservation field's technical infrastructure alignment activities.

Alignment of Infrastructure

This discussion of the alignment of infrastructure begins with a concrete consideration of existing examples of technical implementation, focusing on four specific digital archiving systems and support networks as case studies:

- UK LOCKSS (Lots of Copies Keep Stuff Safe) Alliance;

- kopal (Kooperativer Aufbau eines Langzeitarchivs digitaler Informationen) / koLibRI (kopal Library for Retrieval and Ingest) & DP4Lib in Germany;

- nestor in Germany; and

- LuKII (LOCKSS und KOPAL: Infrastruktur und Interoperabilität) in Germany.

These system infrastructures are highlighted here as one set of exemplars and case studies in the digital archiving field. They are not intended to serve as an exhaustive overview of the field, but rather as a useful subset that can help us to consider some of the principles and criteria that might foster and advance technical alignment.

As we consider these case studies below, we focus on the following questions:

- What infrastructure components comprise these digital archiving systems?

- Are their code bases open source and thus reusable for other archiving systems?

- To what degree do these infrastructures enable and/or foster interoperation?

- To what degree are these systems "complete" or "incomplete" for digital archiving purposes?

Taken together, these case studies exemplify the advantages we may gain through aligning infrastructures across multiple borders and barriers. Though there is some overlap on a software level between these initiatives, the projects and programs themselves have very different national priorities, organizational contexts, and archiving priorities. They are especially useful for the purposes of this discussion of infrastructure for achieving technical alignment because of their developers' insistence upon pushing the limits of the underlying technology's interoperability, and each of the system's corresponding degree of openness and potentials for doing so.

Case Study 1: UK LOCKSS Alliance

The UK LOCKSS Alliance (UKLA)[2] is a cooperative membership organization whose goal is to ensure continuing access to scholarly work in ways that are sustainable over the long term. It represents the collaborative activity of UK libraries that are interested in building national "network-level" infrastructure and coordinating the preservation of electronic material of local and UK interest.

The UKLA seeks to ensure libraries remain central to the process of scholarly information management by enabling its members to take custody of the assets for which they have paid in order to build—not simply lease—local collections of published scholarly material. The UKLA uses the LOCKSS (Lots of Copies Keep Stuff Safe)[3] software to enable UK Higher Education libraries to develop journal preservation infrastructure and collections and to engage with journal preservation issues at a tangible, local level.

The LOCKSS technology is an open source, peer-to-peer, decentralized digital preservation infrastructure. LOCKSS preserves all formats and genres of Web-published content. It works by collecting a direct copy of digitally published scholarly content such that the intellectual content, including the historical context (the look and feel), is preserved. This content is collected by a network of geographically distributed servers that actively monitor the content through iterative cycles of voting and polling (using SHA-1 hashes) to establish the continued authenticity and veracity of the collected content over time.

The strategic goals of the UK LOCKSS Alliance for the period 2010-2013 are to:

1. Identify, negotiate and make available for preservation a collection of journal titles relevant to need;

2. Increase usefulness and relevance of the UK LOCKSS Alliance community activity; and to

---

[2] See UK LOCKSS Alliance: http://www.lockssalliance.ac.uk/ (last accessed 03-14-2012).

[3] See LOCKSS: http://www.LOCKSS.org (last accessed 03-14-2012).

3. Sustain and develop a well-founded UK national cooperative library organization to assist with ensuring continuing access to scholarly material.

EDINA, JISC's National Data Centre at the University of Edinburgh, is leading the provision of support for the UK LOCKSS Alliance. A dedicated team at Stanford University Library develops the LOCKSS software and leads and supports its US and international development.

Libraries are required to supply their own hardware upon which the LOCKSS software is installed. Staff responsibilities tend to be split between librarians responsible for collection development and IT staff responsible for system maintenance. UKLA found that these roles are not always under the same administration structures, and so responsibilities for maintenance are not always clear and well understood. This can lead to the marginalization and neglect of infrastructure. To overcome this, ongoing education and training helps motivate staff and some libraries have found that introduction of an explicit e-journal preservation policy has helped secure the engagement of both library and IT staff and secure commitment of resources, embedding local preservation activity into staff workflows and job descriptions.

For some members, the value of participation in the UK LOCKSS Alliance is best demonstrated through access to content. In early 2012, integration of LOCKSS with link resolver systems was released and the components are now undergoing community test and deployment. Demonstrating access will help secure future funding and resources to add additional functionality and undertake further testing.

A number of e-journal preservation initiatives have emerged over the last decade, and monitoring statements regarding "who is preserving what" is becoming increasingly important. EDINA and the ISSN International Centre have partnered to develop the Keepers Registry, which provides easily accessible information about inclusion of journals in preservation services and will help to identify gaps in coverage. This service aggregates information from archiving initiatives, currently using the information made publicly available (often in spreadsheet formats, with some adhering to the KBART guidelines). As the service develops, it is proposed that journal metadata will be collected using the recent ONIX for Preservation standard.[4]

Testing of LOCKSS in the UK environment has focused on aspects needed to improve service-level qualities of the approach: how to improve coverage and access to content, and how to demonstrate value from participation. All content goes through a quality assurance test process before being preserved in the LOCKSS network. LOCKSS collects content from a wide variety of publishing platforms, and content must be collected according to licensing boundaries (i.e., delimited by volume). A "plugin" defines the URLs to be collected, fetching the relevant full text, PDFs, images, etc. A test process then confirms that everything that should be collected has been collected. We are now at a stage where further testing of the UKLA network is needed, for example to assess the quality and completeness of the content held by UK machines, and of the effectiveness of the software to provide access to content as and when it is needed. Practical tests of this nature will provide libraries with more assurances that a switch to e-only is reliable, and allow the LOCKSS approach to further develop economies of scale to work with a greater range and quantity of material.

Case Study 2: kopal/KoLibRI & DP4Lib

Parallel to these technical alignment developments in the UK, discussions about a digital preservation infrastructure for Germany have from the beginning emphasized a distributed model. The system of memory institutions in Germany is traditionally decentralized with well-established state and regional libraries and archives. Technical alignment is thus critical to cooperation in this environment in order for several disparate organizations to be enabled and empowered to contribute to a larger national directive and initiative for accomplishing digital preservation.

Schwens and Liegmann stated this most eloquently in 2004:

A cooperative structure for digital preservation, corresponding to the structure of the analogue realm, ought to be developed, which ensures preservation and availability of all digital resources published in Germany (in German language or about Germany) [,

---

[4] The ONIX for Preservation Holdings draft standard is available online at http://www.editeur.org/127/ONIX-PH/ (last accessed 07-05-2012).

which] ensures preservation and availability of the most important objects in all scientific fields, no matter if it is text, facts, images, or multimedia, [and which] ensures the preservation and availability of digital archival records.[5]

The *kopal* project ("Co-operative Development of a Long-Term Digital Information Archive") and its successor DP4Lib (see below) represent important building blocks for achieving this alignment.

The aim and purpose of the *kopal* project was to develop and test a long-term preservation system for co-operative use. The system is based on DIAS, at that time a standards-oriented implementation of the OAIS reference model using established IBM software (more on standards and infrastructure implementations below). The DIAS system was designed as an in-house long-term archive for the Koninklijke Bibliotheek (KB) and was extended in the *kopal* project to support co-operative use and remote access. The open source "*kopal* Library for Retrieval and Ingest" (koLibRI) connects individual users with the archival system and it can be configured to meet the needs of those users. As such it allows users with various different selection profiles and with different types of digital objects to share a single archival system, while retaining control of their data.

koLibRI validates the objects' file formats, and packages the objects together with their technical metadata as Submission Information Packages (SIPs) using the Universal Object Format (UOF). The UOF SIP files are imported, and, in OAIS terminology, stored as Archival Information Packages (AIPs) in the DIAS archival storage unit. Each *kopal* user can, via koLibRI, address and retrieve only its own data. Migration was tested as a preservation action within the *kopal* project. Other preservation actions are still to be developed.

After the end of the project, the *kopal* archival system had two active users: The German National Library (DNB) and the Göttingen State- and University Library (SUB). The DNB and SUB have subsequently allied with six different additional partners with varying use scenarios. One partner, the German Institute for International Pedagogical Research, is a research institute with

---

[5] U. Schwens, H. Liegmann: Langzeitarchivierung digitaler Ressourcen, (2004). The paragraph quoted is originally in German.

large specialized holdings, including digitized and born digital journals as well as databases. Another partner, the Library Service Centre of Baden Württemberg, offers long-term preservation as a service to its customers and seeks a safe harbor for the data for which it has assumed responsibility.

The purpose of the DP4Lib project ("Digital Preservation for libraries") is to open up the *kopal* system to these additional users mentioned above and to extend its functionality. The overall goal is to establish and run a ready-to-operate service for long-term preservation. While co-operative use of the *kopal* system is generally technically feasible, various organizational issues had to be clarified and are addressed in the project. The DP4Lib partners are, for example, conjointly compiling a catalogue of requirements for long-term preservation as a service, and are developing business and cost models, as well as process models for co-operative long-term preservation operations. Further work is also being done to enhance functionality, namely evaluating tools for generating technical metadata, and tools for converting and normalizing digital objects. These additional evaluation activities, particularly those focusing on re-use, interoperability, and collaboration factors are made possible and given promising potential thanks to *kopal's and* DP4Lib's intentional emphases on developing a co-operative infrastructure from the outset.

Case Study 3: nestor

Closely associated with *kopal* and DP4Lib, and worth mentioning briefly, is *nestor*, the national competence network for digital preservation in Germany. *Nestor* was originally established in 2003, in the same year that the *kopal* project kicked off. While *kopal* intended to establish the technical preconditions for a co-operative and shared preservation infrastructure in Germany, the *nestor* network aimed at setting the organizational framework and infrastructural foundations. *nestor* brings together experts and institutions active in digital preservation. The *kopal* users and several of the DP4Lib partners take part in *nestor*, as well as the Bavarian State Library, which has implemented a digital long-term archive based on Ex Libris Rosetta. Last not least, the three national subject libraries, which intend to set up a shared digital preservation solution for their purposes together, joined *nestor*. *nestor* contributes to ensuring the conditions through which developers of archiving systems can collaborate to ensure their infrastructures and systems are complete for accomplishing their stated purposes. When considering the value and importance of coalescing trends toward common infrastructures of broad applicability, such groups and models should not be overlooked or undervalued.

nestor hosts several working groups on relevant preservation related questions and standards and it fosters knowledge exchange and advancement. It offers a platform for memory institutions to discuss and align roles and responsibilities in the digital realm. *nestor* also runs a cooperation with the German Institute for Standardisation (DIN), to help crystallize standards in the relatively new field of digital preservation.

Together with several higher education partners, *nestor* develops initial and further training courses in the field of digital preservation in Germany, so that qualified staff are available to deal with the digital preservation challenge.

nestor has also been actively involved in developing an audit and certification system for trusted digital archives. Trust is an important prerequisite for co-operation (more on trust below). Especially in a shared and networked preservation system, partners want to be sure that their information is safe with the respective partners' institution. Because it is impossible to predict in which state a piece of digital information will be in, for example, 50 years, it is important to evaluate the set-up of existing archives.

Case Study 4: LuKii

The LuKII (LOCKSS und KOPAL: Infrastruktur und Interoperabilität) initiative bridges the LOCKSS and KOPAL systems, providing an interoperability model for digital archiving. LuKII is an infrastructure and research project with staffing at Humboldt-Universität zu Berlin and at the German National Library in Frankfurt. The project began in 2009 with funding from the German Research Foundation (Deutsche Forschungsgemeinschaft). The project lists the following goals in its original proposal:

- To establish a cost-effective LOCKSS network in Germany including infrastructure to provide ongoing technical support and management for LOCKSS and its variants (e.g. CLOCKSS);

- To conceptualize and implement interoperability between LOCKSS and KOPAL in order to combine cost-effective bitstream preservation with well-developed usability preservation tools; and

- To test the interoperability prototype by archiving data from German institutional repositories.

An important element of the first goal was to get a minimum of seven partner libraries to be able to implement a Private LOCKSS Network (PLN) within Germany.[6]

A competence center at Humboldt-Universität zu Berlin offers German speaking technical assistance about LOCKSS to the German partners and to others in the German-speaking community. The competence center runs out of the university's computer center (called Computer and Media Service) and is in regular contact with the Stanford LOCKSS team. LOCKSS refers all problems in the German-speaking regions to Berlin.

Programmers are also working at both the DNB and at Humboldt-Universität on modifications to koLibRI and LOCKSS respectively to enable interoperability. One modification is to enable LOCKSS to make use of METS metadata. LOCKSS can, of course, store METS (it can store any form of digital information) but has not previously also used it as actionable metadata. Another modification is to shift the storage containers to the new WARC format. KoLibRI staff have collaborated with the Berlin LOCKSS team to make progress on the WARC conversion, as well as on enabling koLibRI's migration manager to work with LOCKSS. The goal is to introduce prophylactic migration to LOCKSS and to let *kopal* data be able to use on-the-fly migration through LOCKSS. Developing local expertise with the core LOCKSS code also helps to decentralize LOCKSS maintenance and expansion. LuKII is a successful effort to test and validate the value and importance of open source re-use of existing technologies, pursuing interoperability where advantageous, and selecting infrastructure options that are flexible for promoting multi-institutional collaborations on behalf of digital preservation.

The harvesting of works in German open access repositories is about to begin. The first wave of harvesting will be using unmodified LOCKSS software and the second wave will harvest

---

[6] As of mid 2011, LuKII has ten official partners: Bayrische Staatsbibliothek, Deutsche Nationalbibliothek, hbz - Hochschulbibliothekszentrum NRW, Humboldt-Universität zu Berlin, Karlsruher Institut für Technologie, Sächsische Landesbibliothek - Staats- und Universitätsbibliothek Dresden, Universität Konstanz, Universitätsbibliothek Stuttgart, Universitäts- und Landesbibliothek Münster, Niedersächsische Staats- und Universitätsbibliothek Göttingen.

the same sources using LOCKSS in order to be able to test the new programs. This testing will foster a better understanding of the modifications the project team has made to the LOCKSS framework, both within our team and throughout the broader community of digital archiving practice. The empirical data we collect and publish regarding these tests will mark an important development in establishing technical benchmarking for digital archiving systems.

Each of the above case studies demonstrates the advantages gained through aligning technical infrastructures across multiple borders and barriers. In the case of the *UKLA*, use of the open source LOCKSS software has enabled UK Higher Education libraries to build a national "network-level" infrastructure and coordinate the preservation of electronic material of local and UK interest. The focus of *kopal/KoLibRI & DP4Lib* on developing a co-operative infrastructure at the outset models the value of establishing a firm foundation for benefitting later from factors such as re-use, interoperability, and collaboration. *Nestor* demonstrates the organizational dimensions of technical alignment through facilitating interactions across groups to ensure that developers can mutually collaborate to the benefit of their archiving systems. And *LuKII* has demonstrated how to combine open source technologies to enrich preservation activities while bridging multi-institutional environments. In the course of each of these on-going technical alignment developments, iterative testing was recognized as being of critical importance to their maturation and adoption, and remains so. The next sections explore the importance of testing to improve technical alignment.

Towards Testing: Standards and Infrastructure Implementations

The importance of standards to alignment more broadly is discussed in a separate essay within this volume. Here, we focus our discussion specifically on the need for standard approaches to establishing interoperability between digital archiving infrastructures. Such standard approaches ultimately will improve the chances of bridging systems. They make can make ingest and retrieval simpler by reducing the number of choices and special adaptations needed. Standards should also, in an important sense, reduce risk because they represent choices that have in theory undergone extensive design considerations and testing. This is ideal.

There are instances, however, where technical standards for digital archiving have failed to achieve these goals for a variety of reasons. At the ANADP conference a member of the panel on standards admitted that the problem with standards is that there are too many of them. If there are too many "standards" for interoperability and/or for testing of technical components, the result may be no common standards at all. In the technical landscape, some official standards fall into virtual disuse soon after they receive approval, because a new standard supersedes them or because the technical environment changes. This is less the fault of standards-setting organizations like the W3C or ISO than it is the fault of commercial market factors, which determines in fact whether a standard will be used or ignored. Libraries, archives, and other memory institutions have in general too small a market share, even collectively, to influence commercial vendors to accept the standards that the community favors. The exception is firms that market only to memory institutions.

Technical standards tend also to be somewhat misunderstood in the digital preservation community. OAIS (Open Archival Information System) is a classic example. The Consultative Committee for Space Data Systems (CCSDS) documentation about OAIS clearly discusses it as a reference model.[7] That means that it labels the key elements of an archiving system to enable common discourse about the services that that element provides and the role it serves. Many in the digital preservation community continue to conflate this reference function with a system design. A system could be designed specifically with components that use the OAIS model, but more typically it is a matter of changing names on established designs. Commercial vendors use the OAIS label more for marketing than for engineering. This does not make their systems worse, but nor does the label make them better. OAIS compliance has minimal design meaning in most cases, and these claims sometimes obscure as much as they reveal.[8]

Closing the gap between the over-abundance of technical standards that exist today and more widely adopted standards that

---

[7] The OAIS Reference Model document includes a definition of the term Reference Model (page 1-14) and throughout Section 1 refers to the role and significance of reference models (CCSDS, 2009).

[8] Developers are, however, beginning to build and test open source digital archiving systems that aim to be OAIS compliant—DAITSS and DAITSS2, as well as Archivematica, as just a couple of examples. The adoptability and use of these systems is in need of further implementations and tests.

would enhance interoperability and reduce risk involves testing on a large scale. Merely testing to find out whether a proposed standard functions as it should, and whether it has the potential for addressing technical needs, is only a starting point. A more important test is whether multiple system-vendors are willing to adopt a standard, implement it in their software, and then determine whether it meets their needs. This form of testing could also gather actual empirical information about the functioning of a standard. Standards that did not get a minimum number of adopters would fail the test automatically.

The technical standards that matter most for digital preservation can in fact be determined on these empirical levels. For example, formats that are used today to publish contents on the World Wide Web (that is, contents accessed via HTTP services over the Internet) represent de facto format standards after a certain level of adoption, which includes incorporation into established browsers such as Firefox, Internet Explorer, Chrome, and Safari. These browsers have a strong record of enabling backward compatibility. The number of file formats published online and readable by browsers in the 1990s that cannot be read today is negligible. It does not matter whether these formats represent official standards or not—they are the way in which content was and is shared. It is important to distinguish between the longevity of these publication formats and the formats used by text editing systems such as MS-Word. Word was never meant to be a publication format or anything more than an intermediate editor for content. Few MS-Word documents play a publication role except (ironically) in institutional repositories, which are generally run by universities and are meant (at least in part) for digital preservation (Rosenthal 2010).

The long-term use and testing of metadata standards can also contribute to advancing technical alignment on an infrastructure level. However, applying a similar empirical test to metadata is somewhat harder, because metadata tends to be less visible. Clearly, Dublin Core plays a significant role in information exchange on the Internet. METS, and some elements of PREMIS, are increasing in popularity within the digital preservation community, perhaps in part because both schemas are extensible in the capabilities and features that they offer. Whether METS or PREMIS have achieved a similar status more broadly is less likely. In the broader commercial world relatively few METS (and virtually no PREMIS) implementations exist, except among vendors like Rosetta that market directly to the digital preservation community and arguably use METS because of its appeal to customers.

Publication formats and metadata are only two examples of areas where the existence of de facto standards impacts the implementation of digital preservation systems. What is important here is the need to distinguish between those standards established by standards setting agencies that, despite all good intentions, fail to play any functional role as standards, and those that, sometimes without official approval, are in fact so commonly used that digital preservation implementations need to recognize and accept them. In all cases, the role of sound testing is critical for closing gaps, enhancing interoperability, and reducing risk. Testing is needed on a routine basis throughout various implementation phases.

Testing

Testing involves reproducible experiments using, if possible, real data to show whether software and hardware perform under conditions that reflect a reasonable hypothesis about the future. Testing can take several forms and depend on design goals and targeted outcomes (functional vs. non-functional; static vs. dynamic; unit vs. systems, etc.). The first and most basic test is whether a system functions at all—that is, whether the code compiles and runs without errors. A second level test might establish whether the system scales appropriately—the testing should involve not merely storage capacity, but also ingest and access processes. One example would be a stress test, in which large numbers of access requests (including permissions decisions and search/retrieval) are made of a system in a short time. A third and more complex type of test would involve conditions that can be anticipated for future digital environments. One example might be bit rot, which can be predicted mathematically and emulated to age storage systems virtually. Future storage may propose to eliminate bit-rot, but no current evidence suggests such a development. Other examples could be user-tests involving format migration to adapt to evolving e-reader devices.

Testing is one of the key ingredients to making progress in technical alignment in digital preservation. To date, a great deal of the research in this domain lacks the solid ground provided by thorough and consistent testing. Solutions are being developed and presented, yet little is done to ensure that the underlying systems actually address the right problems and address them in ways that have a high probability of long term success.

When it comes to aligning, sharing, and collaboratively furthering tools and infrastructure (both technical as well as knowledge bases) it is essential to be able to rely upon the individual building blocks. This requires reproducible testing of tools and know-how, as well as thorough documentation of the circumstances under which the software was tested. Currently, most tools and most techniques are simply "evaluated" by people without the necessary technical skills or background to judge to what degree it fits the intended purpose.

The problem with this type of evaluation is that it is not replicable, not scalable, not reusable and provides limited (if any) basis for technical alignment and continuous development. The library and archiving community needs to move from ad-hoc evaluation to solid testing and benchmarking. A similar focus on solid and thorough testing has brought huge boosts in other disciplines, specifically information retrieval and machine learning. Testing provides a scientific basis, well-understood measures and limitations, and a sense of the fitness-for-use via its various benchmarks and measurements.

The Role of Trust and the Importance of Distrust

There is a useful tension between trust and distrust in the technical aspects of digital preservation. The *nestor* efforts to certify trusted repositories offer a valuable basis for any form of digital preservation, because certification ensures that basic procedures are followed and that process descriptions exist. A repository whose update or backup procedures are sloppy or one that fails to document key features in system management is not a repository that is likely to provide data with reliable integrity or authenticity over long periods.

Certifying that a repository currently carries out appropriate procedures (opening to review or inspection and expressing conformance to recognized standard practices) does not, however, mean that it should be trusted to reliably preserve digital information over prolonged periods of time. Certification gives a snapshot in time. Typically, organizations make special efforts to clean up their procedures before a certification visit takes place and may let them slide again afterwards. Good practice between certification visits may remain in place, but certification cannot guarantee that. Certification is a form of audit, but one that does not typically include auditing the data for integrity or evidence of authenticity—in part because these are technically complex and difficult issues that the audit teams may not be prepared to handle. The cost in time and effort would increase significantly. Only a few systems, notably LOCKSS, have a built-in integrity-checking process that functions as an ongoing internal audit (described in more detail below and in Rosenthal, 2010).

Distrust presents itself as a much safer basis than trust for designing systems and for planning long term digital preservation, as long as that distrust means building in sufficient redundancy to make reasonable allowance for error, accident, external attack or deliberate internal damage—all of which are known problems. Precisely how much redundancy is needed can currently only be guessed at, since few companies or even non-profit organizations want to admit or publicize their internal problems. The most-cited study in this area (Power, 2002) is now outdated and those with computer center experience believe that the results probably understate the actual magnitude. There is no reason to think that the dangers have changed substantially, though the balance of risks may have changed because of increasing external attacks.

Redundancy also has a geographic component. Recent natural disasters such as the earthquake and tsunami in Japan in March 2011 and even Hurricane Irene in the US in August 2011 show the danger of trusting any one particular location. While no data was known to be lost in either case, electricity was interrupted, services broke down, and the nuclear power plants failed despite extensive and well-tested protections. A repository with all of its data in a single location or even a single geographic area subject to adverse weather, seismic, economic, or political conditions should be considered to be at risk.

The limits of distrust are equally important to recognize. Librarians understand from their experiences with print and microfilm that every additional copy in a different and secure location and on a different physical medium increases the chances of long-term survival. The assurances inherent to static physical mediums that are missing due to the vulnerabilities of electronic content often privilege trust in the physical over the digital. The problem is that information no longer comes exclusively in static text and image formats with clear beginnings, endings, and sequences from start to the finish. They forget also the vulnerability of paper and film to damage by users, to say nothing of a vulnerability to environmental conditions such as humidity or insects. A form of distrust that goes to the extreme of discounting digital archiving errs in its trust of physical media, just as a form of trust in a particular "trusted" archive errs in misjudging the long term vulnerabilities of any one organization. Balance is key.

Requirements for Testing

To achieve effective testing for digital preservation, the digital preservation community needs to begin with a range of scenarios that have:

- CLEAR GOALS: this includes a description of a specific purpose or purposes for the testing.

- BENCHMARK DATA: benchmark data should have the range and complexity of real data and be checked whether they fit the purpose and goals;

- MEASUREMENT SCALES: these scales and measurements need to remain stable over time, even with improvements, so that comparisons are possible;

- KNOWLEDGE BASE: the knowledge base provides a location to collect and make available the test results.

Each of these points will be discussed further below.

Goals for Testing

Testing needs to be specific in terms of what is being tested and what the outcomes mean. Effective testing may have multiple well-focused goals but should not become a catch-all that attempts to cover everything. Defining common goals that are meaningful across multiple software platforms could pose a major challenge to the highly heterogeneous digital preservation community. It may be necessary to focus on some subsets, rather than trying to address too many goals at once.

The goals for testing can exist on multiple levels. At the highest level they should perhaps focus on broad concepts such as establishing how well archiving systems can perform on issues such as:

- maintaining the integrity of the digital content;

- retaining evidence of the authenticity of that content; and

- demonstrating that the content can be used (read) under potential future circumstances.

None of these goals are easy to test, in part because no consensus exists even about how to define terms like *integrity* or *authenticity* in a digital environment. *Use* is particularly problematic because many librarians define use simply as reading the way they read today, without considering how reading has changed over time and without taking other kinds of use (interactive games, for example) into account. *Integrity* comes closest to having an established technical definition based on the comparison of check-sum calculations, though *integrity* is also used in a broader sense by managers of digital content in ways that may confuse this specific technical use of the term.

At a lower level, testing may need to have goals that can vary with particular types of systems, while still enabling broader comparisons among results. A good example of this is the SIP stress test for the Rosetta software, where they tried to find out how many documents they could add in a specific amount of time (Ex Libris, 2010). This was an excellent example of public testing, but to make comparisons with other systems possible, the goals for such tests need to specify the conditions under which they take place. A load test using fiber channels on closely linked systems is, for example, very different than a test loading data via standard Internet services.

Benchmark Data

Standard benchmark data are one of the most important elements in a systematic testing program and are among the hardest to establish. The temptation is to manufacture data that fits a particular system, but artificially manufactured data tend to fail to represent the variety and complexity of real data. This means that systems may work flawlessly with manufactured data and less well with actual cases. Even real data can be flawed if the set does not include the full range of types and formats. In fact, a key first step is defining the range and type of complexity that the benchmark data should have. In some cases this is best done empirically with sampling to avoid overly simplistic assumptions, while in others it may be better to design artificial data sets with well-defined and known characteristics.

Typically library-based digital preservation systems have focused on archiving those text-oriented formats that are successors to print publications.[9] A print-image PDF may seem like a reasonable representation for this form of data, but this may already be an outdated assumption. Publishers typically offer HTML-based versions as well as PDFs. The number of researchers in the UK who get their information from online sources is now up to 85% according to a recent study, and about 45% of them read online rather than print (Tenopir, 2011). Online reading may be PDF, but the screen-friendly online formats using HTML, CSS, Javascript, JPEG, etc. may be more attractive for reading and PDF for printing. The data and the interactions in these HTML-based formats are more complex than content in single file and multimedia data or data from interactive systems are more complex still, especially since the "data" may include executable code.

Knowing what types, varieties, and formats of data to collect still does not mean that it will be easy to gather appropriately representative data. Legal issues may create permissions problems, especially for making the data available as benchmark data to multiple systems. Quantity can also be a problem. A stress test or a scaling test needs relatively large quantities of data.

Measurement Scales

Measuring the success of a test is complex because the scales need to be meaningful in terms of both the goals and the data. There is a strong tendency to approach measurement with a binary mentality: success or failure. This oversimplifies most real situations and is more of a marketing tool than a scholarly assessment. A stress test for an ingest system could have a measurement scale in items per hour, if the items are comparatively homogenous. It could also have MB per hour, if size varies or is a significant factor—though separating performance between large and small items could be necessary too. But if size is relatively stable and the complexity of the digital content varies, then the scale may need to take complexity into account. An overly simplistic scale can show misleading results.

Measurement scales need to be stated in a way that meaningful comparisons are possible when multiple systems run the same test. Anonymous participation in benchmark evaluations

---

[9] With the rapid expansion into research data, this is beginning to change to some degree.

has been shown to be successful in other domains, with only voluntary disclosure of a participant's identity after the evaluation. Commercial vendors may be reluctant to engage in this kind of controlled comparison of systems fearing adverse results.

Knowledge Base

If one of the key reasons for testing is comparison, then the results, the data, the measurement scales, and the goals need to be publicly and openly available. This does not mean in this era of distributed computing that a single server needs to host this information, but it does mean that some form of linkage and easy discovery is needed. While it is tempting to say that there should be established standards for testing and that some institution needs to maintain them, it is also important that testing standards not encounter the same problem as other technical standards where there are so many that actual comparison (the testing equivalent to interoperation) becomes meaningless. It may be better to perform widespread testing first and to build on that experience when establishing standards specifically for digital preservation testing.

In practical terms a subset of the digital preservation community needs to take the lead in creating data, in developing testing scenarios and measures to address specific goals, and in sharing openly all the elements that went into the testing. One incentive for doing this is that the subset that takes the lead could get an advantage of setting the terms by which archiving is tested. It will also be doing the community a service. The task is not trivial, however, and results may take years before the mass is sufficient to be useful.

Learning from Other Domains

In testing, the digital preservation community can also learn from other domains, such as for example the medical domain, where strong compliance requirements exist and are frequently tested beyond mere conformance checks. DICOM standard compliance testing, for example, includes the Connectathon (http://www.ihe.net/Connectathon), which is a week-long interoperability-testing event where system developers must demonstrate their ability to exchange data and to interoperate via common communication protocols using ad-hoc task settings. Similar lessons can be learned from the Machine Learning and Information Retrieval communities, both of which have strong traditions in automated, objective benchmark evaluation, in test data and ground truth compilation, and in scientific competitions, all of which form the basis for scientific progress (Kalgren, 2011).

Examples of Testing for Digital Preservation

So far, several important steps have been made in this direction of establishing a culture of testing for the digital preservation community. Below are a series of case studies that demonstrate progress in this direction and offer approaches that can be built upon and re-applied.

Case Study 1: LOCKSS

LOCKSS has a long history of public testing. Two tests in particular stand out. One looked at measures to resist attacks on LOCKSS as a peer-to-peer preservation system. The issue is especially important for LOCKSS because the LOCKSS servers work in the Internet environment and can routinely be subject to attack. For this reason it was worthwhile to test their robustness and to demonstrate publicly their ability to withstand intrusion attempts (Manaitis, 2004).

The second LOCKSS test of special importance was the test of on-the-fly migration. Migration is a matter of special concern within the library community because of bad experiences with word processing formats. The LOCKSS approach to migration did not rely on converting contents to new formats and storing the resulting version, but built in the ability to convert a format in real time, as the demand arises. LOCKSS demonstrated that the process worked seamlessly and efficiently and published the results (Rosenthal 2005). Storing the code to convert a format is also more space-efficient and makes it easy to implement quality improvements in the migration.[10] That said, format obsolescence remains an area of constant research and particularly for more obscure formats and use cases may require more sophisticated monitoring and migration measures.

Case Study 2: Rosetta

Rosetta (from Ex Libris) did a "scaling proof of concept" for the Church of the Latter Day Saints, and the results of this test are available online. The test used up to 50 million synthetic records of

---

[10] For more on format migration, see David S.H. Rosenthal. "Format Obsolescence: Assessing the Threat and the Defenses," *Library High Tech*, Special Issue, vol. 28, no.2, 2010, pp. 195-210. doi:10.1108/07378831011047613 (last accessed 06-11-2012).

varying sizes. The goal was to demonstrate that they could "meet organizational objectives of loading two petabytes of data within one year" (Ex Libris, 2010). The test was (as Ex Libris explains) a compromise between a full-scale demonstration and one that was economically feasible.

Case Study 3: PLANETS

PLANETS (Preservation and Long-Term Access through Networked Services) offers a test-bed for experiments. The test-bed runs on a Dell PE 2950 III server running Ubuntu with 900 GB of storage. This clearly limits the kind of experiments that are possible and excludes tests involving production-level systems like LOCKSS, Rosetta, or Portico. Its strength is that it offers a standard location and formal methodologies for testing and makes it easy for others to comment. The Planets Preservation Planning Tool PLATO (http://www.ifs.tuwien.ac.at/dp/plato/intro.html) allows testers to share evaluations of the performance of specific preservation actions such as migration and emulation tools, some of which may be called from within a controlled environment.

Case Study 4: CASPAR

CASPAR (Cultural, Artistic and Scientific Knowledge for Preservation, Access and Retrieval) also has a test-bed implementation plan that focuses on "evidence that the CASPAR approach is doing something useful for digital preservation in several different domains in several different organizations." (CASPAR, 2009) CASPAR's goals are, among others:

- Enhance the techniques for capturing Representation Information and other preservation related information for content objects.

- Design virtualization services supporting long-term digital resource preservation, despite changes in the underlying computing (hardware and software) and storage systems, and the Designated Communities.

- Integrate digital rights management, authentication, and accreditation as standard features of CASPAR.

- Research more sophisticated access to and use of preserved digital resources including intuitive query and browsing mechanisms (CASPAR, 2011).

Case Study 5: TRAC

TRAC is the short name for the "Trustworthy Repositories Audit & Certification: Criteria and Checklist" that was produced by a task force convened by the Research Libraries Group (RLG) and the US National Archives and Records Administration Task Force on Digital Repository Certification in 2007 and since maintained by the Center for Research Libraries (CRL). The goal was clearly stated:

> The goal of the RLG-NARA Task Force on Digital Repository Certification has been to develop criteria to identify digital repositories capable of reliably storing, migrating, and providing access to digital collections. The challenge has been to produce certification criteria and delineate a process for certification applicable to a range of digital repositories and archives, from academic institutional preservation repositories to large data archives and from national libraries to third-party digital archiving services.

The TRAC checklist has been used by CRL in performing audits of digital preservation systems. TRAC provided the basis for "ISO standard 16363: Audit and certification of trustworthy digital repositories" (ISO, 2012).

Testing: Opportunities for Technical Alignment

To align, share, and further tools and infrastructure collaboratively, the digital archiving community must mature past ad-hoc evaluations and establish a culture of testing, so that the community can trust the technological solutions being offered. This requires solid evaluation of tools and know-how, as well as thorough documentation of the circumstances under which the software was evaluated. These evaluation strategies need to be replicable, scalable, and re-usable. The purpose of this essay is not to provide a detailed roadmap, but to demonstrate the need for testing and to stimulate thinking about practical solutions. The testing scenarios described and depicted above in the various case studies are a step in the right direction. Building upon their efforts, a couple of further approaches are suggested below.

One approach might be for the cultural memory community to work towards establishing sustainable environments and neutral platform to initiate benchmarking strategies. This could have the added side benefit of creating a market of sorts for emerging solutions. This environment would also serve to drive technical alignment goals such as interoperability. Progress in this direction would require:

- knowing and defining what to test and what is fit for testing;

- thinking about how to test these components and principles;

- defining such tests: including goal specification, measures, data, etc.; and

- running an initial set of pilot tests.

Another approach would be for libraries and other memory institutions, with the help of funding agencies, to progressively and collectively insist on tests and comparisons before they make decisions about choosing long-term preservation solutions. This customer-driven approach might be less systematic and likely many of the tests would turn out to be suspect, but merely insisting on public tests would begin to create a culture of testing and of decision-making based on empirical data that would make systematic benchmarking such as described in the first approach more realistic.

Conclusions

As detailed above, the key technological accomplishments in digital preservation thus far mostly involve the coalescing and maturation of a variety of digital archiving systems, services, and solutions that have demonstrated qualities for achieving technical alignment on national levels across multiple organizational borders and boundaries. This variety should help to protect against the failings of any one system. Two emerging themes demonstrate the power of aligned, heterogeneous approaches: first, initiatives in which data exchanges have been tested between digital archiving frameworks and programs in order to ensure that if a system fails, its data may be safely transitioned into another system option (e.g. MetaArchive and Chronopolis completed a technical bridge between their LOCKSS- and iRODS-based infrastructures for this purpose in 2011, see http://www.metaarchive.org/projects/nhprc). And second, service providers are building technical and organizational partnerships that enable participants to preserve their content in multiple, heterogeneous digital archiving systems (e.g., DuraCloud and Chronopolis are collaborating to offer a combined service). Complimenting this variety of technical approaches, many systems share design features and infrastructure.

This has the advantage of enabling reusability, interoperation, and collaboration.

As we work to align our technical approaches to digital archiving, we also need to design and implement common infrastructure testing practices. This testing needs explicitly to address the technical components and approaches of digital archiving systems. To date, technical testing has largely occurred at the program level. LOCKSS especially has put an emphasis on public testing and peer-reviewed publication of the results. Ex Libris (Rosetta) has also conducted public tests. These are small but significant steps toward establishing an evaluative process for digital preservation that relies on empirical data and reproducible results. This would compliment such audit frameworks as the TRAC standard, and it would provide evidence that libraries and publishers could use as they make decisions to choose one or another archiving system or framework for particular types of content. Significant progress in this area is needed.

Establishing a culture of testing and benchmarking represents a key technical alignment challenge. There are a number of reasons for this. One is that our community currently lacks a culture of testing or using empirical data for decision-making. One reason may be that existing testing scenarios have been poorly developed and that few well-established metrics exist for evaluating success. Another might be that institutions have not yet understood the need and value of such empirical testing, and instead are relying heavily on more qualitative analytic tools such as the TRAC standard or the DRAMBORA approach.

The culture of testing is weak in part because testing is both difficult to do and even more difficult to get funding to implement. Particularly in the early stages of field development, funding agencies are happier to support building a new resource than they are to spend money to test how well the resources they are funding perform. Yet without systematic testing, no archiving system should be considered reliable. Commercial archiving systems have shown little interest in engaging in public testing on their own initiative. They put the emphasis instead on marketing that addresses librarians' concerns and fears. If that trend continues, the risk to digital content will not diminish over time, and our field will not reach appropriate levels of success in our preservation of digital content.

Success is an endlessly moving target, best measured by the continued access to content. Long-term digital preservation ultimately can never be considered complete, because there will (presumably) always be a future with new circumstances and new problems to address. A reasonable five-year goal would be to establish a culture of testing and of basing decisions about digital preservation on empirical data as well as qualitative/organizational data. A major step in that direction would be for funding agencies to encourage, fund, and implement systematic public testing of archiving systems and preservation solutions.

References

Caplan, Priscilla, (2010) "The Florida Digital Archive and DAITSS: a model for digital preservation," *Library Hi Tech*, Vol. 28 Iss: 2, pp. 224 – 234. Available: http://www.emeraldinsight.com/journals.htm?articleid=18 64750&show=pdf (last accessed 07-05-2012).

CASPAR (2009), "CASPAR Draft Testbed implementation Plan." Available: http://www.casparpreserves.eu/Members/metaware/Deliv erables/caspar-draft-testbed-implementation-plan/at_download/file.pdf (last accessed 07-05-2012).

CASPAR (2011), "The CASPAR Project." Available (August 2011): http://www.casparpreserves.eu/caspar-project.html (last accessed 07-05-2012).

DAITSS [Dark Archive in the Sunshine State] (2011) Website. Available: http://daitss.fcla.edu/ (last accessed 07-05-2012).

Ex Libris (2010) "The Ability to Preserve a Large Volume of Digital Assets: A Scaling Proof of Concept." Available: http://www.exlibrisgroup.com/files/Products/Preservation /RosettaScalingProofofConcept.pdf (last accessed 07-05-2012).

Hockx-Yu, Helen (2006), "Establishing a UK LOCKSS Pilot Programme," *Serials: The Journal for the Serials Community, Issue*: Volume 19, Number 1 / March 2006, Pages: 47 – 51. Available: http://serials.uksg.org/content/c431kl9ya6qcpl80/fulltext.

pdf (last accessed 07-05-2012).

International Organization for Standardization, "ISO standard 16363: Audit and certification of trustworthy digital repositories," Edition 1, 2012. Available: http://www.iso.org/iso/iso_catalogue/catalogue_tc/catalog ue_detail.htm?csnumber=56510 (last accessed 07-05-2012).

Karlgren, J. et al., 2011. Use cases as a component of information access evaluation. In Proceedings of the 2011 workshop on Data infrastructurEs for supporting information retrieval evaluation. pp. 19–24.

Knight, Steve, (Preservation Research and Consultancy, National Library of New Zealand, Wellington, New Zealand) 200, Early learnings from the National Library of New Zealand's National Digital Heritage Archive project, *Program*

Koçer, Dipl.-Inf. Kadir Karaca and Dr. Thomas Wollschläger, "Evaluierung von Strategien für lokales Entpacken und Übertragen komprimierter Objekte eines digitalen Archivs," *Frankfurt am Main*, 2005. Available: http://kopal.langzeitarchivierung.de/downloads/kopal_Ev aluierung_Entpacken.pdf (last accessed 07-05-2012).

Library of Congress, "Metadata Encoding and Transmission Standard (METS)." Available: http://www.loc.gov/standards/mets/ (last accessed 07-05-2012).

Library of Congress, "PREservation Metadata: Implementation Strategies (PREMIS) Maintenance Activity." Available: http://www.loc.gov/standards/premis/ (last accessed 07-05-2012).

Maniatis, P. et al., 2004. Impeding attrition attacks in P2P systems. *Proceedings of the 11th workshop on ACM SIGOPS European workshop: beyond the PC*. Available: http://portal.acm.org/citation.cfm?id=1133572.1133601 (last accessed 07-05-2012).

Portico (2011) "Digital Preservation Defined." Available: http://www.portico.org/digital-preservation/services/preservation-approach/ (last accessed 07-05-2012).

Power, R., 2002. CSI/FBI computer crime and security survey, Computer Security Institute.

RLG/NARA Task Force on Digital Archive Certification (2007), "Trustworthy Repositories Audit & Certification: Criteria and Checklist." Chicago: CRL. Available: http://www.crl.edu/sites/default/files/attachments/pages/trac_0.pdf (last accessed 07-05-2012).

Rosenthal , D. S.H et al., (2003), "Economic Measures to Resist Attacks on a Peer-to-Peer Network," *Workshop on Economics of Peer-to-Peer Systems*. Available: http://berkeley.intel-research.net/maniatis/publications/P2P-Econ.pdf (last accessed 07-05-2012).

Rosenthal , David S. H. et al (2005), "Transparent Format Migration of Preserved Web Content," *D-Lib Magazine* 11, no. 1. Available: http://www.dlib.org/dlib/january05/rosenthal/01rosenthal.html (last accessed 07-05-2012).

Tenopir, Carol et al., (2011), "Data Sharing by Scientists: Practices and Perceptions," *PLoS One*, Available: http://www.plosone.org/article/info:doi/10.1371/journal.pone.0021101 (last accessed 07-05-2012).

Schwens, Ute and Hans Liegmann, 2004. "Langzeitarchivierung digitaler ressourcen," In: *Grundlagen der praktischen Information und Dokumentation*. München: K.G. Saur, pp. 567–570, Available: http://nbn-resolving.de/urn:nbn:de:0008-2005110800 (last accessed 07-05-2012).

Walters, Tyler and Katherine Skinner, (2011), "New Roles for New Times: Digital Curation for Preservation," *Association for Research Libraries Report*, March 2011. Available: http://www.metaarchive.org/reading-room (last accessed 07-05-2012).

Economic Alignment

Maurizio Lunghi (Fondazione Rinascimento Digitale)
Neil Grindley (Joint Information Systems Committee)
Bohdana Stoklasová (National Library of Czech Republic)
Aaron Trehub (Auburn University, ADPNet)
Christin Egger (Fondazione Rinascimento Digitale)

Abstract

This essay presents an overview of the economic issues that define, promote, or inhibit effective national and international programs for preserving digital cultural heritage materials. Specifically, it presents and discusses multi-institutional approaches to identifying effective and economically sustainable policies in managed digital information environments, citing current digital preservation initiatives in North America and Europe. The essay will also address related issues, including: service/user relationships, roles and responsibilities throughout the various communities, the choice of suitable business models, and cost analyses as essential components of defining economically sustainable approaches to preservation. In keeping with the aims of the Aligning National Approaches to Digital Preservation conference, the essay concludes by considering what a blueprint for success in this area might look like and offering specific recommendations to that end.

Introduction

Economic sustainability—that is, generating and allocating the resources necessary to support long-term preservation activities—is fundamental for the success of long-term digital preservation programs. If there is disagreement about other aspects of digital preservation, there should at least be agreement on this. And yet, this fundamental point has not received the attention or the analysis it deserves. As the authors of the final report of the Blue Ribbon Task Force on Sustainable Digital Preservation and Access (2010, hereafter referred to as BRTF-SDPA Final Report) have pointed out, while there is a substantial literature on the technical and policy aspects of digital preservation, the economic aspects have, until quite recently, been relatively neglected.

The authors of this essay hope to help remedy this gap by focusing on questions of economic alignment and economic sustainability as they affect digital preservation initiatives in North America and Europe. The essay reflects the views and experiences of its authors, but it also incorporates the results of discussions at the 2010 "Aligning National Approaches to Digital Preservation" (ANADP) conference in Tallinn, Estonia. The conference organizers posed three general questions to the participants, with a view to formulating an action plan for the international digital preservation community. The first question was to consider the most important alignment accomplishments that have taken place in the digital preservation field. The second was to examine the current challenges and gaps that represent barriers to establishing sustainable digital preservation activities. And the third asked where the panel thought the digital preservation community should plan to be in five years' time and what would success in this area look like? These questions conveniently encompass many of the issues that have a bearing on economically sustainable digital preservation strategy and action. There are a number of additional questions and issues, however, that relate more specifically to economic alignment. They include: the nature of costs and business models, the effectiveness and demand for services, strategies for selection and appraisal, requirements for partnership and training, and the general need for clarity around roles and responsibilities.

Digital Preservation: A Value Proposition

The long-term preservation of digital materials is an issue that has global relevance. It has become generally understood since the publication in 1996 of the landmark Garrett-Waters report on preserving digital information that engagement with preservation is an unavoidable corollary to the creation and use of nearly all forms of digital content.

Individuals, organizations and businesses are usually highly motivated to think about the issues and challenges they are likely to face in the next phase of planning, which generally means three to five years. Five years is not that long in digital preservation terms, however, and this short-term perspective is probably the single most critical reason that making a business case or economic argument for preservation is a difficult proposition. Therefore, the first and most important concept to argue is that some digital information *does have implicit enduring value*; or alternatively, that it can be used to create entities that will have value. Whilst a case can and should more often be made for the short-term benefits of preservation, it is this long-term value proposition that underpins all other arguments and evidence for engagement in this area. Digital preservation often looks to its equivalent in the physical realm and cites the maintenance of manuscripts over centuries as proof of the impact and worth of caring about the integrity, complexity, intricacy and context of materials produced by human endeavor. The starting point for this paper, therefore, is that digital preservation is an important activity that will enable this generation and subsequent generations to make choices and exploit opportunities that they would otherwise be unable to take advantage of. It is ultimately these human outcomes, rather than technical or bureaucratic ones, that make the economic and every other case for digital preservation.

Putting the ideological view to one side and given the understandable focus of most people on short-term goals, persuading a wide range of information professionals that digital preservation ought to be an essential and embedded part of their daily work is always going to be a challenge. Given that issues span technical, legal, educational, organizational, and of course economic categories, there is an innate complexity to tackling digital preservation that many find a disincentive to engagement. For the minority that find this complexity stimulating, digital preservation continues to present rewarding intellectual opportunities. For the vast majority, however, continuing "access to" or future "use of" the preserved materials will always be the principle motivation for continuing to fund preservation activity. This level of interest from the user community is crucial. Preservation, whether physical or digital, is going to seem like wasted investment without any current or future usage intention. If the demand for access to preserved digital objects and their permanent storage is well articulated, then economic sustainability becomes far more likely. If those arguments originate from the community, and even across national boundaries, then so much the better.

The difficulty of assigning accurate value to digital information is a global problem and sharing that problem is a good mitigation measure. Whilst it may be possible in hindsight to judge that people made errors of judgment in assigning substantial resources to preserving material that was subsequently never used or was considered of negligible value, it will be a compelling defense to cite community, national, or international precedent as proof of good faith.

Economic Alignment: Core Approaches

The first core task is to consider where progress has already been made, either nationally or internationally, to help ameliorate problems relating to the economics of digital preservation. The topic itself encapsulates a lot of complexity in that there are various perspectives that need to be factored into any discussion of what constitutes economic issues in this field. The focus could conceivably be on the cost of maintaining digital material over time, the budget strategies of organizations obliged to engage with preservation, the economic framework in which preservation may effectively occur, or the type and extent of funding required for effective preservation to flourish. The aforementioned BRTF-SDPA Final Report represents a notable accomplishment in this area, in the sense that it was the first—and to date the only—comprehensive examination of digital preservation from an economic perspective. Among other things, the report offered a succinct definition of economically sustainable preservation[1] and analyzed the economic factors involved in the preservation of four types of digital content: scholarly discourse, research data, commercially owned cultural content, and collectively produced Web content. (We would add a fifth category to this list: digital content produced and owned by libraries, archives, museums, and other cultural heritage organizations.) In the course of disentangling and classifying the different elements of digital preservation, the report's authors posited five conditions for sustainable digital preservation:

1. Recognition of the benefits of preservation by decision makers;

2. A process for selecting digital materials with long-term value;

3. Incentives for decision makers to preserve in the public interest;

4. Appropriate organization and governance of digital preservation activities; and

---

[1] "[A] means of keeping information accessible and usable over time by ensuring the ongoing and efficient allocation of resources to its maintenance" (BRTF-SDPA Final Report, 2010, p. 107).

5. Mechanisms to secure an ongoing, efficient allocation of resources to digital preservation activities (p. 12).

This paper takes the view that all of these perspectives and the criteria for economic sustainability are valid areas for discussion, though some have been subject to more development and attention than others in terms of the amount of alignment that may have occurred.

The first of those options—the work that has been done on the lifecycle cost of information management—is arguably the most widely understood interpretation of any question about the "economics of preservation" and probably makes the most immediate sense to the non-specialist who may be concerned to know whether preservation constitutes a "nice-to-have" but dispensable layer of assurance, or whether it is an information management necessity. Knowing the cost of preservation does not necessarily decide this question, but it may focus the enquirer's mind on how seriously he or she needs to contemplate the question.

In the United Kingdom, the cost of preservation has recently been the focus of various phases of the LIFE project[2] undertaken by the British Library and University College London. The project developed and refined a lifecycle model that primarily relates to materials that may be found in a (digital) library context (e.g. text and images) and developed a complex spreadsheet tool to help with calculating the cost over time of storing, managing, and preserving that material. This work has also been picked up and further developed by the Danish National Archives and the Royal Library of Denmark[3] and an online version of the costing tool is being developed and piloted by the Humanities Advanced Technology & Information Institute (HATII) at the University of Glasgow in collaboration with the Open Planets Foundation (OPF). Further detailed work looking at the long-term cost of preserving materials, in this instance research data, was carried out in the first two phases of reporting by the Keeping Research Data Safe (KRDS) project (the third and final phase defined a taxonomy for identifying direct and indirect benefits of long-term digital

---

[2] Lifecycle Information for E-Literature: http://www.life.ac.uk/ (last accessed 03-08-2012).
[3] Anders Bo Nielsen and Ulla Bøgvad Kejser. 2008. "Using the LIFE Costing Model: Case Studies from DK." Available at: http://discovery.ucl.ac.uk/9313/ (last accessed 03-08-2012).

preservation).[4] As well as relying on new research in collaboration with data centers to assess the real costs of keeping data over long periods, the KRDS project drew on both the LIFE Project modeling work and the Cost Estimation Tool (CET) developed by NASA, and other resources such as: the TRAC (Transparent Approach to Costing) Model, the Open Archival Information System (OAIS) Reference Model, and the Digital Curation Centre (DCC) Lifecycle Model in order to create an effective generic framework to discover the cost of managing research data. More generally, the cost of digital preservation figured prominently in the eSpida Project at the University of Glasgow, an initiative aimed at "exploring how intangible assets might be valued in order to make a sound business case to ensure the longevity of information objects; in other words, achieve truly sustainable digital preservation" (Currall and McKinney, 2006). In the United States, Serge Goldstein and Mark Ratliff (2010) of the Office of Information Technology at Princeton University have devised a cost model for the long-term preservation of research data. Dubbed "DataSpace," the model includes a "Pay Once, Store Forever" (POSF) funding formula. The price schedules for community-based digital preservation initiatives like HathiTrust, Chronopolis, and the Private LOCKSS Networks as well as proprietary preservation services like Portico and Tessella also embody assumptions about the cost of long-term preservation.

So the stewardship cost of keeping digital material over time has been demonstrably addressed by various projects, both recently and in the past, and it seems appropriate to declare that some alignment around this work, and the initiatives of other organizations and projects on this topic, has taken place—if not around the precise cost of various preservation tasks, then at least around some of the digital lifecycle information models on which they are based. These models are themselves significant as the digital equivalent to earlier examples from the realm of archival practice and records management, the former a discipline that goes back hundreds of years and the latter an activity that emerged in response to the burgeoning amount of documentation being produced during the middle of the 20th century. There is plenty of evidence to suggest that the lifecycle of information and its management is well understood by now, and there is also reason to

---

[4] Keeping Research Data Safe (KRDS) Web site: http://www.beagrie.com/krds.php (last accessed 03-08-2012).

believe that the main components of digital preservation have been successfully described and categorized. Whether every component in a diagram such as the DCC Lifecycle model[5] is understood and implementable (or even practical to contemplate) for many organizations is another question, but there does appear to be some alignment and agreement about the nature of, and the relationship between, preservation tasks.

Slightly more contentious, particularly beyond the edges of the broad preservation community, is the notion that there is alignment or consensus around the principle of appraisal and selection. This is a deeply significant point in relation to the economics of preservation since the amount of material that one chooses to keep does, of course, have an impact on the infrastructure that one needs to manage it—a point made repeatedly in the BRTF-SDPA Final Report. It is indeed true that at least amongst communities that have spent time thinking hard about the consequences of information management policies (economic and otherwise), there is alignment about the value— indeed the necessity—of selecting and appraising digital information: in effect, assigning value to it and prioritizing some data as more valuable than others. There is, however, less alignment about the practicality and processes for actually carrying out selection and appraisal routines. This point will be addressed in the "Gaps and Challenges" section below.

Another highly visible area of alignment that must surely result in enhanced economic sustainability for digital preservation is the amount of community-building and the national and international collaborations that have occurred, not only as a result of the numerous seminars, workshops and conferences that take place around the world, but also from the open exchange of information that takes place between preservation practitioners, many of whom are based within public and non-profit institutions such as universities, libraries, and archives. Whilst it would be banal to spell out the benefits of cooperation and discussion between theorists and practitioners in any given field, the exchange of experience and good and bad practice; wide participation in advocacy and awareness raising; and the development of common terminology and common approaches have all been key components of establishing digital preservation as a sub-discipline.

---

[5] DCC Lifecycle model, see http://www.dcc.ac.uk/resources/curation-lifecycle-model (last accessed 03-08-2012).

International cooperation has not simply been a by-product or an extension of the peer-review process: it has been critical for the establishment of practice and policy in a field where many onlookers are still waiting to hear and understand what a convincing and robust long-term business case for preservation looks and sounds like.

As well as providing opportunities for forming useful contacts and becoming more closely acquainted with the concerns of peer practitioners, attending and participating in meetings is a way of accelerating the learning and training process for staff who are developing knowledge in the field. This is of very practical economic benefit to organizations that might otherwise have to contemplate expensive training and staff development. National and international preservation-related conferences, workshops, seminars, symposia, and other events are numerous, occasionally free, and increasingly focused on communicating and delivering practical preservation outcomes.

In addition to standalone or annual events such as International Conference on the Preservation of Digital Objects (iPres), and International Digital Curation Conference (IDCC), funded projects have made an enormous contribution to aligning policy, strategy and practice in the field, not only through dissemination meetings funded as part of project work plans, but also through their associated reports and deliverables. One of the outstanding contributions in this area has been made by the European Commission, which has funded a number of major European projects that continue collectively to have a significant impact on digital preservation. These include the following:

- ERPANET: Electronic Resource Preservation and Access Network

- DPE: Digital Preservation Europe

- PLANETS: Preservation and Long-Term Access through Networked Services

- CASPAR: Cultural, Artistic and Scientific Knowledge for Preservation, Access and Retrieval

- KEEP: Keeping Emulation Environments Portable

- PrestoSpace: Preservation Towards Storage and Access. Standardised Practices for Audiovisual Contents in Europe.

- PARSE Insight: Permanent Access to the Records of Science in Europe

- APARSEN: Alliance for Permanent Access to the Records of Science Network

These are all ambitious multi-partner institutional undertakings where many participants from all over Europe (and in some cases beyond) have been given an opportunity to hone or develop their skills in an emerging area. Whilst it is not training as such, there will almost certainly have been ample requirement for many participants to learn quickly "on the job," and this accelerant factor, bringing people up to speed within finite deadlines, is of broad economic benefit.

Similar work is being carried out at the national level in the United States under the auspices of the National Digital Information Infrastructure and Preservation Program (NDIIPP) of the Library of Congress. The NDIIPP's mission is "to develop a national strategy to collect, preserve and make available significant digital content, especially information that is created in digital form only, for current and future generations,"[6] and to that end it has focused on three areas: capturing, preserving, and making available digital content; building a nationwide network of preservation partners, including the MetaArchive Cooperative and the Chronopolis digital preservation network; and directly supporting or promoting a technical infrastructure of tools and services, including BagIt, Heritrix, and the JSTOR/Harvard Object Validation Environment (JHOVE). Perhaps the NDIIPP's most important accomplishment to date has been articulating a convincing case for the importance of long-term digital preservation, one that bears the imprimatur of the closest thing that the US has to a national library. An endorsement by the Library of Congress carries weight for organizations working in related fields and the Library has succeeded at least in making the argument that digital preservation ought to be a national priority. This can be seen, for example, on the Web site for the National Digital Stewardship Alliance (NDSA[7]), an outgrowth and extension of the NDIIPP.

---

[6] NDIIPP Web site: http://www.digitalpreservation.gov/ (last accessed 03-08-2012).
[7] NDSA Web site: http://www.digitalpreservation.gov/ndsa (last accessed 03-08-2012).

In addition to the Library of Congress, the Institute of Museum and Library Services (IMLS), a federal funding agency, has also supported digital preservation initiatives in the United States, most notably the establishment of the Alabama Digital Preservation Network (ADPNet), a statewide LOCKSS-based network. Aaron Trehub discusses this initiative and the challenge of achieving economic sustainability elsewhere in this volume.

Finally, the National Science Foundation (NSF), the National Archives and Records Administration (NARA), and the National Historical Publications and Records Commission (NHPRC: a unit of NARA) have supported work on "implementing solutions to the challenges of preserving electronic records with permanent historical value."[8] This work includes the development of the Integrated Rule Oriented Data System (iRODS) at the Data Intensive Cyber Environments (DICE) Center at the University of North Carolina at Chapel Hill and the Institute for Neural Computation at the University of California San Diego.

Despite these tangible proofs of progress, however, it can be incredibly difficult to persuade library administrators and other decision makers to embrace the requirements of digital preservation and to get it embedded into organizational strategies and thought processes. Bohdana Stoklasová addresses some of the challenges of advocating for preservation at these levels later in this volume. She argues that the gradual introduction of both effective technology and skilled personnel is a critical requirement, but it is not cheap or easy to accomplish.

Once momentum is achieved, however, and the backing of powerful advocates secured, a great deal of progress can be made and partnerships can be brokered and usefully exploited. Returning again to North America, the Library of Congress, IMLS, and other funding organizations have supported efforts to define best practices and procedures for digital preservation. They have also supported the development of governance instruments (a crucial but often-overlooked precondition for creating economically sustainable and scalable preservation networks, especially among different kinds of institutions in different states, provinces, and countries), and have actually created functioning preservation networks. For example, the NDIIPP supported the creation of the

---

[8] See http://www.archives.gov/nhprc/apply/eligibility.html (last accessed 03-08-2012).

Data-PASS network; the Persistent Digital Archives and Library System (PeDALS) project; and the MetaArchive Cooperative, which was the first Private LOCKSS Network (PLN) explicitly designed for the preservation of locally created (and locally owned) digital content. For its part, the IMLS-supported ADPNet was the first statewide PLN and served as the model for the Council of Prairie and Pacific University Libraries (COPPUL) PLN in western Canada. Indeed, the ADPNet-COPPUL relationship represents a working example of economic alignment and offers proof that it is possible to create affordable and sustainable preservation networks in very different environments.

In the UK, the Joint Information Systems Committee (JISC) has been influential in funding innovation and building capability through preservation programs and projects (most often based within UK universities) that have supported a wide range of activity including feasibility and scoping work, technical development, policy and legal studies, and network and partnership support. The Dutch National Library and the National Archives have been an influential force in the Netherlands driving preservation practice there and being influential around the world, as have their UK, Australian, New Zealand, German, and Danish counterparts (in association with those responsible for their core and capital funding). It is worth noting that this partial and arbitrary list exclusively describes publicly funded organizations and this goes some way to underpin the next point of alignment, which is around the theme of "openness." It is tempting to think that the natural tendency of all publicly funded organizations would surely be towards the open: i.e. open source (software), open access (content), open standards, and indeed open communities, where participants from all sectors are welcome and encouraged to join in the discussion and add value. But on reflection, this is taking an influential core value of a group of mostly large and powerful institutions and extending it across a whole diverse community.

Intuitively, the adoption of "open" approaches, in particular open-source software in the context of technical preservation solutions, seems like a tactic designed to appeal to cash-strapped organizations with little by way of resources and funding to engage with the complexities of preservation. But as anyone who works with a range of software will state, "open source does not mean free." Whilst the source code may be accessible and reusable, there may be a cost for distribution, for support, or for particular license conditions. Additionally, to actually implement, use, and locally maintain the software in a way that is useful for one's own organization, there may well be significant costs down the line that are inherent to a community-owned resource. In some cases, it may be valid to argue that such costs would be usefully subsumed within a service-level agreement on a piece of proprietary software from a commercial vendor. That said, there has nonetheless been great progress in establishing an array of open and free tools, toolkits, models, frameworks, and guidance that have removed many of the financial barriers to engaging with preservation, at least up to a certain level. Resources such as Archivematica (a comprehensive digital preservation system); the California Digital Library's Data Management Planning Tool (DMP Tool) and suite of microservices for data curation; The Curator's Workbench (University of North Carolina at Chapel Hill pre-ingest tool); and HOPPLA (Vienna University of Technology) may indicate the path to further progress in this direction. Other tools such as DRAMBORA (a risk audit tool), AIDA (Assessing Institutional Digital Assets), and DAF (the Data Asset Framework) are being combined in an integrated suite to tackle sophisticated work in the area of long-term data management practice.[9] This approach emulates various projects over the years that have built on and integrated various robust preservation components such as DROID and PRONOM (The UK National Archives); JHOVE (JSTOR and the Harvard University Library); and the NLNZ Metadata Extractor (National Library of New Zealand).

In terms of open standards, probably the most widely referenced and influential standard reference point in Digital Preservation is ISO 14721, better known as the Open Archival Information System (OAIS) reference model.[10] The OAIS model is an excellent framework for defining the inputs, processes, and outputs of an eligible preservation system and it is this flexibility, combined with a collection of canonical terms and an easily reproducible graphic, which has earned it a ubiquitous role throughout the preservation literature and a place in almost every entry-level presentation ever given about the topic. But alongside

---

[9] See the IDMP: Integrated Data Management Planning & Support Project at the DCC:
http://www.jisc.ac.uk/whatwedo/programmes/mrd/supportprojects/idmpsupport.aspx (last accessed 03-08-2012).
[10] ISO (International Organization for Standardization) 14721:2003; originally proposed by the Consultative Committee for Space Data Systems.

its usefulness, particularly in the areas of teaching and training, the OAIS model has an economic relevance precisely because it is an open and free framework. One of the great benefits of the model is that it describes a workflow and environment that adheres to good and effective working practices without being too prescriptive about compliance with detailed implementations of (and therefore investments in) particular forms of infrastructure.

Economic Alignment: Gaps and Challenges

The alignment accomplishments alluded to above signal that preservation, and more particularly economic positions in relation to preservation, have either purposefully been developed (e.g. cost models, dedicated preservation funding programs, and institutional policy development) or have realized some oblique benefits from the tendency towards "openness" in many public institutions, and also perhaps the general move towards e-only provision of resources (a trend that is particularly apparent in the area of scholarly journals).

But despite the many advances there is still a great deal to be done to ensure that we have sustainable economic strategies for preservation. This is especially important precisely because digital preservation can be a financially demanding undertaking whose benefits may not be immediately apparent. A large number of digitized volumes is eye-catching proof of a project's "success;" the substantial investment required to ensure their long-term availability is invisible to users and less likely to generate enthusiasm among decision makers. As a result, long-term preservation is still not perceived as an indispensable part of digitization projects and its cost is often underestimated or entirely ignored in favor of digitizing more materials. The ability to build effectively on previous and current investment is therefore a powerful argument for digital preservation and evidence of its economic sustainability.

Building on Current Investment

Given the wide variety of institutions that should be concerned about digital preservation and the differences among them in culture, policies, laws, regulations, and resource levels, it would be misleading to speak of economic alignment in terms of a single, uniform approach. What may work for one type of institution in a given country would not work at all for the same type of institution in another country. That said, there are general principles that are useful in designing economically sustainable digital preservation networks, and some of them can be discerned from working examples in North America and Europe. One task, therefore, might be to compile an international library of recommended practices that can be modified and applied to different situations; in other words, national resource pages writ large.

Fortunately, there are a growing number of working examples to draw on, some of them of fairly lengthy provenance. The San Francisco-based Internet Archive (IA) was founded in 1996 as a non-profit organization by Internet entrepreneur Brewster Kahle and now contains almost five million texts, moving images, live music concerts, and audio recordings. A number of Private LOCKSS Networks (PLNs) have been established in North America, the United Kingdom, and Germany in order to preserve locally created digital content.[11] The oldest of them, the MetaArchive Cooperative, was founded in 2004 under the auspices of the NDIIPP and now numbers almost fifty member institutions in the United States, the United Kingdom, Brazil, and Spain. The aforementioned Integrated Rule Oriented Data System (iRODS) was launched in 2006; it is now based at the Data Intensive Cyber Environments (DICE) Center at the University of North Carolina at Chapel Hill and the Institute for Neural Computation at the University of California San Diego and is in use at the Carolina Digital Repository, the Texas Digital Library, the Bibliothèque nationale de France (BnF), and other cultural heritage organizations in the United States and Europe. One iRODS-based network, Chronopolis, is based at the San Diego Supercomputer Center and the University of California San Diego and offers a suite of distributed preservation services to other institutions. HathiTrust is a large-scale collaborative repository of digitized content from the Google Books initiative, the Internet Archive, and local digital collections. Established in 2008 by the thirteen member libraries of the Committee on Institutional Cooperation (CIC), the HathiTrust partnership now includes over sixty research libraries in the United States and Europe and has

---

[11] Examples include the MetaArchive Cooperative (http://www.metaarchive.org); the Alabama Digital Preservation Network (ADPNet: http://www.adpn.org/); the Council of Prairie and Pacific University Libraries Network (COPPUL: http://coppullockssgroup.pbworks.com/); the UK LOCKSS Alliance (http://www.lockssalliance.ac.uk/); and LuKII (http://www.lukii.hu-berlin.de/) (all last accessed 03-08-2012).

digitized almost ten million volumes, almost 30 percent of which are in the public domain. The University of California Curation Center (UC3) recently launched Merritt, a digital repository and preservation service for the University of California community. Finally, in November 2011, DuraSpace—a non-profit organization formed by the merger of DSpace and Fedora—announced DuraCloud, a cloud-based service aimed at "providing preservation support and access services for academic libraries, academic research centers, and other cultural heritage organizations." Among those organizations are Hamilton College, Indiana University-Purdue University Indianapolis, the Inter-University Consortium for Political and Social Research (ICPSR), and the Massachusetts Institute of Technology.

All of these initiatives are generating useful information on pricing models and the economics of digital preservation. The LOCKSS networks are especially interesting from the point of view of economic alignment and economic sustainability. The North American networks in particular—the MetaArchive Cooperative, ADPNet, and COPPUL—are financially self-sustaining and have devised membership fee schedules that are affordable for smaller, poorly resourced institutions. Taken together, their experience suggests that using open-source software, aiming for lightweight administrative structures, and delegating as much decision-making power as possible to the member institutions contribute to economic sustainability and can promote economic alignment among otherwise very different networks. Whichever approach or solution one chooses, however, it is advisable to keep it as simple and inexpensive as possible. Simplicity contributes to economic sustainability; complexity undermines it. This maxim rings true across a whole spectrum of activity as there is a great deal of anecdotal evidence to suggest that preservation is a hard sell because of the perceived complexity of its processes. It is true that without recourse to technical effort and knowledge a non-specialist will struggle to gracefully embed current preservation tools into a local infrastructure, let alone be able to wrestle with the complexities of developing an emulated environment for legacy software to run in. But these issues are a distraction from the fact that all the principle preservation issues, certainly at a managerial level, are almost exclusively non-technical.

What is required is clear and attractive advocacy material that focuses on the issue of what decisions are required *to effectively deal with content.* At some stage, someone in the institution will have to take responsibility for technology choices but those decisions will be inordinately easier, and will be taken more effectively and probably more economically, if they are working from a clear specification, with clear policy guidelines, and in the context of a considered, responsible, and joined-up set of information policies.

In a risk-averse atmosphere, trust is a valuable commodity and audit and certification of preservation environments and processes can be helpful as assurance for organizations to make investments they would otherwise be nervous of making. The development of standards is a form of assurance and as mentioned above, the OAIS model sits alongside other ISO entities (such as ISO 15489:2001 for records management) to offer a useful formal framework to build on. There are a number of models, such as: the DINI (Deutsche Initiative für Netzwerkinformation = German Initiative for Networked Information) framework and DINI-Certificate (2002); the DANS (Data Archiving and Networked Services) Data Seal of Approval (2005-2006); the DRAMBORA (Digital Repositories Audit Method Based on Risk Assessment) audit tool (2006-2007); and the TRAC (Trustworthy Repositories Audit and Certification) checklist (2007).[12] There is also now an ISO-approved process for preservation certification, the TRAC standard (ISO 16363:2012), which may provide the basis for an audit/assessment option that is both effective and affordable, especially once the audit component can be delivered by a trusted and sustainable agency.[13] Thanks to collaborative work between the TRAC Task Force, the Consultative Committee for Space Data Systems (CCSDS), and the Alliance for Permanent Access (APA), individuals and agencies may soon be able to be certified to provide TRAC assessments. If this comes to pass, it will represent significant progress.

---

[12] See DINI: http://www.dini.de/; DINI-Certificate: http://www.dini.de/dini-zertifikat/; DANS: http://www.dans.knaw.nl/; DRAMBORA: http://www.repositoryaudit.eu/; TRAC: http://www.crl.edu/archiving-preservation/digital-archives/certification-and-assessment-digital-repositories (all last accessed 03-08-2012).

[13] See "Space data and information transfer systems—Audit and certification of trustworthy digital repositories" (ISO 16363:2012): http://www.iso.org/iso/iso_catalogue/catalogue_tc/catalogue_detail.htm?csnumbe r=56510 (last accessed 05-16-2012).

The challenge of reducing complexity and streamlining preservation functions also applies to metadata. The PREMIS Data Dictionary is a comprehensive and exhaustive catalogue of nearly all of the fields that one might need for the purposes of preservation and is one of the standard works of reference in the field.[14] Combined with various work that examined the significant properties of information (e.g. the CEDARS and INSPECT projects in the United Kingdom[15]), and work on representation information (carried out in the context of the PLANETS and CASPAR projects amongst others), there has been a great deal of progress made in understanding what technical, descriptive, and administrative data may be required to effectively describe digital material for long-term preservation purposes.

But a gap remains between understanding the ideal metadata requirements for digital objects and choosing to implement that metadata in real-world situations. That gap has to do with time and resources and is therefore an economic issue. Metadata is currently laborious to comprehensively and effectively assign to digital objects in a manner that is likely to satisfy all of their potential future use scenarios. Manual tasks, or even semi-automated tasks, of this nature will not scale up to the level that most organizations require. Whilst technical metadata extractors such as DROID, JHOVE, and the NLNZ Metadata Extractor can harvest useful information, work is still required to work out ways of either automatically extracting or intelligently tagging objects such that they align with institutional policies around value and retention. Automated ways of managing digital objects require machine-readable protocols, which in turn require reliably and persistently identified components. There are different views on the best identifier sets for all sorts of purposes, including file formats, subject classification terms, organizational identity, researcher identity, and so on and so forth, but the overarching issue once again is one of trust—which in turn often depends on prospects for sustainability, which ultimately leads back to economics.

---

[14] See PREMIS Data Dictionary: http://www.loc.gov/standards/premis/ (last accessed 03-08-2012).

[15] See The CEDARS Project: http://www.ukoln.ac.uk/services/elib/projects/cedars/; and INSPECT: http://www.significantproperties.org.uk/ (both last accessed 03-08-2012).

Learning from failed initiatives

It is important to build on success in designing economically sustainable digital preservation programs. It is equally important to learn from unsuccessful initiatives. For example, the Preserving Access to Digital Information (PADI) project was a digital preservation subject gateway set up and maintained by the National Library of Australia (NLA) from the mid-1990s until late 2010. The project was discontinued in that year, primarily because of business decisions about resourcing. "Subject interest, expertise and enthusiasm are vitally important but not sufficient," one of the project participants later observed. "Ongoing sustainability of a service like PADI over a long period probably also requires some dedicated discretionary budget funds, not just a few dedicated individuals. It also requires some available expertise in the means of communication, not just the content." Another important element contributing to sustainability is sharing the "ownership" of a program among a number of institutions and building community engagement in it, even at the expense of managerial efficiency. Again, the fate of the PADI project illustrates the dangers of concentrating ownership in one institution: "The other significant development that came with, and contributed to the growing success of PADI as an information gateway, was a local decision against collaboration, taking control of PADI away from a diverse committee of organizations, and investing it in one institution.[...] A case of making it much more easy to manage, but closing off local commitment to its survival and usefulness."[16] This lesson has been absorbed by the Private LOCKSS Networks in North America, whose governance policies were designed to ensure that management of the networks is shared by or rotates among the participating institutions, thereby building a sense of shared ownership.

Services and (more) business models

As stated in various ways previously, preservation is not an activity that easily lends itself to being configured for delivery as a business practice or commercial enterprise. One of the conclusions of the BRTF-SDPA Final Report (2010, p. 1) argued that devising strategies for preserving digital materials was made difficult by four inherent factors:

---

[16] Personal communication between Maurizio Lunghi and Colin Webb, January 2011.

- Long time horizons;

- Diffused stakeholders;

- Misaligned or weak incentives; and

- Lack of clarity about roles and responsibilities among stakeholders

This may explain why the demand for preservation services is still relatively weak, and consequently why the list of commercial vendors offering to supply those services is still fairly short. The United Kingdom-based technology company Tessella has had success, principally (in this area) with its Safety Deposit Box (SDB) system, which is in use in major national archives around the world and has recently been implemented by the Church of Jesus Christ of Latter-Day Saints to deal with their ingest challenge for the Family Search archive. OCLC launched its Digital Archive Service in 2001 and has been marketing it to state libraries and archives, especially those that are already using CONTENTdm, another OCLC product, to manage their digital collections. Ex Libris has a digital preservation product called Rosetta and is building up its customer base. Ex Libris is pursuing an interesting collaboration model with the National Library of New Zealand, which takes the view that working with a commercial vendor offers the best chance for creating and sustaining some of the core services that a preservation system will require, including a file format registry that will sit at the heart of the product and supply an identification function.

It is clear that, if handled in the right way and set up as a mutually beneficial partnership, relationships between vendors and public-sector institutions can bring enormous benefits to client organizations in terms of economic efficiencies and clarity of business processes. There is a strong argument for saying that organizations should play to their strengths. Taking a slightly different approach, it is possible to engage with technology but only on terms that are advantageous to one's own organization. In telecommunications, banking, health-care and most other sectors of society, organizations set out their principles and mission; and then establish their rights, values and basic rules. They then define the components, functionalities, workflow, and models and terms of specific services, and invite competitive tenders to bid for aspects of the work. An example from Italy is the *Magazzini digitali* ("Digital Stacks") project, in which the Ministry of Culture set up the global architecture and functions of a trusted digital depository (complete with ingest rules and selection criteria for long term preservation) and then put out a call to tender (or, in American usage, a Request for Proposal or RFP) to private companies.[17] Similarly, Auburn University has outsourced the actual digitization of large analogue collections to external vendors. When it comes to digital preservation, however, the librarians at Auburn have been reluctant to entrust such a crucial part of the library's mission to an external vendor, taking the view that the primary responsibility for ensuring the long-term preservation of the human record in digital form ought to rest with public institutions or alliances of public institutions. That view is shared by many other research universities in the United States.[18] That said, there may be room to explore the topic with some major commercial players in the digitization field (e.g. Google). Conversations of this nature being undertaken by the HathiTrust partnership and the Digital Public Library of America (DPLA) initiative at the Berkman Center for Internet & Society at Harvard University will be worth monitoring.

In common with the broadly accepted view that preservation is an international concern and should be tackled using broadly collaborative working methods, preservation is also increasingly being viewed as a process and a workflow that need not be dealt with by an end-to-end local process. The cost efficiencies and the accelerated development processes that accompany collaborative working can enhance the preservation workflow and can relieve institutions of training and technical overheads that they may not be equipped to meet.

Disaggregated services for preservation were much in vogue several years ago (service-oriented architectures), but the focus has now moved to the potential for cloud services to offer preservation and curation capacity using elastic storage and computing provision. "Trust" remains an issue for organizations contemplating cloud services and whilst one could imagine most services, e.g., replication, hashing, identification, characterization, validation, ingest, migration, verification, authentication, etc., being offered as some form of service, these would need to be

---

[17] Magazzini digitali: http://www.rinascimento-digitale.it/projects-digitalstacks.phtml (last accessed 03-08-2012).

[18] See for example the emerging Digital Preservation Network (DPN) initiative.

underpinned by the type of trusted certification processes mentioned previously (e.g. TRAC, DINI-Certificate).

When faced with hard economic choices about service provision, organizations may inevitably run through a fairly universal set of questions:

- Is this something that we really need?

- How much will it cost?

- How much money have we got?

- How much of what we've got do we want to spend on this?

- Can we get someone else to pay for it?

And in the unlucky event that the answers to all those questions are unsatisfactory, the final question becomes:

- How can we adapt what we already have to do what we need to do?

This is a somewhat long-winded way of illustrating that most organizations are generally forced to make very pragmatic decisions, but in terms of gaps and challenges, it follows that the clearer the arguments are for the value of digital materials, the easier it will be to win the argument about funding. This is true irrespective of whether the chosen solution is an entirely outsourced approach (let's pay someone else to do this for us), or an entirely self-managed one (let's do this ourselves, or with a group of like-minded institutions). In either and all cases, the goal should be the same: to codify long-term digital preservation in institutional (or consortial, or national) policy, and incorporate it into an institution's regular workflow.

If the ideal is to embed digital preservation in the core institutional function so firmly that it becomes a line item in the institution's operating budget, then there is also a pressing need to acknowledge and understand all of the steps short of that ideal. Practically speaking, all organizations (except those for whom preservation is the core mission) are probably going to find themselves somewhere down the rungs of that particular ladder for the immediate future. There remain large challenges and gaps in both defining the business case and the business models for preservation but interesting work has emerged in recent years to start classifying and examining possible options. The BRTF-SDPA Final Report (2010, p. 45) lists five "common funding models for digital preservation." Ithaka S+R has also done some very useful work in producing case studies on sustaining digital resources.[19]

Roles and Responsibilities

When considering what we might refer to as the preservation interrogatives: the "who," "what," "where," "when," and "how" of digital preservation, the question "who" is probably the most interesting (and sometimes the most intractable) question for many people, focusing as it does on the human aspect and drilling down into the detail of who is actually responsible for preserving material.

There is currently uncertainty within many institutions about who ought to take responsibility for the long-term stewardship of digital content. This is also reflected at the macro-level, where funding bodies, government agencies, institutions and individuals are looking from one to the other trying to work out their moral and financial responsibilities *vis-à-vis* content that is of interest to them.

In terms of building *capability* to preserve, this could be characterized as a problem that funders are interested in. Organizations such as JISC, the Library of Congress, the Institute of Museum and Library Services (IMLS), the Deutsche Forschungsgemeinschaft (DFG), the SURF Foundation in the Netherlands, and various other agencies that support research and innovation have a vested interest in ensuring that the communities that they support have the tools and frameworks and infrastructure that they need to manage the information that they produce in the course of their largely education-related activities. When focusing on the *capacity* to preserve, this is arguably more likely to devolve to institutions and organizations whose responsibility it is to deal with the logistics of having staff in place with the right skills to do the work that the institution requires of them.

When it comes to the *sustainability* of both of the above, then this is where the gap or challenge becomes identifiable. A funder may be able to commission the creation of a useful tool or resource but ensuring that the transfer of that capability into the institution

---

[19] See for example Maron, Nancy L., Kirby Smith, K., & Loy, Matthew. (2009). Sustaining Digital Resources: An On-the-Ground View of Projects Today, *Ithaka Case Studies in Sustainability, Strategic Content Alliance*. Available at: http://www.ithaka.org/ithaka-s-r/research/ithaka-case-studies-in-sustainability (last accessed 03-08-2012).

actually happens is an uncertain proposition, particularly given that short-term "soft" funding often results in the loss of staff at the end of a project, (thereby also affecting the organization's capacity to preserve). But these are not extraordinary problems. Staff members come and go all the time. Perhaps the answer to this sustainability challenge lies with the sorts of membership bodies that are formed to represent and support different types of organizations. For example, the Digital Preservation Coalition (DPC), the Open Planets Foundation (OPF), and the Alliance for Permanent Access (APA) are all designed to support the transfer of knowledge within and beyond the different domains of activity where digital preservation is a live issue. By the coordination of activity in (and between) areas such as science, humanities, publishing, archives, museums, libraries, galleries, government, etc., it should be possible to establish a more effective collective understanding of how information professionals working in a great variety of different contexts can more effectively preserve digital materials. In economic terms, the issue revolves around how to ensure that the benefits of membership justify the cost of joining.

As already stated above, preservation issues for the majority of people revolve around non-technical issues and when focusing on roles and responsibilities in this domain, the discussion at some point needs to drill down to a granular level, and ultimately requires someone to take some form of position on the nature and the value of the content in question. In any discussion of the economics of preservation, "value" is an interesting word: different from "cost;" and not as practical as "benefit." But if we can establish who regards the content as valuable, then we may arrive at a better understanding of who the potential beneficiaries of the preservation process are. We may then be able to find out if anyone is likely to benefit from that preserved content without contributing to the cost of its preservation, which is of course a ubiquitous scenario in a digital world where instant global access to a dazzling universe of material has become not only common but expected. This is what the BRTF-SDPA Final Report (2010, p. 45) (and the language of economics) calls the "free rider" problem.

In some contexts, universal permanent access is not only a convenient by-product of digitized material finding its way into an open preservation environment, but is the intended and funded outcome. Legal deposit arrangements in various countries are the logical conclusion to the information as "public goods" arrangement, where taxes pay for comprehensive tranches of material to be made available in perpetuity (sometimes under particular access conditions) by trusted public repositories. But in many other contexts and for the vast majority of institutions and organizations, this is an irrelevance. These bodies have budgets to balance and priorities to define and are very conscious of the opportunity costs of assigning precious resources to an enterprise as currently ill-defined as long-term preservation. At some point, the question will be asked, "Who is going to pay for this?" Should the creator pay? Should the user pay? Should responsibility fall to the institution? Or is it a public problem?

Perhaps one way to examine this problem is to take a step back and look at the creation or acquisition process and work through the decisions that are involved at the instigation of this whole process. In some instances, the case for acquiring a digital file is straightforward. Where the original analogue object is unique or at risk, there is a clear justification for creating a surrogate and this also indicates ownership and interest in the digital file. As a surrogate, the physical object and its digital manifestation are related. In cases where a physical object needs to be copiously used by a great variety of people, there is also a clear justification for digitization, although given that the original is probably sturdy and common, the subsequent stewardship issues begin to get murky when questions are asked about the point of storing something that can be easily accessed in a number of other ways.

The following represent four selection criteria elements that might help inform policy-making:

- Are we allowed to preserve it? (Who owns it?)

- Is there someone (right now) that wants to use it?

- Can we carry on making it accessible? (Will it be technically possible?)

- How interesting is the information? (Will someone want it in the future?)

As stated before, selection is an absolutely key part of effective preservation practice, particularly as we exist in a period where analogue material is likely to be with us for some time to come whilst the amount of new digital material requiring storage grows all the time.

It may be possible for some organizations to settle on fairly loose or general policies towards responsibility for material, such as forming the view that any decision to ingest material into a given preservation environment implies the acceptance of responsibility, and therefore the acceptance of ongoing cost. Other general statements of this nature may be applicable also, but there is a potential problem with this approach in that the stewardship of digital material and collections is not a static and tidy problem. As digital objects progress through a lifecycle, their value—like any investment—may rise and fall. Perhaps what is needed is some low-overhead administrative (or even just conceptual) way to keep track of three vital pieces of information that will assist content owners with the ongoing challenge of appraisal, which can be defined as the iterative selection process that ideally takes place at various points subsequent to the initial selection decision.

The role of *creator* of the digital object/collection/dataset is fairly clear and should often be reflected in the metadata associated with an object, or will be known to those managing the environment that the object is destined to be stored in. This is often a key piece of information for a great variety of reasons but may also be important for appraisal purposes. What is less obvious, and not by any means likely to be the same as the *creator* is the identity of a person who might be referred to as the *principal keeper*. This would refer to someone who has appropriate authority and is interested in knowing that the object(s) in question are supposed to be residing in the preservation environment. The third piece of information that might be useful to know is who the *principal user* is. This would refer to someone who had self-identified themselves as a person who was interested in the object(s) in question and who had a vested interest in seeing that they continued to be stored safely.

In many environments, one suspects that these designations would not make much sense as two, or perhaps all three, of the designations would be the same person. But in other cases— particularly perhaps where special collections of digital material were stored for long periods of time (at some expense) and the original motivations for archiving the material had become unclear—designations of this type may be helpful in determining ongoing value.

In order for this proposal to be valuable, refinements would need to be introduced whereby the identity of the keeper or the user would be passed on as appropriate to new incumbents or to others taking on the mantle of research or teaching in that area (if that was the use case). An action would be triggered however if at any point the keeper or the user identity changed or became blank—that is, if one or other of those roles became vacant in relation to an object. This would alert the host organization to the fact that either somebody thought that the object was no longer worth storing, or that the file was no longer worth using, either of which represents a strong case for disposal. A number of other refinements (e.g. designated community alerts and automatic retention periods) could be introduced as safeguards but the point would be to try and tackle the problem of unmanaged persistence.

What Success Looks Like: A Five-Year Forecast

One measure of success will be that analogue and digital documents are considered and treated equally in any preservation regime. The current practice of acquiring, cataloguing, protecting, and making available predominantly or even only analogue materials while postponing similar treatment for digital content entails possibly irrecoverable losses to the corpus of cultural heritage materials and important research resources.

Of course, given limited resources, selection and prioritization will have to be applied to both types of resources. This will require fundamental changes in strategic planning and organization at many institutions. Cultural heritage institutions are by nature conservative, and transforming them will be far from easy. However, the authors agree that these changes will be necessary to achieve success in this field. When normal practice within an organization automatically factors in the whole lifecycle costs of acquiring or creating a digital collection (including the opportunity costs) and the institution has a clear view of the likely short, medium, and long-term benefits of doing so, then it might be possible to claim that the role of digital preservation is as innately understood within an organization as (analogue) archival practice or records management. Fortunately, as the body of this paper shows, there are a growing number of successful transformations underway. Taken together, they suggest that momentum is building in the right direction.

In that connection, success in this area will begin with an institutional recognition that long-term digital preservation is a high-priority activity that requires an ongoing commitment of time and resources. This will involve having policies that are broadly meaningful across institutions and model governance instruments that can be adapted to reflect local conditions and practices. It will mean that staff members are trained in basic preservation competencies, ranging from digitization best practices and optimal file organization to writing instructions for digital preservation software (e.g. LOCKSS manifests and plugins). And it will mean that digital preservation is embedded into the institutional way of behaving and operating (i.e. linked to policy and workflow measures) and embodied in an optimum balanced budget from the start.

In short, we will have achieved success when long-term digital preservation becomes a routine and economically sustainable activity and a generally accepted part of the mission of cultural heritage organizations and other stakeholders—that is, when most institutions have incorporated the long-term stewardship of digital materials into their day-to-day operations, preferably with some degree of mutual assistance and coordination. This may happen as a result of national policy and government mandates, or because of a series of local initiatives. The main thing is that it happens—and in a sustainable way, with long-term institutional commitment, public understanding and support, budget lines, and dedicated personnel.

To that end, the authors propose the following guiding principles:

- Digital preservation should be an integral part of all of projects dealing with the digitization of analogue documents and/or the acquisition of born-digital documents having to do with the national cultural heritage.

- Digital preservation is not a luxury. Ensuring adequate protection for digital content should be just as much a part of an institution's workflow as protecting analogue materials from water, fire, or careless handling.

- More broadly, digital preservation should also figure in national public policy. Recipients of public funding (libraries, museums, archives, etc.) should be required to include digital preservation in their activities, build and share a knowledge base, and pool resources to develop or add to preservation tools and services. The recent requirement by the National Science Foundation (NSF) in the United States that grant applicants submit a long-term data management plan is just one example of this.[20]

- Sufficient funding should be dedicated exclusively to digital preservation. Large-scale publicly funded digitization initiatives that do not also include a budget and a clearly defined strategy for digital preservation are disasters waiting to happen and an unwise use of public monies.

As was pointed out at the beginning of this paper, digital preservation is a relatively new area of activity for most cultural heritage organizations. It is all the more important, therefore, to share experiences, tools, and successful approaches across institutions and countries.

Towards Economic Alignment: Ten Recommendations

The following set of ten recommendations is intended to address economic and cost issues and to promote economic alignment among digital preservation initiatives in different countries. It reflects the cumulative experience of the authors and incorporates discussion points that arose at the ANADP conference.

- Develop and launch a coordinated international campaign to make Archive/Library/Museum (ALM) directors and administrators aware that long-term digital preservation requires stable funding and a continuous allocation of resources. ALMs and scientific institutions need specific, practical suggestions for incorporating digital preservation into their budgets. Some of this work is already being done by national libraries and archives in individual countries (e.g. the National Digital Stewardship Alliance in the United States). These efforts need to be coordinated.

- Establish a Digital Preservation Resource Centre (DPRC). Decision-makers at ALMs need a single place where they can find current information on various digital preservation solutions. Ideally, this resource centre—which we are provisionally calling a Digital Preservation Resource Centre (DPRC)—should address three key areas: awareness, tools,

---

[20] See NSF Data Management Plan Requirements:
http://www.nsf.gov/eng/general/dmp.jsp (last accessed 03-08-2012).

and hosting. It should include case studies (including best practices as well as failed initiatives), data from benchmarking exercises, and technical evaluations of systems performance. It should also contain information on a palette of economic approaches and solutions, ranging from proprietary commercial and vendor solutions (e.g. Ex Libris Rosetta, or Tessella SDB, the OCLC Digital Archive, Portico) to community-owned, member-managed solutions (e.g. the HathiTrust or the MetaArchive Cooperative). These solutions could be arranged by format, with transparency about costs, rights, and responsibilities being essential. In designing the portal, we can take a lesson from the IT industry. In the late 1980s, as the market for desktop workstations and enterprise servers was taking off, a small number of workstation vendors formed the System Performance Evaluation Corporation (SPEC). Based in Gainesville, Virginia, SPEC defines its goal as "ensur[ing] that the marketplace has a fair and useful set of metrics to differentiate candidate systems"[21] by providing standardized source code based on existing applications that can be used in benchmarking exercises. Another possible model is The Keepers Registry based at the University of Edinburgh. This is currently a registry of e-journal preservation services but could be developed further to address issues related to metrics. Questions for further discussion include the level of detail, openness, and transparency (e.g. whether the portal should include specific information about failed preservation efforts or the neglect or loss of materials), as well as funding and sustainability.

- Share experience, objectives, tools, documentation (including governance policies), and practices with other preservation initiatives and communities. The additional effort and cost of doing so should be understood as a prudent investment in the sustainability of digital preservation in general. Given the growing body of successful experience, no institution, consortium, or country should have to navigate the challenges of digital preservation in isolation. Similarly, every institution should be prepared to contribute knowledge and experience back to the general preservation community. Specific recommendations for promoting partnerships and cooperation

---

[21] System Performance Evaluation Corporation (SPEC): http://www.spec.org/ (last accessed 03-08-2012).

include periodic conferences like ANADP and other events at the national or international level (e.g. iPres); the aforementioned Digital Preservation Resource Centre (DPRC); and Distributed Preservation Development Networks (DPDNs). The DPRC could include a "technology watch" section and a brokerage service for open-source developers and users to share experiences and solutions.

- Assemble and make available case studies of digital preservation costs. Although costs cannot be predicted with certainty, benchmark figures and real-life cost scenarios are useful. Case studies of cost and business models are emerging in particular from some of the projects funded by JISC, which is committed to supporting research on cost issues and making this information and the methods of organizing and obtaining it as widely available as possible.

- Develop a matrix of selection criteria for digital preservation—in other words, a digital-preservation "triage chart." Digital content is easy to produce. Preserving it can be complex and expensive. For this reason, ALMs must decide what they want to preserve, why, for how long, and for what level of use. Appraisal and selection must reflect user requirements (both actual and anticipated) and legal constraints, if any. As part of this effort, the community should compile a list of selection best practices for specific types of institutions, types of content, and user communities.

- Study and (where appropriate) promote community-owned solutions. Community-owned digital-preservation initiatives are gaining currency and credibility. For example, the MetaArchive Cooperative is an international LOCKSS-based network with a good track record and relatively low barriers to entry. The same could be said of ADPNet, COPPUL, and other community-owned networks in North America. HathiTrust is another interesting example of an international community-based partnership in action. Initiatives like these enable practitioners to pool resources and share experience. That said, the community still needs viable business models to create a financially sound digital-preservation development community (e.g. JHOVE and JHOVE2). The Open Planets Foundation (OPF) may be a possible model for this. The community also needs mechanisms for billing, hosting, and assigning prices to digital-preservation products and services. Here it is important to recognize that "sweat equity" (i.e. in-kind contributions by member institutions) can be a useful currency. The OPF relies on this model: the charter members pay for the administration and organizational costs and the associate members provide the "sweat." The authors propose setting up a brokerage mechanism, perhaps in the form of a registry of developers who are willing to trade expertise with others through the aforementioned Distributed Preservation Development Networks (DPDNs). Skillshare—a Web-based teaching and learning exchange—could be a possible model for the DPDN brokerage.

- Explore opportunities for public-private partnerships. Public institutions and private businesses have very different missions and priorities, but there may be areas in which they can cooperate in mutually beneficial ways. Google Books and HathiTrust in the United States are two examples of apparently successful public-private partnerships; *Maggazzini digitali* in Italy is another. Building successful partnerships depends on standardizing the preservation needs of public-sector institutions and creating conditions in which private companies can compete to meet those needs against an agreed-upon set of benchmarking criteria. It also depends on persuading private companies to participate in preserving society's patrimony and cultural heritage, perhaps through public recognition or even preferential fiscal (read: tax) policies. The BRTF-SDPA Final Report identified incentives and business models for public-private cooperation, but the solutions tend to be country-specific and the state of research in this area is still undeveloped. The community needs to identify other activities and suggest new initiatives to tackle the topic of public-private partnerships. The current large-scale EU-funded initiatives in whcih a range of organizations (including commercial partners) are looking at preservation issues might serve as a good starting-point.

- Add digital preservation to the library-school curriculum. Adding a standardized course on digital preservation to the curriculum and investing in post-graduate professional development in digital preservation are good ways to inculcate an understanding of the economics of digital preservation and promote international alignment in this area. Training programs in digital preservation should focus on common technologies and standards and should culminate in the awarding of an international certificate in digital preservation.

This will help to facilitate cooperation in this area by inculcating a common understanding of key concepts and a common skill set.

- Define core services. We have argued that a clear definition of roles and responsibilities is crucial for digital preservation. The same thing goes for core services, an area in which we need to take our cue from the larger user community. We should look to the user community to identify key services, coordinate initiatives, promote common standards, implement policies and recommendations, and encourage the use of basic services like Trusted Digital Repositories (TDR) and Persistent Identifiers (PI) for preservation networks and preserved materials. It would be strategically useful to "standardize" some key services across user communities in order to offer tested, universally applicable solutions for end-users and to stimulate competition among technology providers, which should in turn lead to lower prices. Certification tools for trusted digital repositories include TRAC in the United States and DINI in Germany; DOI, Handle, NBN are examples of protocols for persistent identifiers.

- Support research and development. Finally, encourage research and development (R&D) in digital preservation in order to identify tools and services that yield the best return on investment. This is an area in which external support from government or private funding agencies can play a useful— indeed, a crucial—role, and ALMs should work together across national boundaries to identify and apply for suitable opportunities. Research and development on various aspects of digital preservation could also be added to the curricula at schools of library and information science in North America, the United Kingdom, Europe, and around the globe. Indeed, we need to move beyond our focus on North America and Europe and make connections with digital preservation initiatives in Latin America, Africa, Asia, Australia, and New Zealand.

Conclusions

In a 2004 article whose title was inspired by American poet Wallace Stevens' "Thirteen Ways of Looking at a Blackbird," Brian Lavoie and Lorcan Dempsey recognized that digital preservation is "an economic process, in the sense of matching limited means with ambitious objectives." They were right on both counts: the means are limited and the objectives are indeed ambitious. As this paper shows, however, an impressive—one might even say "ambitious"—amount of work has already been done in Europe, North America, and elsewhere on identifying the costs of digital preservation and devising tools, techniques, and procedures for absorbing those costs into ongoing preservation programs. Moreover, this work has been accomplished in large part by realizing economies through collaboration among institutions. Despite their different origins, missions, and management structures, the preservation initiatives identified in the body of this paper: the *Maggazzini digitali* project in Italy; HathiTrust, the MetaArchive Cooperative, and the Alabama Digital Preservation Network in the United States; the COPPUL PLN in Canada; the Digital Curation Centre in the United Kingdom; the Open Planets Foundation; and so forth—prove that it is possible to take advantage of accumulated experience and community-based effort to build working, economically sustainable digital preservation networks across states, provinces, and even countries. In Lavoie's and Dempsey's (2004) words, digital preservation "is an ongoing, long-term commitment, often shared, and cooperatively met, by many stakeholders." The task facing us now is to build on the collaborative work that has been done.

References

AIDA: http://aida.jiscinvolve.org/wp/ (last accessed 06-06-2012).

Alabama Digital Preservation Network (ADPNet): http://adpn.org/ (last accessed 06-06-2012).

Alliance for Permanent Access (APA): http://www.alliancepermanentaccess.org/ (last accessed 06-06-2012).

Archivematica: http://www.archivematica.org/wiki/index.php?title=Main _Page (last accessed 06-06-2012).

Blue Ribbon Task Force on Sustainable Digital Preservation and Access. (2008). *Sustainable the Digital Investment: Issues and Challenges of Economically Sustainable Digital Preservation.* Interim Report of the Blue Ribbon Task Force on Sustainable Digital Preservation and Access. Retrieved July 29, 2011 from http://brtf.sdsc.edu/biblio/BRTF_Interim Report.pdf (last accessed 06-06-2012).

Blue Ribbon Task Force on Sustainable Digital Preservation and Access. (2010). *Sustainable Economics for a Digital Planet: Ensuring Long-Term Access to Digital Information.* Final Report of the Blue Ribbon Task Force on Sustainable Digital Preservation and Access. Retrieved July 29, 2011 from http://brtf.sdsc.edu/biblio/BRTF_Final_Report.pdf (last accessed 06-06-2012).

Borgman, C.L. (2007). Scholarship in the digital age: Information, infrastructure, and the Internet. Cambridge, MA: MIT Press.

Borgman, C.L., Wallis, J.C., & Enyedy, N. (2006). Building digital libraries for scientific data: An exploratory study of data practices in habitat ecology. *10th European Conference on Digital Libraries. Alicante, Spain*: Berlin: Springer.

California Digital Library (CDL): http://www.cdlib.org/ (last accessed 06-06-2012).

Chronopolis: https://chronopolis.sdsc.edu/ (last accessed 06-06-2012).

Council of Prairie and Pacific University Libraries (COPPUL) Private LOCKSS Network: http://www.coppul.ca/pln.htmlEconomic-v2.docx (last accessed 06-06-2012).

Curator's Workbench: http://www.lib.unc.edu/blogs/cdr/index.php/2010/12/01/announcing-the-curators-workbench/ (last accessed 06-06-2012).

Currall, J., & McKinney, P. (2006). Investing in Value: A Perspective on Digital Preservation. *D-Lib Magazine* 12 (4). http://www.dlib.org/dlib/april06/mckinney/04mckinney.html (last accessed 06-06-2012).

Data Asset Framework (DAF): http://www.dcc.ac.uk/resources/tools-and-applications/data-asset-framework (last accessed 06-06-2012).

Deutsche Initiative für Netzwerkinformation: http://www.dini.de/ (last accessed 06-06-2012).

DICE Center: http://www.diceresearch.org/DICE_Site/iRODS_Uses.ht ml (last accessed 03-08-2012).

Digital Curation Centre. (2005). *Digital curation and preservation: Defining the research agenda for the next decade.* In Report of the Warwick Workshop, November 7-8, 2005. Digital Curation Centre: Warwick, UK. Retrieved July 27, 2007, from http://www.dcc.ac.uk/events/warwick_2005/Warwick_W orkshop_report.pdf (last accessed 06-06-2012).

Digital Preservation Coalition (DPC): http://www.dpconline.org/ (last accessed 06-06-2012).

Digital Public Library of America (DPLA): http://dp.la/ (last accessed 06-06-2012).

DRAMBORA: http://www.dcc.ac.uk/resources/tools-and-applications/drambora (last accessed 06-06-2012).

DROID and PRONOM: http://www.nationalarchives.gov.uk/PRONOM/Default.as px (last accessed 06-06-2012).

DuraCloud: http://www.duracloud.org/ (last accessed 06-06-2012).

Esanu, J., Davidson, J., Ross, S., & Anderson, W. (2004). Selection, appraisal, and retention of digital scientific data: Highlights of an ERPANET/CODATA workshop. *Data Science Journal* 2004, 3. Retrieved July 30, 2007, from http://www.jstage.jst.go.jp/article/dsj/3/0/227/_pdf (last accessed 06-06-2012).

Effective Strategic model for the Preservation and disposal of Institutional Digital Assets (espida): http://www.gla.ac.uk/espida/ (last accessed 06-06-2012).

Ex Libris Rosetta: http://www.exlibrisgroup.com/category/RosettaOverview (last accessed 06-06-2012).

Garrett, J. and Waters, D. (1996). *Preserving Digital Information: Report of the Task Force on Archiving of Digital Information.* Washington, D.C.: Commission on Preservation and Access; Research Libraries Group.

Retrieved July 29, 2011, from
http://www.clir.org/pubs/reports/pub63watersgarrett.pdf
(last accessed 06-06-2012).

HathiTrust: http://www.hathitrust.org/ (last accessed 06-06-2012).

HOPPLA: http://www.ifs.tuwien.ac.at/dp/hoppla/ (last accessed
06-06-2012).

Internet Archive: http://www.archive.org/ (last accessed 03-08-
2012).

ISO/IEC Guide 73. (2002). Risk management. Vocabulary.
Guidelines for use in standards.

JHOVE: http://hul.harvard.edu/jhove/ (last accessed 06-06-2012).

The Keepers Registry: http://thekeepers.org/thekeepers/keepers.asp
(last accessed 06-06-2012).

Keeping Research Data Safe (KRDS):
http://www.beagrie.com/krds.php (last accessed 06-06-
2012).

Lavoie, B., and & Dempsey, L. (2004). Thirteen ways of looking
at: digital preservation. *D-Lib Magazine* 10 (7/8).
doi:10.1045/july2004-lavoie (last accessed 06-06-2012).

Lifecycle Information for E-Literature (LIFE):
http://www.life.ac.uk/ (last accessed 06-06-2012).

LOCKSS und KOPAL Infrastruktur und Interoperabilität:
http://www.lukii.hu-berlin.de/ (last accessed 06-06-2012).

Maggazzini digitali (Digital Stacks): http://www.rinascimento-
digitale.it/projects-digitalstacks.phtml (last accessed 06-
06-2012).

Maron, N.L., Kirby Smith, K., & Loy, M. (2009). Sustaining
Digital Resources: An On-the-Ground View of Projects
Today, Ithaka Case Studies in Sustainability, Strategic
Content Alliance. Retrieved April 28, 2010, from
http://www.ithaka.org/ithaka-s-r/research/ithaka-case-
studies-in-sustainability (last accessed 06-06-2012).

Mayer-Schönberger, V. (2009). *Delete: The Virtue of Forgetting in
the Digital Age.* Princeton, NJ: Princeton University
Press.

Mayernik, M.S., Wallis, J.C., Borgman, C.L., & Pepe, A. (2007).

Adding context to content: The CENS Deployment Center. *Proceedings of the American Society for Information Science and Technology* 44 (1). Milwaukee, WI: Information Today. doi:10.1002/meet.1450440388 (last accessed 06-06-2012).

MetaArchive Cooperative: http://www.metaarchive.org/ (last accessed 06-06-2012).

National Digital Information Infrastructure and Preservation Program (NDIIPP): http://www.digitalpreservation.gov/ (last accessed 06-06-2012).

National Digital Stewardship Alliance (NDSA): http://www.digitalpreservation.gov/ndsa/ (last accessed 06-06-2012).

National Library of New Zealand (NLNZ) Metadata Extraction Tool: http://www.natlib.govt.nz/services/get-advice/digital-libraries/metadata-extraction-tool (last accessed 06-06-2012).

National Science Foundation. (2003). *Report of the National Science Foundation Blue-Ribbon Advisory Panel on Cyberinfrastructure.* Retrieved July 29, 2011, from http://www.nsf.gov/publications/pub_summ.jsp?ods_key=cise051203 (last accessed 06-06-2012).

National Science Foundation Data Management Plan Requirements: http://www.nsf.gov/eng/general/dmp.jsp (last accessed 06-06-2012).

Nielsen, A.B. & Kejser, U.B. (2008). Using the LIFE costing model: case studies from DK. Retrieved July 29, 2011, from http://discovery.ucl.ac.uk/9313/ (last accessed 06-06-2012).

OCLC and CRL. (2007). *Trustworthy Repositories Audit & Certification: Criteria and Checklist.* Retrieved July 29, 2011, from http://www.crl.edu/sites/default/files/attachments/pages/trac_0.pdf (last accessed 06-06-2012).

OCLC Digital Archive: http://www.oclc.org/digitalarchive/ (last accessed 06-06-2012).

Open Planets Foundation (OPF): http://www.openplanetsfoundation.org/ (last accessed 06-

06-2012).

Payette, S., Staples, T., & Wayland, R. (2003, April). The Fedora Project: An Open-source digital object repository management system. *D-Lib Magazine* 9 (4). Retrieved September 30, 2006, from http://www.dlib.org/dlib/april03/staples/04staples.html (last accessed 06-06-2012).

PADI Archive: http://pandora.nla.gov.au/tep/10691 (last accessed 03-08-2012).

Portico: http://www.portico.org/digital-preservation/ (last accessed 06-06-2012).

Preserving Access to Digital Information (PADI): http://pandora.nla.gov.au/tep/10691 (last accessed 06-06-2012).

Rusbridge, C. (2008, July, 29) Re: "Digital preservation" term considered harmful? [Web log message from *Digital Curation Blog*]. Retrieved September 7, 2009, from http://digitalcuration.blogspot.com/2008/07/digital-preservation-term-considered.html (last accessed 06-06-2012).

Santini, M. (2004a). A shallow approach to syntactic feature extraction for genre classification. Proceedings of the 7th Annual Colloquium of the UK Special Interest Group for Computational Linguistics.

Santini, M. (2004b). *State-of-the-art on automatic genre identification*. (Technical Report ITRI-04-03). University of Brighton, UK, Information Technology Research Institute (ITRI).

Skillshare: http://www.skillshare.com/learn (last accessed 06-06-2012).

Skinner, K., & Schultz, M., eds. (2010). *A Guide to Distributed Digital Preservation*. Atlanta, GA: Educopia Institute. Retrieved April 28, 2011, from http://www.metaarchive.org/GDDP (last accessed 06-06-2012).

Smith, M., Barton, M., Bass, M., Branschofsky, M., McClellan, G., Stuve, D., et al. (2003, January). DSpace: An open source dynamic digital repository. *D-Lib Magazine 9 (1)*.

Retrieved September 30, 2006, from
http://www.dlib.org/dlib/january03/smith/01smith.html
(last accessed 06-06-2012).

System Performance Evaluation Corporation (SPEC):
http://www.spec.org/ (last accessed 06-06-2012).

Tessella SDB Digital Preservation: http://www.digital-preservation.com/ (last accessed 06-06-2012).

UC3Merritt: http://merritt.cdlib.org/ (last accessed 06-06-2012).

UK LOCKSS Alliance: http://www.lockssalliance.ac.uk/ (last accessed 06-06-2012).

Witten, I. H., & Frank, E. (2005). *Data mining: Practical machine learning tools and techniques*. (2nd ed.). San Francisco, CA: Morgan Kaufmann.

ECONOMIC SUSTAINABILITY AND ECONOMIC ALIGNMENT: EXAMPLES FROM NORTH AMERICA

Aaron Trehub (Auburn University)

Abstract

Much of the literature on digital preservation focuses on technical solutions. However, recent experience from North America suggests that questions of governance and economic sustainability are equally if not more important than technical issues. This paper examines how three community-owned and community-governed digital preservation networks in North America have crafted policies aimed at achieving long-term economic sustainability and discusses their relevance for digital preservation initiatives in other countries.

Introduction

Digital preservation is the corollary to digital collection building. Like many things having to do with infrastructure, it's invisible, unglamorous, and absolutely necessary. Although precise figures are hard to come by, it is generally recognized that most of the world's information is currently being produced in digital form, not as print documents or analogue artifacts. This poses a serious challenge to libraries, archives, museums, and other cultural memory organizations, as well as government agencies. Unlike their analogue counterparts, digital files are inherently susceptible to decay, destruction, and disappearance. Given the vulnerability of digital content to fires, floods, tornadoes, hurricanes, power blackouts, cyber-attacks, and a variety of hardware and software failures, cultural heritage organizations need to start incorporating long-term digital preservation services for locally owned and created digital content into their routine operations, or risk losing that content irrevocably.

A number of countries have recognized the challenge and embarked on ambitious digital preservation programs at the national level. In the United States, the Library of Congress initiated the National Digital Information Infrastructure and Preservation Program (NDIIPP) almost ten years ago, and recently launched the National Digital Stewardship Alliance (NDSA). In the United Kingdom, the Digital Curation Centre of the Joint Information Systems Committee (JISC) provides a national focus for digital preservation issues. Similar initiatives are underway in Canada, New Zealand, France, Germany, Italy, the Netherlands, and other European countries.

Several lessons have already emerged from these initiatives. One of them concerns the importance of collaboration among institutions, states, and even countries. In digital preservation, as in many other endeavors, there is strength in numbers. With numbers comes complexity, however, and comprehensive digital preservation programs inevitably raise difficult technical, administrative, financial, and even legal questions. That said, these questions are not unsolvable. Indeed, they are being solved, or successfully addressed, by a number of preservation programs in the United States, Canada, and other countries. There is a growing body of empirical experience that shows that it is possible to build technically and administratively robust digital preservation networks across institutional and geographical borders without compromising those networks' long-term viability through excessive complexity and cost.

Economic Sustainability: One Approach

The authors of the final report of the Blue Ribbon Task Force on Sustainable Digital Preservation and Access (2010) have written that "economically sustainable preservation—ensuring the ongoing and efficient allocation of resources to digital preservation—is an urgent societal problem" (p. 9). Proceeding from that assertion, they posited five conditions for economic sustainability:

1. Recognition of the benefits of preservation by decision makers;

2. A process for selecting digital materials with long-term value;

3. Incentives for decision makers to preserve in the public interest;

4. Appropriate organization and governance of digital preservation activities; and

5. Mechanisms to secure an ongoing, efficient allocation of resources to digital preservation activities. (p. 12)

Fortunately, digital preservation solutions that satisfy most or all of those five conditions have started to emerge in the past several years. One especially promising approach combines Distributed Digital Preservation (DDP) with LOCKSS ("Lots Of Copies Keep Stuff Safe") peer-to-peer software in so-called Private LOCKSS Networks (PLNs). As its name implies, DDP is based on the idea of distributing copies of digital files to server computers at geographically dispersed locations in order to maximize their chances of surviving a natural or man-made disaster, power failure, or other disruption. DDP networks consist of multiple preservation sites, selected with the following principles in mind:

- Sites preserving the same content should not be within a 75-125-mile radius of one another;

- Preservation sites should be distributed beyond the typical pathways of natural disasters, such as hurricanes, typhoons, and tornadoes;

- Preservation sites should be distributed across different power grids;

- Preservation sites should be under the control of different systems administrators;

- Content preserved in disparate sites should be on live media and should be checked on a regular basis for bit-rot and other issues; and

- Content should be replicated at least three times in accordance with the principles detailed above. (Skinner, 2010, pp. 12-13)

LOCKSS was developed and is currently maintained at the Stanford University Libraries. It is ideally suited for use in DDP networks. Originally designed to harvest, cache, and preserve digital copies of journals for academic libraries, LOCKSS is also effective at harvesting, caching, and preserving multiple copies of locally created digital content for cultural memory organizations in general. LOCKSS servers (also called LOCKSS boxes, LOCKSS caches, and LOCKSS nodes) typically perform the following functions:

- They collect content from target Web sites using a Web crawler similar to those used by search engines;

- They continually compare the content they have collected with the same content collected by other LOCKSS boxes, and repair any differences;

- They act as a Web proxy or cache, providing browsers in the library's community with access to the publisher's content or the preserved content as appropriate; and

- They provide a Web-based administrative interface that allows the library staff to target new content for preservation, monitor the state of the content being preserved, and control access to the preserved content.

LOCKSS is open-source software and therefore theoretically available for further development by the open-source community. In practice, however, its design and development have been confined to the LOCKSS team at Stanford.

Although there are LOCKSS-based digital preservation networks in Europe (e.g. the UK LOCKSS Alliance and LuKII), most of the Private LOCKSS networks are currently based in North America.[1] Auburn University, a large land-grant university in east-central Alabama, is a founding member of two of them: the MetaArchive Cooperative, an international preservation network which began in 2004 with support from the Library of Congress' NDIIPP Program; and the Alabama Digital Preservation Network (ADPNet), a statewide preservation network which began in 2006 with a two-year grant from the Institute of Museum and Library Services (IMLS), a federal funding agency. ADPNet also served as the model for a third LOCKSS-based network in North America: the Council of Prairie and Pacific University Libraries (COPPUL) PLN in western Canada.

The MetaArchive Cooperative is an independent, international membership association administered by the Educopia Institute, which is based in Atlanta, Georgia. The Cooperative's purpose is to support, promote, and extend the MetaArchive approach to distributed digital preservation practices. The Cooperative is responsible for preserving member organizations' content in a decentralized, distributed preservation network consisting of subject- and genre-based archives (e.g.

---

[1] Private LOCKSS Networks listing:
http://www.lockss.org/lockss/Private_LOCKSS_Networks (last accessed 03-05-2012). This may be changing, as seen through emerging PLNs in Italy and Belgium.

Southern Digital Culture, Electronic Theses and Dissertations, etc.), as well as maintaining and extending its methodology and approach to distributed digital preservation. MetaArchive is growing quickly and currently preserves content for more than fifty member institutions in the United States, the United Kingdom, Brazil, and Spain. MetaArchive is also engaged in exploratory work with several statewide digitization efforts to build a new preservation network and infrastructure that is based on the model of a "preservation hub." The network currently has 16 terabytes of storage at each of the member institutions and has harvested over 900 archival units totaling over six terabytes.

The Alabama Digital Preservation Network (ADPNet) is a statewide digital preservation network that serves cultural heritage organizations in Alabama. ADPNet currently has nine members: the Alabama Department of Archives & History in Montgomery, Auburn University, the Birmingham Public Library, the Huntsville-Madison County Public Library, Spring Hill College in Mobile, Troy University in Troy, the University of Alabama in Tuscaloosa, the University of Alabama in Birmingham, and the University of North Alabama in Florence. Inspired in large part by Auburn University's experience with the MetaArchive Cooperative, the Alabama network began in 2006 with a two-year National Leadership Grant from the Institute of Museum and Library Services (IMLS). The grant provided support for equipment and associated expenses to the seven founding institutions; crucially, it also covered those institutions' annual membership fees in the LOCKSS Alliance for the same period. For their part, the participating institutions split the equipment costs with the IMLS and contributed staff time and other in-house resources to the project. A LOCKSS staff member was assigned to the project to provide technical support and guidance. The IMLS grant ended in September 2008, and ADPNet is now a self-sustaining, member-owned DDP network operating under the auspices of the Network of Alabama Academic Libraries (NAAL), a department of the Alabama Commission on Higher Education in Montgomery. All of the original member institutions have contributed content to the network, which currently contains over 400 archival units totaling over four terabytes. The network plans to harvest several terabytes of new content in 2012, including content from the public libraries in Birmingham and Huntsville.

The COPPUL PLN is a digital preservation network that operates under the auspices of the Council of Prairie and Pacific

University Libraries, a consortium of twenty-two academic libraries in western Canada. The COPPUL PLN began work in 2006 as a two-year pilot initiative among eight member institutions: Athabasca University, Simon Fraser University, and the universities of Alberta, British Columbia, Calgary, Manitoba, Saskatchewan, and Winnipeg (a ninth institution, the University of Victoria, joined the network in late 2010). The pilot initiative was approved by the COPPUL consortium in 2008; and the network has been financially self-supporting since 2010. The COPPUL PLN focuses its preservation efforts on digital collections of local or regional interest that would not be preserved elsewhere. These include: locally hosted open-access journals, especially those that use Open Journal Systems (OJS), an open-source journal management and publishing system developed and managed by the Public Knowledge Project (PKP) at the University of British Columbia and Simon Fraser University; locally digitized collections; small university press publications; digitized journals with a regional focus; and Web sites and online resources from the member institutions' local collections.[2] The COPPUL PLN based its governance policy and administrative structure on ADPNet's, and the two networks have discussed swapping LOCKSS servers to increase geographic dispersion and improve the preserved content's survivability in the event of a major mishap. The COPPUL PLN has harvested over 500 archival units (mostly articles from Open Journal Systems) and 100 gigabytes of content to date. Plans are in place to begin harvesting digital objects from DSpace, CONTENTdm, and other digital content-management systems.[3]

Why Alabama?

ADPNet is the first working statewide PLN in the United States. Alabama was an attractive candidate for a geographically distributed digital preservation network for several reasons. The first is the frequency of hurricanes, tornadoes, flooding, and other natural disasters, especially on and around Alabama's Gulf coast. In the past ten years, Alabama has been hit by at least four major hurricanes and many more tropical storms. In 2005, Hurricane Katrina devastated the coastal communities of Bayou la Batre and

---

[2] Personal communication from Andrew Waller, University of Calgary, March 11, 2011.
[3] Personal communication from Mark Jordan, Simon Fraser University, March 20, 2012.

Coden and flooded downtown Mobile. The coastal communities are not the only parts of the state that have suffered from natural disasters, however. The interior of the state is vulnerable to tornadoes. In March 2007 a tornado swept through Enterprise, Alabama, destroying a high school and causing nine deaths.[4] In April 2011, a string of powerful tornadoes hit the cities of Tuscaloosa, Birmingham, and Cullman, destroying entire neighborhoods and killing over 250 people.[5]

The second factor is Alabama's economic status and financial situation. An historically poor state, Alabama ranked 47th out of 51 states and territories in median household income in 2010.[6] The lack of state and institutional resources in Alabama means that technical solutions have to be simple, robust, and above all inexpensive to implement and maintain.

Finally, despite its economic challenges, Alabama is home to a rich and growing array of digital collections at libraries, archives, and museums. Many of these collections can be found in AlabamaMosaic, a statewide repository of digital materials on all aspects of Alabama's history, geography, and cultures.[7] AlabamaMosaic currently contains over 40,000 digital objects from more than twenty institutions around the state, and the number continues to grow. This combination of circumstances—extreme weather, meager state financial resources, and rich digital collections—made Alabama an ideal test case for a simple, inexpensive, but effective digital-preservation solution like LOCKSS.

Although ADPNet was originally inspired by and has some similarities with the MetaArchive Cooperative, there are important differences between the two initiatives. First and most importantly, the Alabama network is a single-state solution. This has simplified governance and allowed the network to be absorbed into an existing legal and administrative entity, one with bylaws and a

---

[4] For more about the 2007 tornado in Enterprise, Alabama, please see:
http://en.wikipedia.org/wiki/Enterprise,_Alabama (last accessed 03-05-2012).
[5] For more about the "2011 Super Outbreak" http://en.wikipedia.org/wiki/April_25-28,_2011_tornado_outbreak (last accessed 03-05-2012).
[6] U.S. Census Bureau (2010), "Table R1901: Median Household Income (In 2008 Inflation-Adjusted Dollars)," available at
http://factfinder2.census.gov/faces/tableservices/jsf/pages/productview.xhtml?pid=ACS_10_1YR_R1901.US01PRF&prodType=table (last accessed 03-06-2012).
[7] AlabamaMosaic repository: http://www.alabamamosaic.org/ (last accessed 03-06-2012).

committee structure already in place. Second, the Alabama network was designed to be a practical solution to a pressing statewide problem, not a research-and-development project (although the network has worked with the LOCKSS technical team on ingesting large archival units and other technical issues). In order to attract participants, ADPNet had to be simple, robust, and above all inexpensive. This, and the fact that only one or two institutions in Alabama had had any prior experience with LOCKSS, meant that the members opted for the simplest, least expensive hardware and software solutions available, in the hope that these would be easier to deploy and manage and more attractive to other institutions in the state. Finally, unlike the MetaArchive Cooperative, ADPNet is not a service organization with a separate administrative office. Rather, the preservation network was intended to be sustained primarily by in-kind contributions from its participating institutions. In other words, ADPNet was designed from its inception to run on relatively small expenditures and "sweat equity." To some degree these differences reflect Alabama's expense-averse institutional culture. They also reflect a preference for simplicity, self-sufficiency, and informality where administrative arrangements are concerned.

Economic Sustainability: Practical Issues

Auburn University's experience with the MetaArchive Cooperative and especially with ADPNet suggests that LOCKSS-based distributed digital preservation networks are a relatively simple and affordable way to preserve locally created digital content, regardless of the type of institution or the nature of the content to be preserved. If a group of institutions in one of the poorest states in the United States can set up and sustain a robust digital preservation network, then presumably other institutions in other states and countries can do it too.

This raises a practical question: How does a group of institutions go about setting up a LOCKSS-based preservation network? A good first step would be to download and read a copy of the *Guide to Distributed Digital Preservation*, the MetaArchive Cooperative's first book—it was published in 2010 by the Educopia Institute, and it is the first comprehensive guide to the subject. The *Guide* is available for free as a PDF file from the MetaArchive Web site.[8]

The first requirement for a PLN is a quorum of at least six institutions that have locally created digital content they would like to preserve and that have agreed to work together to create the network and to allocate sufficient resources to sustain it over the long term. A PLN may have more than six members— MetaArchive, COPPUL, and ADPNet all do—but six is the recommended minimum to ensure network robustness in the event that one or two nodes experience a simultaneous failure.

The second requirement is a policy or governance document. This document contains the rules for running the network and spells out the rights and responsibilities of the network members. When the MetaArchive Cooperative began its work in 2004-2005, there were no governance documents for collaborative digital preservation networks to use as models, so the members had to draft their own from scratch, with some help from legal counsel at one of the member institutions and *pro bono* contributions from a private law firm in Atlanta. Thanks to MetaArchive's work and work by other preservation initiatives in North America, there are now at least three publicly available governance documents that nascent preservation networks can copy or adapt to their purposes: the MetaArchive Cooperative Charter, the ADPNet Governance Policy, and the COPPUL PLN Governance Policy. All of these documents are publicly available on the Web sites of the three PLNs.[9] Other institutions are encouraged to use them as models.

Finally, setting up a distributed digital preservation network requires money, either in kind or in cash. Distributed digital preservation is less expensive than re-creating damaged or destroyed collections, but it is not without cost. In general, the costs can be divided into four categories: hardware, staff time, communication, and membership fees.

Hardware first. Every preservation site in a PLN needs a dedicated LOCKSS server computer, or LOCKSS box. LOCKSS

---

[8] The Guide to Distributed Digital Preservation: http://www.metaarchive.org/GDDP (last accessed 03-06-2012).

[9] These governance policies are publicly available at the following locations: http://adpn.org/resources.html; http://coppullockssgroup.pbworks.com/w/page/11478105/FrontPage#Governance Policy; http://www.metaarchive.org/documentation (all last accessed 03-06-2012).

will run on inexpensive, even surplus or superannuated equipment, but we have found that it runs best on up-to-date servers with at least several terabytes of expandable storage capacity. Although prices are falling, these servers typically cost between USD$2,000-USD$4,000. Remember too that as a digital preservation network grows, additional storage space needs to be purchased and that hardware must be refreshed at regular intervals.

Staff time is needed is manage the LOCKSS equipment and to write the documentation and instruction sets (manifest pages and plugins) that LOCKSS uses to identify available content and harvest it into the network. The total commitment in staff time is not very large—typically the equivalent of one quarter-time staff person or even less—but it is an expense and needs to be considered at the outset. Communication costs are negligible, at least in our experience. The MetaArchive Cooperative conducts weekly conference calls and holds an annual meeting of the cooperative's Steering Committee. ADPNet conducts monthly conference calls and holds an annual meeting of the network's Steering Committee. COPPUL conducts "mostly monthly" Skype calls. All three networks have listservs, and most routine business is conducted by e-mail.

This brings us to membership fees, the single most expensive item on the list. There are two types of membership fees in PLNs: the annual LOCKSS Alliance fee, which is usually required but may be waived at the discretion of the LOCKSS administration, and network membership fees, which are optional. The LOCKSS Alliance fee is based on the Carnegie Classification system for colleges and universities in the United States and currently ranges from USD$1,080 per year for small, two-year institutions to USD$10,800 per year for large research universities. Obviously, this is a substantial expense, and it has put LOCKSS-based digital preservation beyond the reach of smaller, poorly resourced institutions—that is, precisely those institutions whose digital collections are most vulnerable to loss.

In an attempt to eliminate this obstacle to membership, the Alabama network worked out an agreement with LOCKSS that will permit institutions to join the network for a graduated annual membership fee without also having to join the LOCKSS Alliance, as long as the network delivers an previously agreed-upon amount for the year to LOCKSS to pay for continued software development and technical support. The product of negotiations between the LOCKSS administration and Thomas C. Wilson,

Associate Dean for Library Technology at the University of Alabama, the new ADPNet membership system consists of four membership categories with progressive annual membership fees, base storage allocations in the network and fees for increasing that allocation, different levels of technical and administrative responsibility, and different levels of representation on the ADPNet governance bodies. Specifically, the four ADPNet membership categories are: Anchor (base annual membership fee: USD$5,000; base local data allotment: 1.5TB); Host (base annual membership fee: USD$2,400; base local data allotment: 500GB); Participant (Large) (base annual membership fee: USD$800; base local data allotment: 1.5GB); and Participant (Small) (base annual membership fee: USD$300; base local data allotment: 500MB).[10]

The new four-tiered ADPNet membership system was designed to address three issues. First, by divorcing membership in ADPNet from membership in the LOCKSS Alliance, it was designed to make participation in the network possible for smaller, poorly resourced institutions that cannot afford the LOCKSS Alliance membership fees. Second, it was designed to enforce the principle of "use more, pay more" by making membership fees commensurate with usage of the network. Third, and in that connection, it was designed to address the "free rider" problem that was identified by the authors of the Blue Ribbon Task Force on Sustainable Digital Preservation and Access Final Report and which they defined this way:

> **free-rider problem:** a situation arising when goods are nonrival in consumption, when benefits accrue to those who don't pay for them. For example, the costs of preserving digital assets may be borne by one organization, but the benefits accrue to many. (p. 107)

The new ADPNet membership system ensures that all the members pay something in order to belong to the network. At the same time, the less-expensive membership categories were designed to persuade institutions that might otherwise opt out to participate. Evidence to date suggests that the system is working as intended. Two public libraries—the Birmingham Public Library and the Huntsville-Madison County Public Library—joined the network at the end of 2011, the first at the Host level, the second at the Participant (Small) level. The network now consists of a state

---

[10] For details on the different levels of membership, see the "ADPNet Membership Model" at http://adpn.org/resources.html (last accessed 03-06-2012).

agency, five large or medium-sized research universities, a small liberal-arts college, and two public libraries—a fairly diverse membership. This early evidence suggests that the system of graduated membership fees will be successful; we hope that it can serve as a model for other digital preservation networks that are facing the same problem.

The MetaArchive Cooperative has been grappling with some of the same issues. The Cooperative encourages but does not require members to pay the LOCKSS Alliance membership fee. In addition, it charges an annual membership fee of USD$5,500 (for Sustaining Members—the highest level of membership) or USD$3,000 (for Preservation Members—a lower level of membership). These fees are used to support the Cooperative's administrative, collaborative, and software-development activities. The Cooperative recently added a Collaborative Member category that has enabled consortia of institutions to join the network through a lead institution for USD$2,500 per year, with nominal annual fees—typically USD$100 per year—for each of the consortium member institutions.[11] It is hoped that this will broaden participation in MetaArchive.

It is important to repeat that membership fees are not required for LOCKSS-based networks. For example, the COPPUL PLN in western Canada does not charge a separate membership fee. Instead, every member pays the annual LOCKSS Alliance membership fee (the same arrangement that ADPNet used to have).

Economic Sustainability: Some Guiding Principles

Auburn University's experience as a founding member of two digital preservation networks and the model for a third has enabled it to identify a number of principles that contribute to economic sustainability. Briefly, the main ones are as follows:

- Whenever possible, use open-source solutions (e.g. LOCKSS)—not necessarily because they cost less than commercial solutions, although generally they do, but because they can be managed and modified locally. This is an

---

[11] Please see: http://www.metaarchive.org/how-to-join (last accessed 03-05-2012). Starting in 2012, the membership fee for the Collaborative category is calculated on a case-by-case basis in accordance with the number of member institutions in each consortium: see http://www.metaarchive.org/costs (last accessed 03-05-2012).

important consideration if one believes that cultural heritage organizations should retain control of and access to the digital content they want to preserve while minimizing their dependence on third-party solutions.

- Whenever possible, take advantage of existing administrative infrastructure. There is a corollary here: whenever possible, avoid creating new administrative infrastructure. As was mentioned above, ADPNet is part of the Network of Alabama Academic Libraries (NAAL), an existing state agency. The COPPUL PLN is part of the Council of Prairie and Pacific University Libraries, an existing consortium of academic libraries in western Canada. For various reasons, the MetaArchive Cooperative decided to create a new administrative entity (the Educopia Institute in Atlanta, Georgia) to manage that network, but that decision was necessitated by the network's geographic dispersion across a number of states and the absence of a satisfactory existing administrative home. In the MetaArchive event, this arrangement does not seem to have impeded the network's growth. On the contrary, basing the administration of the network with a neutral agency seems to have allayed concerns about institutional favoritism (and fluctuations in institutional commitment) and increased the network's attractiveness to potential members.

- Aim for a lightweight administrative structure. Like any other form of administration, administering a digital preservation network costs time and money, and it is therefore advisable to keep the administrative structure as simple as possible. ADPNet and the COPPUL PLN each have just two committees: a steering committee for policy questions and a technical committee for hardware and software issues. The MetaArchive Cooperative has a similar administrative structure. The networks have different communication schedules: due to its size and relative complexity, MetaArchive holds weekly conference calls, the COPPUL PLN meets via Skype every other week, and ADPNet has monthly conference calls. A lot of business in all three networks is conducted by e-mail. The idea is to make digital preservation a routine, low-maintenance, and integral part of an institution's information-management activities.

- Delegate as much decision-making power as possible to the individual member institutions. They know their digital collections best, and are best able to set preservation priorities.

- Broaden "ownership" of the network by involving all the network members in management and administration. The chair of the ADPNet Steering Committee—the network's policy-making body—rotates among the participating institutions every year or two. This helps to ensure a flow of fresh ideas and approaches and gives all of the members a stake in the network's success. The same arrangement obtains in the COPPUL PLN. Management of the MetaArchive Cooperative tends to be concentrated in the central office that was created for that purpose, but the member institutions are represented on the network's steering committee.

- Finally, a perhaps-controversial and counterintuitive principle: resist spending a lot of time working on "business models" or devising detailed financial justifications for digital preservation. Such activities may be necessary at the national level or for very large and complex organizations (e.g. national libraries and archives), but they are less useful at the local level. The very fact that institutions have invested substantial resources in creating digital collections and have a professional and fiduciary interest in protecting that investment by preserving those collections is reason enough to institute a digital preservation program. Doing so will require planning and the apportionment of responsibilities, but it should not require elaborate and time-consuming justifications. If it does, that itself may be a sign that long-term institutional commitment is lacking.

Whichever preservation model one chooses, it is advisable to keep it as simple and cheap as possible. Simplicity contributes to economic sustainability; complexity undermines it. This maxim rings true across a whole spectrum of activity, especially since anecdotal evidence suggests that digital preservation can be a tough sell precisely because of its perceived complexity and cost.

Robert Fox (2011) of the University of Notre Dame has identified a number of "key advantages" of peer-to-peer digital preservation networks, including "garner[ing] support from like-minded institutions and rais[ing] the awareness level regarding the preservation of key digital assets"; "the potential to increase the knowledge base required to maintain the preservation systems being used"; and "increas[ing] the opportunity for validity checking, especially in systems that use 'voting' as a mechanism for checking file integrity" (p. 268). In addition to those benefits, distributed digital preservation networks also offer excellent opportunities for international collaboration. Geographic separation of LOCKSS nodes is one of the core principles of DDP, and the more far-flung the LOCKSS servers are, the more survivable the network will be. It is hoped that the points raised in this paper will help to persuade other institutions that distributed digital preservation is an affordable option for their digital collections. The members of the MetaArchive Cooperative, ADPNet, or the COPPUL PLN would be happy to help interested institutions—in the United States, Canada, or other countries—get started on setting up their own DDP networks.

Conclusion: Toward Economic Alignment?

Digital preservation is widely perceived to be a complex and expensive undertaking, requiring years of planning and large infusions of money and other resources. As Fox (2011) put it, the issues surrounding long-term digital preservation "are daunting not only owing to the complexity of the topic, but also the time commitment that would be required to implement very robust preservation systems" (p. 271). This perception may be true in some cases, but it need not be. The experience of the LOCKSS-based DDP networks in North America suggests that it is possible to build robust, scalable, and economically sustainable preservation solutions with relatively modest resources. Moreover, it is possible to extend this solution across different kinds of institutions in different states, provinces, and countries. The MetaArchive Cooperative is a truly international preservation network, with institutional members in Brazil, Spain, and the United Kingdom. The ADPNet-COPPUL relationship is an example of two self-sustaining DDP networks that are collaborating fruitfully across national borders. Taken together, these initiatives represent working examples of economic alignment and offer proof that it is possible to create affordable and sustainable preservation networks internationally.

References

Alabama Digital Preservation Network (ADPNet): http://adpn.org/ (last accessed 03-05-2012).

AlabamaMosaic: http://www.alabamamosaic.org/ (last accessed 03-05-2012).

Blue Ribbon Task Force on Sustainable Digital Preservation and Access. (2008). *Sustainable the Digital Investment: Issues and Challenges of Economically Sustainable Digital Preservation.* Interim Report of the Blue Ribbon Task Force on Sustainable Digital Preservation and Access. Retrieved July 29, 2011 from http://brtf.sdsc.edu/biblio/BRTF_Interim_Report.pdf (last accessed 03-05-2012).

Blue Ribbon Task Force on Sustainable Digital Preservation and Access. (2010). *Sustainable Economics for a Digital Planet: Ensuring Long-Term Access to Digital Information.* Final Report of the Blue Ribbon Task Force on Sustainable Digital Preservation and Access. Retrieved July 29, 2011 from http://brtf.sdsc.edu/biblio/BRTF_Final_Report.pdf (last accessed 03-05-2012).

Council of Prairie and Pacific University Libraries (COPPUL) Private LOCKSS Network: http://www.coppul.ca/pln.html (last accessed 03-05-2012).

Digital Curation Centre (DCC): http://www.dcc.ac.uk/ (last accessed 03-05-2012).

Educopia Institute: http://www.educopia.org (last accessed 07-06-2012).

Fox, R. (2011). Forensics of digital librarianship. *OCLC Systems & Services* 27 (4): pp. 264-271. doi: 10.1108/10650751111182560 (last accessed 03-05-2012).

Joint Information Systems Committee (JISC): http://www.jisc.ac.uk/ (last accessed 03-05-2012).

Lavoie, B., and & Dempsey, L. (2004). Thirteen ways of looking at: digital preservation. *D-Lib Magazine* 10 (7/8). doi: 10.1045/july2004-lavoie (last accessed 03-05-2012).

LOCKSS: http://www.lockss.org/ (last accessed 03-05-2012).

MetaArchive Cooperative: http://www.metaarchive.org/ (last accessed 03-05-2012).

National Digital Information Infrastructure and Preservation

Program (NDIIPP): http://www.digitalpreservation.gov/ (last accessed 03-05-2012).

National Digital Stewardship Alliance (NDSA): http://www.digitalpreservation.gov/ndsa/ (last accessed 03-05-2012).

Network of Alabama Academic Libraries (NAAL): http://www.ache.state.al.us/NAAL/ (last accessed 03-05-2012).

Public Knowledge Project Open Journal Systems: http://pkp.sfu.ca/?q=ojs (last accessed 03-05-2012).

Skinner, K., & Schultz, M., eds. (2010). *A Guide to Distributed Digital Preservation*. Atlanta, GA: Educopia Institute. http://www.metaarchive.org/GDDP (last accessed 03-05-2012).

Czech National Digital Library: Economic, Strategic, and International Aspects of Digital Preservation

Bohdana Stoklasová (National Library of the Czech Republic)
Jan Hutař (National Library of the Czech Republic)
Marek Melichar (National Library of the Czech Republic)

Abstract

This essay reflects digital preservation experience gained by the authors over several years in the National Library of the Czech Republic (NL CR) as well as through participation in international projects. The first part of the article deals with the development of digital preservation at the NL CR in connection with the digitization of analogue documents and archiving of born-digital documents. After a short description of the main projects related to digital preservation, the primary accent is on the strategic-economic and international aspects of digital preservation in a memory institution financed by the state. At a time of budget cuts, the relatively new area of digital preservation is not easy—and for many difficult—to understand, to reach one of the foremost places in the list of strategic priorities and attain the necessary financial and personnel provisions. In the area of digital preservation, the NL CR has moved in a relatively short period of time from having nothing in place to a achieving a good level of practice, chiefly thanks to the utilization of the results of international projects and the best practices of foreign national libraries and other institutions. In this paper, the authors evaluate, categorize, and describe the most useful projects, products, and practical experiences acquired during visits of workplaces abroad as recommendations for digital preservation beginners.

Introduction

This paper describes how the National Library of the Czech Republic (NL CR) began its digital preservation efforts. As a memory institution, the NL CR has dealt with the preservation of paper documents for several centuries but turning its attention to the preservation of digital documents has not been easy. We believe that a number of national libraries or other memory institutions have had or will soon have similar experiences. In the following pages, we reflect upon the fundamental effects of digital preservation's introduction on various library processes, on financing, and on staffing.

Digital Collections at the NL CR

The NL CR started to learn about digital preservation rather long after the institutions' infrastructure housed many terabytes of digital data. The data were generated mainly in the digitization of paper documents. The NL CR digitized all of its card catalogues (approximately 5,000,000 cards) in the middle of 1990s. Later, the digitization moved to the library documents—both historical and modern. The routine digitization of manuscripts began in 1996 and the digitization of endangered newspapers (at the beginning based on microfilms) began in 2000, the year in which the NL CR began to harvest and archive Czech Internet content. The NL CR created three digital libraries: Manuscriptorium (historical collections), Kramerius (modern books and periodicals), and WebArchiv (archiving the Czech Web) and built a unique national access point, the Uniform Information Gateway (UIG).

However, in recent years, the budget available for digitization has continually declined. In response, the NL CR has undertaken two projects: The National Digital Library project, financed mainly from the EU Structural Funds, which will digitize and store primarily modern documents (issued after 1800) and the Google Books project, which will focus on digitization of early prints. These projects will result in approximately 500,000 volumes or 100,000,000 pages of digitized analogue documents by 2020.

In 2011, the NL CR also launched a pilot project aimed at the acquisition and processing of born-digital documents and of the digital preprints of printed documents. The pilot program relies on voluntary cooperation with the publishers; the obligation to deposit electronic publications should be anchored in new legislation.

As the amounts of data in the digital repository of the NL CR have grown, its administration has required ever more attention and finances. The library management decided first to stabilize the hardware infrastructure of the repository, which improved at least the bitstream level preservation of the data. More sophisticated logical preservation via data and metadata management should be fully serviced by the Long-term preservation system solution, which the NL CR should build in the National Digital Library project.

National Digital Library Project

In February 2010, the NL CR applied along with the Moravian Library (ML) as its partner for the "Creation of the National Digital Library" (NDL, Czech initials: NDK) project. The project was submitted within the Call 07 of the Integrated Operational Programme "Electronisation of Public Administration." In June 2010, the project was approved. It is one of the cornerstones of the eCulture concept, through which the sector of culture significantly contributes to the fulfillment of the aims of Smart Administration.

The budget of the project is ca. EUR 12 million, of which 85 percent comes from the ERDF structural fund and 15 percent from the Czech Republic state budget.

The NL CR and ML each have been deposit libraries for more then 200 years. In their collections are most documents published in the CR (*Bohemica* in the narrow sense of the word), a great number of documents related to the CR published abroad (*Bohemica* in the broad sense of the word), and abundant historical collections. The libraries cherish extensive and unique materials of cultural and factual value.

The NDL project has three main aims:

1. The digitization of a significant part of the *Bohemica* of the 19th–21st Centuries, i.e. books issued in the Czech Republic, written in Czech or discussing the Czech Republic. By the end of 2019, we will have digitized in total more than 50 million pages, approximately 300,000 volumes. The digitization will continue beyond the scope of the project (2014) and also beyond the mandatory sustainability of the project.

2. Building a reliable digital repository for the long-term preservation of digital documents. The system will provide an environment for the management and preservation of documents digitized in previous years and ingest also the digital documents created during the NDL project.

3. Provide a single point of access to all these digital documents, in user-friendly interface with advanced personalization options. The system should overlay digitized documents,

online scholarly journal databases, and all other information resources.

Strategic and Economic Aspects

The complexity of the NDL project is enhanced by its relationship to two physical construction projects: the reconstruction of the historical building of the Klementinum in the centre of Prague and the construction of a new building on Prague's periphery, which should house the major part of the technology and staff of the NDL project. The NDL project will affect many activities, and sometimes will require profound transformations of processes and workflows.

The context and expectations of the NL CR stakeholders are naturally changing too. Users expect more off-site services and are not ready to bridge the traditional library barriers. Users expect single place of access with Google-type indexes. The NL CR has to fulfill also coordination functions—for example, in the digitization project, the NL CR has to publish standards and requirements on the quality of its metadata. During the NDL project, also other institutions will start new larger digitization projects financed in the regions.

In the following section, we will explain how the NDL project has affected and will yet affect the NL CR's budgeting, staff decisions, and also organizational issues. This will set our digital preservation efforts into an appropriate context.

Financing and Staffing

The funds from the EU Structural Funds for the NDL project cover the expected expenditures only partially. In the area of human resources, the project must be heavily subsidized from the internal resources of the NL CR (as well as our partner, the ML). The project will have to integrate so far individually managed organization units and will absorb several projects which existed rather independently in the past.

The project will integrate the departments involved in in-house digitization, management of external digitization, and administration of digital libraries as well as the Web archiving department and the recently established digital preservation department. As the NDL project will build digitization infrastructure in-house in the NL CR and the ML, the information technology (IT) team will have to be strengthened too.

Both Manuscriptorium and Kramerius were independent projects based on cooperation with external entities supported by small teams on the part of the NL CR. The teams were constituted at a time when the NL CR had enough staff available and their creation did not require any reductions in other departments.

The Web Archiving Department was created in a different atmosphere—the decision to begin with this new activity required reorganization, brought new requirements for library processes, and required new library content types. Web archiving brought heterogeneous activities into the institution that had until then dealt exclusively with traditional library analogue documents. Besides the technical part of the harvesting, which remains even for many librarians blurred, other aspects required attention too: first the legal conditions of this project and then also the new curatorial processes (selecting, acquiring, describing and archiving of the documents is rather different in a Web archive then in the rest of the Library). This all caused some misunderstandings and tensions around this department.

The Digital Preservation Division emerged slowly. The embryo was one full-time equivalent with a single employee. Later, during the participation of the NL CR in the Digital Preservation Europe project in 2006–2009, the NL CR invested all of the financial means acquired from the DPE project into building the digital preservation team. The preparation of the NDL project began in 2008. Without the existence of a high-quality digital preservation team, the NL CR would not have been capable of preparing and submitting the project with one part focused on building a trusted digital repository.

The departments most affected by this change were the departments involved in the development of the Kramerius digital library system, the departments running current in-house digitization, the departments managing our current digital content in the archive and digital libraries, the Web archive department, and a substantial part of the IT department (augmented by several new employees form the new NDL team). Other departments like the cataloguing department and administration of the library catalogue will be substantially affected by both the Google Books project and the NDL. All of this will change the long-time established balance in the staff structure. Less pure librarian skills will be required and more technically oriented system librarians, or only partly library-oriented technical experts, will be needed.

The NDL project, like other projects dealing with digital data, requires skills and an organizational culture that traditionally did not exist in the pre-digital library. In the scope of the NDL, the NL CR and the ML will have to cooperate with large numbers of suppliers, project managers, and administrators from external commercial institutions. This will bring the need to accommodate the standard project management processes. The librarians can be overly vigilant about adhering to standards and accumulating sufficient metadata, which may cause friction in dealing with external (non-librarian) partners.

Strategic Planning

The strategic aspects are very closely connected with economic and staffing aspects. A widespread myth is that digital preservation can be reduced to the purchase of hardware and basic software, pushing digital preservation somewhere into the area of IT. Digital preservation instead fundamentally influences various processes in the institution, pervading them and requiring deep changes of the organizational structure as well as the strategies of the institution's direction.

Limiting digital preservation first to the work of one organizational unit and gradually pushing this topic to entire organization was not the ideal approach. Precisely this was the NL CR's experience: beginning with one singular department of digital preservation and moving to whole institutions devoted to digital curation. This process of growing from one department requires a number of small organizational and budgetary changes. A better approach would be that of the "enlightened ruler" in upper management who would set digital preservation as one of the main strategic priorities and then would steer the entire institution in this direction. However, the "enlightened ruler" approach is seldom possible in practice within the traditionally directed memory institutions. The NL CR's experience is that at the moment digital preservation has started to influence the basic processes of the institution, the well-worn routines can be very resistant to change and the qualifications of existing employees may be hard to improve. Without explicit support in the strategic documents of te institution, organizational inertia may weaken or dismiss the whole area of digital preservation, as happened several times at the NL CR. With the installment of the new general director of the NL CR, digital preservation has become one of the main priorities of the institution, but this does not mean complete victory yet.

Digital preservation is a financially demanding area in which the benefits are not visible at first sight. The number of digitized volumes is eye-catching evidence of the project's success, but the investment in the preservation of metadata or building a whole preservation system is hard to sustain. The future savings of finances or documents are not realized immediately. Digital preservation will therefore be vulnerable for some time to funding cuts, much as digital documents are vulnerable to technological and environmental changes.

Hardly any national library today can venture to deposit millions of paper books or periodicals forming the national cultural heritage in spaces unprotected from water, fire, or the entry of unauthorized persons. A number of national libraries have begun large digitization projects and collect born-digital documents without having instruments for ensuring the long-term preservation of the digital content. Long-term preservation has not been perceived so far as an indispensible part of the digitization projects and when setting project budgets it is usually underestimated or entirely ignored in order to digitize more documents.

International Context

The National Library of the CR joined the DigitalPreservationEurope (DPE) project in April 2006. Library management approved the NL CR's participation in this project with the aim of developing staff qualifications and learning from the emerging European digital preservation community. The main target of DPE was to "raise the profile of digital preservation" (DPE, 2006), which was exactly what was needed. One of the main benefits of involvement in the DPE was personal contact, the possibility to ask and to see what others were doing. In addition, there was a unique chance to organize a week-long WePreserve training in Prague with people from other European projects like PLANETS, CASPAR, Nestor, DRAMBORA, and JISC, presenting the basic concepts of digital preservation. Some 25 librarians and archivists from across the country's culture heritage institutions profited from this workshop. Following the DRAMBORA training in Prague, it had the same impact for the NL CR and for the memory-institution community in the Czech Republic.

During the DPE project, the NL CR published a number of DPE papers in Czech translation, chiefly the document called PLATTER, co-authored by one of the NL CR's staff. This was the first document in the Czech language to explain digital preservation issues to a wider audience. The impact of this document reached beyond culture heritage institutions. PLATTER (Planning Tool for Trusted Electronic Repositories) is one of the main outcomes of the DigitalPreservationEurope project. Both PLATTER and DRAMBORA were presented in a one-day Archiving Digital Documents workshop, part of the largest conference in the field of culture heritage institutions.

The DPE partners were also asked to test a first version of the DRAMBORA, tool developed by the DPE and Digital Curation Centre. At the NL CR, the DRAMBORA self-audit took place in the summer of 2007, while a second audit was run in the repository of Charles University in Prague. The audit outcomes were used in negotiations about the future repository budget, and led to the initiation of the first steps aimed at mitigating the principal identified risks. The outcomes were also widely published across Czech memory institutions, and DRAMBORA was adopted by several other institutions. The National Technical Library for example uses DRAMBORA annually for the audit of the repository of grey literature.

Besides the DPE project, the NL CR participated in other projects related to digital preservation like Living Web Archives (LIWA, 2008–2010) and in less formal projects and cooperation like the project called the "LTP Group," initiated by the National Library of the Netherlands. In this project, the NL CR could follow the experience of a number of other European national libraries, better understand the tenants of the OAIS mapping and its practical implementations, and see the achievements of other institutions in a less-formal environment. This project led the NL CR to reconsider its Long-Term Preservation system requirements and to realize that wider integration of its electronic and traditional library processes will be needed.

From the beginning, the NL CR followed the development in the CASPAR and PLANETS projects, using in its day-to-day process the PLANETS tools—the PLANETS testbed and mainly PLATO for preservation planning. Other tools like JHOVE and DROID are used in our current workflows as well, as we believe that adding technical metadata and performing format characterization and validation of all of the data coming to the repository is the necessary first step in building a repository with a long-term preservation mission.

As the logical next step, the NL CR tried to establish partnerships with universities and other institutions. The first intention was to spread knowledge about digital preservation issues. We worked attract interest in digital preservation at conferences and inter-institutional working groups in the Czech Republic. The NL CR also endeavored to involve more university library experts in certain fields (specifically: file formats and metadata). A strong connection to Charles University in Prague and Masaryk University in Brno was established. The NL CR's staff now holds regular courses at Charles University's Institute of Information Studies and Librarianship at the Faculty of Arts as well as proposing and supervising relevant thesis topics. In this way, the NL CR can profit from the work of young professionals, get tools developed, and find motivated new employees.

Onsite Visits and NDL Planning

As the planning for the NDL project proceeded, the leading team visited several institutions with digital preservation experience. Reading articles and reports was useful, but personal visits and chats with the staff and managers provided even more. We selected the National Library of the Netherlands (The Hague), the New Zealand National Library (Wellington), the German National Library (Berlin) and the Wellcome Trust Library (London) for visits with the aim of discussing their digital preservation experience and strategies. We saw running systems and heard a great deal about their experiences and future plans. All of this information was used in the preparation of the requirements for the future Long-Term Preservation system, which was planned as one of three main parts of the NDL project (NDK, 2011).

As a second step, the NL CR also tried to conduct a market survey based on initial long-term preservation system requirements. The aim was to receive feedback from potential commercial suppliers. The NL CR does not have a strong IT development team, so the NDL Long-Term Preservation system was from the beginning planned as a chance to purchase a commercial solution. Two rounds of RFI with IBM, Ex Libris, and (later) with Tessella have taken place in 2008 and 2009. All of the companies were very welcoming, readily presented their systems, and provided access to all of the relevant documentation.

Finally in 2010, the NL CR ran a small "proof of concept" project. At that time, the staff had more-or-less only theoretical knowledge, which was not enough. The team needed to see what the commercial systems really could do and how complex it was to set the systems up, configure them, manage them, and ingest data into them. The three above-mentioned companies were asked for cooperation. Only Ex Libris (Rosetta) and Tessella (SDB) agreed to run through proof of concept and let the NL CR's staff more deeply understand their systems.[1] The NL CR has invested development work and using the API of each system, performed the necessary transformations and ingested data into the systems. We realized that Rosetta and SDB bring different approaches to building a complete solution in the area of digital preservation and that both solutions have strong points. Thanks to the "proof of concept," the NL CR was able to better specify the staff skills and other requirements on the organizational structure needed to run one of the systems in a real-life setting.

Besides the "proof of concept," the NL CR became active in a digital preservation community and made use of the newly developed tools. Many of the individual preservation tools are freely available, but until recently no free complete digital preservation repository solutions existed. This has changed. The preservation department has experimented with Archivematica, has seen Digital Preservation Software Platform from the Australian National Archive, and has monitored the news and improvements of other tools like Mopseus, RODA, ePrints, and Fedora with its preservation extensions.

Our knowledge of recent achievements and innovations in digital preservation comes from personal contacts, tracking relevant Web sites, and projects. We have also drawn great benefit by monitoring relevant mailing list subscriptions.[2]

Conclusions

Strategic and Economic Thoughts and Recommendations

- Digital preservation should be an inseparable component of all of the projects dealing with the digitization of analogue

---

[1] For an overview of Rosetta, see: A New Way of Preserving Cultural Heritage and Cumulative Knowledge at:
http://www.exlibrisgroup.com/category/RosettaOverview. For additional information about the Safety Deposit Box from Tessella see: The Safety Deposit Box at: http://www.digital-preservation.com/solution/safety-deposit-box/.

[2] See e.g. DigLib Listserv: diglib@infoserv.inist.fr; JISC-Repositories Listserv: jisc-repositories@jiscmail.ac.uk; Digital Preservation Listserv: digital-preservation@jiscmail.ac.uk

documents and/or the acquisition of born-digital documents that form the national cultural heritage.

- Digital preservation is not a luxury that can be postponed until later or even entirely jettisoned. Ensuring adequate protection for digital documents should be just as natural as protecting a physical library space for the deposition of analogue documents from water, fire, or intrusion of undesired persons.

- There are several substantial differences between the securing of analogue and digital documents: digital documents are more vulnerable than analogue documents—digital preservation has not only a physical but also a logical level.

- Whereas the preservation of analogue documents is locally limited to the areas of their deposition and movement, the idea that digital preservation takes place somewhere on the grounds of IT and begins and ends with the procurement of suitable hardware and software is mistaken.

- Invest in the hardware and IT staff, but do not dismiss the project management part. Strategies, preservation plans, setting-up processes, and documentation writing are time-consuming. The stakeholders have to acknowledge that digital preservation is not solely an IT issue; it is also an issue of management and financing. Often librarians, archivists, and other memory institutions' representatives in different countries still believe the back-up policy is a sufficient means of long-term preservation.

- Digital preservation affects an institution very complexly and creates the need for a transformation of the routine approaches and organizational changes.

- Cooperation between publishers and cultural heritage organizations (e.g., libraries) in building a trusted digital repository for the deposit of digital versions of publications is extremely important for long-term management and for short-term savings on the cost of digitization.

- The unpreparedness of the institution for relatively fundamental changes could become a more serious hurdle for digital preservation than a lack of financial means for investment.

- Preservation policy is more important than one would think at the beginning of one's digital preservation efforts. The preservation policy should meet the needs of your projects, workflows, and data types, and it should be in line with the strategy of the institution as a whole. Advocating for digital preservation related budget items always runs more smoothly when the goals are explicitly stated in strategic documents. This may be common practice in some countries, but it is less usual in others.

- From the broader perspective, the strategy and coordination of digital preservation on a national level are crucial as well. The recipients of public funding (libraries, museums, archives) should be impelled to concentrate on digital preservation, share results and lessons learned, and develop tools collaboratively among institutions.

- Some funding should be clearly focused on archiving and preserving only the digital data. When all of the national programs and funding schemes "produce" just digital data without relying on a clearly defined and adequately resourced national strategy for digital preservation, it is a disaster and a waste of money.

- Considering that it is a relatively new area with which a number of memory institutions are only now beginning, it is exceptionally important to share experience and the results achieved on the international level.

Practical Conclusions and Recommendations

- Starting with digital preservation now will take less time than a couple years ago.

- Tools, systems, and experience in the form of papers, case studies, and reports are available and their number is increasing. It is ever harder for a novice to become acquainted with the field of digital preservation. Although it is still a research area, the number of the "best practices" found around the world for novices to study constantly increases.

- Do not hesitate to arrange an onsite visit. Colleagues who are engaged in digital preservation are usually keen to share their knowledge.

- Become part of the digital preservation community—follow listservs, blogs, conference proceedings, and relevant project outcomes.

- Contact commercial producers. The NL CR's experience was extremely positive. They provided the library with access to various testing sites, documentation, training materials, and presentations.

- Develop a committed IT staff. Both developers and managers for the IT part of your digital preservation project are vital.

- Test and start using the available tools for format validation, metadata extraction, etc.

- A profound planning of a digital documents' lifecycle is not a waste of time and money. The term "data curation" (Harvey, 2010), which covers the whole lifecycle of a digital document, is virtually unknown to Czech libraries.

- The systems themselves are inefficient if the data does not flow in well-designed workflows. It is fairly easier to find money for building one system than running a rationally (inter)connected workflow.

References

Archivematica: http://archivematica.org (last accessed 03-12-2012).

Archiving Digital Objects: http://skip.nkp.cz/akcArch09.htm#work (last accessed 03-12-2012).

CASPAR: http://www.casparpreserves.eu/ (last accessed 03-12-2012).

Digital Curation Centre: http://www.dcc.ac.uk/ (last accessed 03-12-2012).

Digital Preservation Software Platform (DPSP): http://dpsp.sourceforge.net/ (last accessed 03-12-2012).

DigitalPreservationEurope (DPE) (2006). *About DPE*. Retrieved on 16 March 2011, from

http://www.digitalpreservationeurope.eu/about/

DRAMBORA: http://www.repositoryaudit.eu/ (last accessed 03-12-2012).

ePrints: http://www.eprints.org/software/ (last accessed 03-12-2012).

Ex Libris, Rosetta Overview: A New Way of Preserving Cultural Heritage and Cumulative Knowledge: http://www.exlibrisgroup.com/category/RosettaOverview (last accessed 03-21-2012).

Harvey, R. (2010). *Digital Curation. A How-To-Do-It Manual*. Neal-Schuman Publishers, New York.

Hutař, J., Fojtů, A., Pavlásková, E. (2008). DRAMBORA – tool for internal audit of digital repositories (version 2) and relevant information from the carried out audits. In *Inforum 2008, 28–30 May 2008 VŠE Prague.* http://www.inforum.cz/archiv/inforum2008/en/proceeding s/45/ (last accessed 04-10-2012).

JISC: http://www.jisc.ac.uk/ (last accessed 03-12-2012).

Kramerius: http://kramerius-info.nkp.cz/welcome/view?set_language=en (last accessed 03-12-2012).

Living Web Archives: http://www.liwa-project.eu/ (last accessed 03-12-2012).

Manuscriptorium: http://www.manuscriptorium.com (last accessed 03-12-2012).

Mopseus: http://www.ifs.tuwien.ac.at/dp/ipres2010/papers/gavrilis-34.pdf (last accessed 03-12-2012).

National Digital Library Project: http://www.ndk.cz/narodni-dk/podrobnejsi-popis-projektu/ndk-context/view?set_language=en (last accessed 03-12-2012).

Nestor: http://www.langzeitarchivierung.de/ (last accessed 03-12-2012).

PLANETS: http://www.planets-project.eu (last accessed 03-12-2012).

PLATTER: http://www.digitalpreservationeurope.eu/platter/ (last accessed 03-12-2012).

RODA: http://www.fedora-commons.org/about/examples/roda (last accessed 03-12-2012).

Stoklasová, B., Hutař, J, Krbec, P., (2007). Preservation of digital cultural heritage in Europe and in Czech Republic. In Communication of Memory in Archives, Libraries and Museums: The Interaction of Science, Policy and Practices, Vilnius, 4 –5 October 2007, Vilnius: Vilnius University Press, 2008, pp. 213–230 (ISBN 978-9955-33-314-2)

Stoklasová, B., Hutař, J. Krbec, P., (2008) Long-term preservation and accessing of digital documents in national and international context. Paper presented at the UNICA Scholarly Communication Seminar: Partnership in Academic Excellence, Prague, 15–16 May 2008, from http://www.ulb.ac.be/unica/docs/Sch-com-2008-Bohdana_Stoklasova.ppt (last accessed 03-21-2012).

Stoklasová, B., (2007). Strategy and Cooperation on Long-Term Preservation in the Czech Republic. Paper presented at The Challenge: Long-term Preservation, Frankfurt, April 20, 2007, from: http://lza.ddb.de/eu2007/modules.php?op=modload&name=PagEd&file=index&page_id=45 (last accessed 03-21-2012).

Tessella, The Safety Deposit Box: http://www.digital-preservation.com/solution/safety-deposit-box/ (last accessed 03-21-2012).

Uniform Information Gateway: http://info.jib.cz/welcome-to-uniform-information-gateway-uig?set_language=en (last accessed 03-12-2012).

WePreserve: http://web.archive.org/web/20100704025757/http://www.wepreserve.eu/events/prague-2008/ (last accessed 05-16-2012).

WebArchiv: http://en.webarchiv.cz (last accessed 03-12-2012).

EDUCATION ALIGNMENT

Joy Davidson (Digital Curation Centre, Humanities Advanced Technology
and Information Institute, University of Glasgow)
Sheila Corrall (University of Sheffield)
George Coulbourne (Library of Congress)
Andreas Rauber (Vienna University of Technology)

Abstract

*This essay reviews recent developments in embedding data
management and curation skills into information technology,
library and information science, and research-based
postgraduate courses in various national contexts. The essay
also investigates means of joining up formal education with
professional development training opportunities more
coherently. The potential for using professional internships as a
means of improving communication and understanding between
disciplines is also explored. A key aim of this essay is to identify
what level of complementarity is needed across various
disciplines to most effectively and efficiently support the entire
data curation lifecycle.*

Introduction

Over the last decade we have seen a vast increase in the
general awareness about the need for data management, curation,
and preservation activities. Indeed, many funding bodies are now
seeking assurances at the bid stage from prospective recipient
organizations and researchers that they are ready and able to
manage access to their digital information over time. But just who
is responsible for data management, curation, and preservation and
how do those charged with responsibility get the skills they need to
do the job? There is no single role within an organization that can
take on the effective management of digital information from
creation through to reuse in isolation. Researchers, information
professionals, and information technologists all have roles to play.
We need to determine how the various stakeholders can get the
skills they need to effectively work together to undertake their

specific roles within the digital curation lifecycle.[1] While many of the essays in this volume look specifically at the topic of digital preservation, this essay will explore the broader concept of data management, curation, and preservation, which deals with data conceptualization and creation as well as preservation and access.

This essay will explore what educational alignment is needed—across disciplines as well as across nations—to support the digital curation lifecycle most effectively. In particular, the essay will focus on the skills of computing scientists, information science professionals, and researchers and how these may be progressed and supported through existing and emerging educational frameworks and knowledge transfer opportunities. There are views that data curation should be a profession in its own right as well as views that aspects of data management, curation, and preservation should be integrated to some degree into all disciplines.[2] To complicate matters further, we are beginning to see the emergence of new tools and applications that will significantly simplify, and in some cases automate, aspects of data management, curation, and preservation. As these tools are developed, the amount of specialist knowledge required by many of the stakeholders may be greatly reduced. As such, there is a real risk that some of the content covered in the new courses currently being developed may become immediately obsolete. Greater join-up between educators and those building infrastructure will be necessary.

This essay will look at where the community is now by highlighting some of the recent developments in embedding data management and curation skills in information technology, library and information science, and research-based postgraduate courses in various national contexts; move on to explore some of the challenges that we collectively face as well as some of the opportunities we might collectively exploit; and conclude with a series of recommendations for progressing the alignment of data management, curation, and preservation education within a number of disciplines. The authors would like to make clear that this essay

---

[1] See Digital Curation Centre (DCC) Curation Lifecycle model:
http://www.dcc.ac.uk/resources/curation-lifecycle-model (last accessed 03-26-2012).

[2] It is important to note here that the authors did not cover education of the general public in our deliberations, however we recognize that this is a key area that requires investigation.

is not intended to represent a comprehensive investigation into the topic, but rather provides a snapshot of current national and disciplinary activities that may be of relevance as we attempt to improve the alignment of various curricula.

Where Are We Now?

Information Science

The UK has been at the forefront of developments in e-research as a result of its substantial investment in a national e-science program that has led to multinational collaborations and active participation by researchers at national, regional, and local levels. We have also seen significant national investment in research studies, development projects, and other initiatives intended to raise awareness, build understanding, develop policy, and enhance practice in the management of research data. The UK has the Digital Curation Centre, recognized internationally as a center of expertise and a catalyst for change, which has worked energetically and effectively with other key players in the UK and internationally, particularly the Higher Education Funding Councils' Joint Information Systems Committee (JISC), UKOLN, and the Research Information Network (RIN).

However, developments in the UK library and information science community have generally lagged behind other countries, notably the US. The tradition of library involvement in facilitating access to social science data is less well developed here than in North America. There is a small group of committed data librarians in the university sector who have responded positively to the current agenda[3] but we have not seen the creation of new positions, launch of initiatives, or development of services that has occurred in the US. Librarians have engaged in discussion through working groups and meetings initiated by Research Libraries UK and they have collaborated with others in exploring the need for a national research data service[4] but the lack of investment targeted specifically at university libraries combined with the funding cuts

---

[3] Macdonald, S. and Martinez, L. (2005) "Supporting local data users in the UK academic community," *Ariadne,* 44: http://www.ariadne.ac.uk/issue44/martinez/ (last accessed 03-26-2012).

[4] Lewis, M. (2010), "Libraries and the management of research data," in McKnight, S. (ed.), *Envisioning Future Academic Library Services: Initiatives, Ideas and Challenges,* pp. 145-168, Facet, London.

experienced by these libraries over the last few years has been a serious constraint.

While several universities across the EU have introduced digital preservation into their masters' level information science and library courses,[5] far fewer have started to include aspects of data management and curation. Part of the reason for this may be financial, with many schools of information and library studies experiencing cutbacks and lacking the funding for curriculum development that US counterparts have obtained from the Institute of Museum and Library Studies (IMLS) and National Science Foundation (NSF).[6] Current UK educational provision is limited and uneven, with minimal progress since the review conducted by Pryor and Donnelly in 2009.[7] Since then, UK-based library and information science educators have discussed the need for curriculum development at meetings of their subject association, the British Association for Information and Library Education and Research (BAILER), and have expressed interest in working collaboratively to meet needs for both initial professional education and continuing professional development (CPD). CPD provision is particularly important in the short term, but will be difficult to develop in the current UK situation unless additional funding is available.

Information Technology

To date, the majority of data management and curation research and development undertaken by information technology professionals has focused on preserving individual data objects. While some information technology programs do cover digital preservation topics—such as those offered by the Technical University of Vienna[8]—this is the exception rather than the rule.

---

[5] See e.g. the Information Management and Preservation (IMP) course at the Humanities Advanced Technology and Information Institute (HATII) at the University of Glasgow http://www.gla.ac.uk/postgraduate/taught/informationmanagementpreservationdig italarchivesrecordsmanagement/ (last accessed 03-26-2012).

[6] Ray, J. (2009) "Sharks, digital curation, and the education of information professionals," *Museum Management and Curatorship,* 24 94), 357-368.

[7] Pryor, G. and Donnelly, M. (2009) "Skilling up to do data: whose role, whose responsibility, whose career?," *International Journal of Digital Curation,* 4 (2),158-170: http://www.ijdc.net/index.php/ijdc/article/view/126 (last accessed 03-26-2012).

[8] Technical University of Vienna http://www.ifs.tuwien.ac.at/~andi/pr_thesis_topics.html (last accessed 03-26-2012).

What we need are information technology professionals who are capable of working collaboratively with other institutional stakeholders to develop scalable application chains and business processes that seamlessly integrate data management, curation, and preservation functionality over the entire lifecycle. Information technologists will need to be able to build bridges between disparate operational systems to ensure that data is generated and managed in a "preservation-ready" manner.

It is also vital that emerging information technology professionals are trained to think of the issues on a much grander scale. So far, we have been thinking in terms of gigabytes and terabytes, but new professionals need to be able to understand how error rates might scale as the amount of data that is produced on a daily basis increases exponentially.

At the moment, we are training information technologists to simply keep data alive through active intervention. We need to instigate a major shift in this way of thinking and emphasize the need for ongoing maintenance of end-to-end systems that are capable of producing and managing preservation-ready data. Essentially, there is a distinct need to produce information technology graduates who are fluent in enterprise architecture and interoperability. Indeed, these are areas that data curation and preservation practitioners are eager to progress and we need information technologists who can understand the problems and develop innovative approaches to meet these needs.

Data-centric Disciplines

In recent years, significant effort has been put into defining data management, curation and preservation roles and responsibilities for data authors, data scientists, and data mangers. In a 2005 report, the US National Science Foundation (NSF) defined data authors as "the scientists, educators, students, and others involved in research that produces digital data," and suggested that that data authors have a responsibility to:

- conform to community standards for recording data and metadata that adequately describe the context and quality of the data and help others find and use the data;

- allow free and open access to data consistent with accepted standards for proper attribution and credit, subject to fair opportunity to exploit the results of one's own research and appropriate legal standards for protecting security, privacy and intellectual property rights;

- conform to community standards for the type, quality, and content of data, including associated metadata, for deposition in relevant data collections;

- meet the requirements for data management specified in grants, contracts, and cooperative agreements with funding agencies; and

- develop and continuously refine a data management plan that describes the intended duration and migration path of the data.[9]

Although these recommendations have been around for some time, there is little evidence that these skills are being embedded within UK postgraduate courses. Indeed, the data management skills and capacity session at the JISC Innovation Forum 2008[10] confirmed that while there were pockets of data management training within some UK universities' postgraduate courses, much more needed to be done to embed data management training into all postgraduate programs. To improve this situation, JISC recently funded the development of disciplinary-specific research data management training programs through their RDMTrain strand.[11] Researchers also have increasing access to a number of high quality support materials like those being produced by the UK Data Archive and the DCC[12] to assist them with their data management and curation activity.

Continuing Education

There has been a lot of work in recent years to develop intensive continuing education and training courses for data custodians and digital preservation practitioners, such as the

---

[9] See NSF report *Long-Lived Digital Data Collections: Enabling Research and Education in the 21st Century*:
http://www.nsf.gov/pubs/2005/nsb0540/nsb0540_5.pdf (last accessed 03-26-2012).

[10] See JISC Innovation Forum 2008: http://jif08.jiscinvolve.org/wp/theme-2-the-challenges-of-research-data/sub-page-2/ (last accessed 03-26-2012).

[11] See JISC RDMTrain programme that is managed by the Managing Research Data Programme (MRD):
http://www.jisc.ac.uk/fundingopportunities/funding_calls/2010/03/410dataskills.aspx (last accessed 03-26-2012).

[12] See the Digital Curation Centre (DCC) resources: http://www.dcc.ac.uk/resources (last accessed 03-26-2012).

Digital Preservation Management (DPM) Workshops, the Digital Preservation Training Programme (DPTP) that builds on the core concepts developed by DPM workshops, DigCCurr Institute, Digital Curation 101, and Digital Futures. A key objective of these courses is to bring together participants from a range of professional backgrounds to ensure that a wide variety of perspectives are shared and that viable curation approaches can be jointly developed and implemented at the institutional level. These courses have been quite successful to date and have led to some real changes in working practice within institutions.[13] However, the bulk of professional development training to date has focused on training those at the middle-management level with awareness-raising skills and the capacity to meet more immediate challenges. We also need to ensure that we target senior management staff and equip them to plan strategically over the longer term as well as furnishing those at the coal face with the practical skills they need on a daily basis.

Risks Presented by the Absence of Alignment on Core Competencies

The identification of basic data management skills for the various roles has been investigated by a number of ongoing working groups and initiatives (e.g., DigCCurrII, International Digital curation Education Action Group,[14] European MSc in Digital Curation working group, Knowledge Exchange, and DigCurV). Some progress has been made by these groups but the range of skills identified varies widely across these groups—ranging from very technical aspects to more traditional library and information sciences skills. To effectively embed data management and curation skills into a range of professions, agreement is still needed regarding: 1) what constitutes core data management and curation skills for each group; 2) a means of consistently describing and assessing these skills, and 3) a framework that supports the progression of skills development over time. Without agreement on core skill-sets and responsibilities for each of these groups along with an overall understanding of how they should all

---

[13] For example, the DigCCurr Institute and DC101 conduct post-course follow-up with participants and have learned about new activities that have been undertaken at their home institutions as a direct result of taking part in these courses.

[14] Hank, C. and Davidson, J. (2009) "International Data curation Education Action (IDEA) Working Group: a report from the second workshop of the IDEA," *D-Lib Magazine*, 15 (3/4): http://www.dlib.org/dlib/march09/hank/03hank.html (last accessed 03-26-2012).

fit together into the curation lifecycle we collectively face a number of risks. A selection of these risks are described below.

Relevance of Information Science Professionals

If education and professional development training in the library and information science sector do not evolve to cover data management and curation, there is a risk that librarians and other information specialists will not be able to contribute appropriately to the management of research data. Roles that library and information science staff are in other respects well qualified to fulfill may be assigned to other staff, who may have relevant and necessary subject and/or IT competencies, but lack the informational, managerial, and personal competencies that are required to apply the required specialist competencies successfully. The result could be that library services and information careers do not evolve in line with institutional needs and service provision is sub-optimal, being neither fit for purpose nor cost-effective. There could also be wider effects as stakeholders might lose confidence in the library and information science profession as a result of its perceived failure to respond appropriately to data management and curation needs and this might influence decisions on allocation of responsibilities and resources in other areas.

Capacity of Information Technology Professionals

Data management, curation, and preservation is not merely an evolution of "conventional" curation—complex and diverse as it may be—but rather an entirely new arena, requiring very different skills in completely new areas. This requires a completely new approach and new curricula to ensure we can educate information technology experts who will be able to develop and progress this field. There is a risk that we are not equipping information technologists with enough strategic development skills to produce appropriate systems to support researchers and information professionals in data management and curation activity. A solid foundational education and practical training opportunities are vital to ensure that information technology professionals can develop scalable, future-proof technical solutions and are also able to work with the tools and systems we already have in place to manage the less complex settings that we are currently confronted with.

Engagement of Researchers in the Curation Lifecycle

Managing and curating data requires dedicated effort. As such, researchers will want to ensure that their effort is being allocated only to the items that they need to keep. Accordingly, researchers need to be educated to make effective selection and appraisal decisions about what they can keep and what they must not retain for legal reasons. The researchers themselves are best placed to determine just how much contextual information needs to be kept along with their data to enable validation of their research results, to provide evidence of good research practice, to meet their funding body and institutional requirements, and to facilitate reuse amongst their own community in the first instance.

Researchers have a key role to play during the conceptualization and creation stages of the curation lifecycle. Many of the decisions made during these early stages have major consequences for the curation and preservation of the data over the longer term. A particular area of risk for researchers is data licensing. Less ambiguity about what can—and more importantly cannot—be done with the data both in the short and longer term means that preservation actions may be more easily undertaken by preservation practitioners and restrictions on reuse are made clear to other researchers. If the data cannot be reused, there may be little value in curating and preserving it for the longer term.

Licensing, selection, and appraisal activities will involve several stakeholders in the curation lifecycle. Unless we can reach some agreement on specific data management roles, responsibilities, and (subsequently) skills, there is a real risk that we will duplicate effort across disciplines while failing to equip any of the stakeholder groups with anything but a thin veneer of knowledge across the lifecycle. Instead of educating the various groups on general issues we need to focus on specific areas where each group can make the best contribution and develop a deeper understanding of concrete actions and approaches. However, while there needs to be an emphasis on educating researchers in particular areas, it will also be essential that each stakeholder group understands how their own actions and those of the others fit into the bigger picture.

Development of Practitioners' Skills

There are many risks to be anticipated if data management, curation, and preservation skills are not covered by continuing education programs, field experiences, and professional internships. A major area of risk is in the ability to provide effective, market-ready graduate education in fields requiring management and curation of large digital collections, such as library and information science (LIS), archival science, and museum studies. Within the LIS field, for example, researchers have noted gaps at times, e.g., between theory and practice[15] and between preservation studies, administration, and digital content.[16] These types of gaps must be bridged if tomorrow's corps of data management and curation experts is to be developed. In addition, the field has a need for professionals with expertise in advanced digital technologies, combined with other LIS expertise. In a 2006 study in librarians in academic and research libraries, participants identified digital topics (e.g., Web design, digital imaging, XML standards and technologies, and programming and scripting languages) as among the top areas in which their education had not prepared them adequately.[17]

A second major risk is that without optimal data management, curation, and preservation training, there will not be a cadre of experts able to provide support to users (including in libraries, museums, and archives) on digital resources in order to obtain maximum benefit. This is something that must be done as a daily service in addition to adequately planning and mapping the digital future for these collections and organizations. Thus, these needs are near-term and long-term. If collections cannot be managed, they will not be used and will lose value.

Another major risk is that of damage, deterioration, and/or loss of individual and shared heritage (or "memory") if individuals and organizations are not aware of the urgent need for data management and curation, are not able to support and conduct it, and if a workforce of data management and curation experts is not developed. One helpful analogy that has been drawn is between data management and curation preparedness and emergency preparedness.

---

[15] Ball MA. "Practicums and service learning in LIS education," *Journal of Education for Library* and Information Science. 2008;49(1):70-83.

[16] University of Michigan School of Information. *Engaging communities: fostering communities for preservation and digital curation.* Narrative by Elizabeth Yakel, Ph.D., of project proposal to the Institute of Museum and Library Services.

[17] Choi Y, Rasmussen E. "What is needed to educate future digital librarians: A study of current practice and staffing patterns in academic and research libraries," 2006. *D-Lib Magazine*, 12 (9): http://www.dlib.org/dlib/september06/choi/09choi.html (last accessed 5-21-2012).

Obstacles in Mitigating Key Risks

To mitigate the key risks described above, several obstacles need to be addressed in the short term. A selection of these is described below.

Limited Resources for Developing New Courses

Unsurprisingly, a lack of staff and/or financial resources can hinder efforts to embed data management and curation skills and activity into education, training, and the workplace. In the UK there have been substantial reductions in funding across the higher education sector as a result of the economic downturn. This general trend has been amplified for the LIS sector by government policy to concentrate resources on STEM subjects. Over the last two years, most information schools have experienced staff reductions through not being able replace departing staff, while student intakes at Masters and Doctoral levels have either stayed the same or increased. Many schools have also suffered cuts in the quality-related QR research funding[18] allocated on the basis of their performance in the Research Assessment Exercise because of the switch of resources from arts, humanities, and social sciences to STEM subjects. In addition, all academics face a continuing challenge in trying to balance the demands of research, teaching, and administration. There is constant pressure on faculty members to produce research publications and generate research income, which both tend to be prioritized over curriculum innovation—unless the latter is accompanied by significant external funding. Designing, developing, and delivering data management and curation curricula/courses that will meet identified education and training needs requires dedicated and sustained academic effort. Finding this academic staff time in light of these additional pressures can be difficult.

Modifications to Existing Curricula

Accommodating new content within existing educational curricula is a challenge, particularly in the core courses/modules/units taken by all students, where it is essential for data management and curation to be embedded so that all graduates gain the necessary knowledge and skills. There is pressure from employers and practitioners to extend or add

---

[18] For more information about quality-related research funding see: http://www.hefce.ac.uk/data/year/2011/quality-relatedfundingdata2011-12/name,67493,en.html (last accessed 3-27-2012)

coverage of specific topics to meet current needs (such as pedagogical knowledge and skills for development of information literacy), but rarely any suggestions of topics that could be dropped or given lower priority to make space for the desired new content. This problem is particularly acute in the UK, where the typical duration of a Masters programme is only one year and the taught element generally has to be squeezed into two 12-week semesters, with the remaining time devoted to an independent research project. The alternative strategy of embedding new competencies in specialist electives, pathways, or programmes (an individual course/module/unit or set of courses/modules/units) would in theory be easier to manage, but some UK schools do not currently offer electives and many others are under pressure to reduce the number of electives offered to students as a result of staffing cuts. Institutions would be unlikely to support new specialist programmes in the current economy—unless a critical mass of funded participants could be guaranteed.

Access to Practical, Hands-on Experience and Training

In supporting the growth of a skilled digital curation workforce, it is imperative that these professionals are able to activate the theory they learn in academic programs with practice. Internships and residencies address this key risk by tying theory with direct experience in the field. A number of challenges reside within the endeavor of planning and executing data management and curation internship programs, such as finding host organizations that are both actively practicing curation activity (as distinct from "digitization") and are geographically accessible to students; deciding where in academic programs it is best to incorporate internships (e.g., during the classroom experience or as a separate, freestanding component, such as a residency); establishing optimal length; determining who should lead planning and content (e.g., the home institution, the host, or guidelines from one or more professional bodies); and finding funds, apart from the currently small number of projects funded by agencies such as the US-based NSF, IMLS, and the National Endowment for the Humanities (NEH). The Laura Bush 21st Century Librarian Program of IMLS has funded a number of initiatives addressing the digital curation and electronic records needs of rural, underserved libraries. Other 21st Century projects focused on developing graduate certificates in digital curation and digital management and developing internship opportunities for the curation and stewardship of digital public information. These projects support the need to address the future of libraries and the digital nature of their services. However, funding methods for field experiences in this area must evolve to include those other than just grants and government funding.

Among the components that will be important to include in field experiences are:

- Clear objectives;

- Short-term and long-term goals;

- Diverse skill sets, including in information technology; data creation (e.g., incentives, preservation, curation, and use agreements); data management (e.g., selection/evaluation, interoperable architecture, metadata standards, and maintenance); and data use (e.g., exploration, search/retrieval, authentication/verification, and use/reuse). Other desirable skills include policy, economics, project design, project and financial management, data rights/ownership, financial management, workforce development, and communications;

- An international component, e.g., through exchanges of professional data management and curation interns between the US and other regions such as Europe or Africa;

- Decisions on-site versus virtual components;

- One or more shareable final deliverables for interns, beyond the typical, brief exit summary—such as presenting at a meeting, writing a blog entry, or drafting a manuscript for journal submission;

- Means of assessing whether interns have acquired the skills during their internship;

- Providing community for interns, including through developing virtual communities and maintaining strong ties with home institutions; and

- Developing a training academy for internship supervisors and mentors, recognition in one or more ways for their efforts, and ways to build community.

The Office of Strategic Initiatives (OSI) at the Library of Congress has hosted interns for the past six years from several national internship programs and has seen the need for these principles firsthand. A major challenge in providing field experiences is financial. In the Digital Preservation Outreach and Education (DPOE) Training Needs Assessment Survey[19] 34 percent of respondents said they did not have money for professional development or training. Studies have found that internships are highly advantageous—including to students, graduates, colleagues in the workplace, supervisors/mentors of interns, employers, academic institutions, and professionals—and that their return on investment is positive.[20,21] Internships do involve significant financial costs, but this is a challenge that can be addressed collaboratively; economic factors are a driver that can often bring people together.

There is also a lack of real-life, practical examples that can be located and easily repurposed for teaching and training to demonstrate the theoretical concepts taught about data management and curation in a meaningful and practical way. We need to be able to illustrate how data management relates to day-to-day activities in a range of disciplines. The work being carried out by the University of Michigan on graduate profiles and the DaMSSI career profiles[22] may be of value in addressing this challenge.

Supply and Demand

Most organizations are not devoting enough staff resources to data management and curation. In a 2010 national survey conducted by the Library of Congress's DPOE initiative, out of the almost 900 respondents, representing organizations of various types and sizes, only 33 percent had full-time or part-time paid staff dedicated to digital preservation duties. Eighty-four percent of respondents said, however, that their organizations consider it very important to preserve digital information for 10 years. The digital materials needing preservation included Web sites, architectural

---

[19] Library of Congress. Digital Preservation Outreach and Education (DPOE) Training Needs Assessment Survey: Executive Summary. 2010: http://digitalpreservation.gov/education/documents/DPOENeedsAssessmentSurve yExecutiveSummary.pdf (last accessed 03-26-2012).

[20] Sides CH, Mrvica A. *Internships: Theory and Practice*. Amityville, NY: Baywood Publishing; 2007.

[21] Lanier D, Henderson C. "Library residencies and internships as indicators of success: evidence from three programs," *Bulletin of the Medical Libraries Association*. 1999;87(2):192-199.

[22] University of Michigan graduate profiles, http://www.si.umich.edu/academics/pathways-success and DaMSSI career profiles, http://www.dcc.ac.uk/training/data-management-courses-and-training/career-profiles (last accessed 03-26-2012).

and design drawings, research data files, digital image files, PDFs, geographic information files, and audiovisual files. Challenges arising from the larger environment include the rapidly evolving digital landscape; issues related to shifts from analogue to digital; the uncertain economy and shrinking funding sources, the effects of which are being seen everywhere from local libraries to state archives to federal agencies; and the questions of where and for how long graduates trained in data management and curation can be employed, beyond the small number of projects based upon grants of limited duration.

This would seem to indicate that there is a market for graduates from a range of disciplines with data management and curation skills. However, recruiting sufficient participants to justify the time and effort required to develop new curricula/courses that include data management, curation, and preservation is a problem. The new student fees regime in the UK combined with the current depressed employment market is likely to affect recruitment at both undergraduate and postgraduate levels. Reductions in library budgets have affected both staffing levels and training support. The type of provision most likely to appeal to busy practitioners interested in CPD is flexible distance learning or an intensive immersion program (such as a short summer school). Both models could be costly to prepare and deliver, so providers would need to be confident that take-up would be sufficient for the fee income to cover their costs. The current financial situation is likely to deter potential providers from taking such initiatives—unless special funding were provided to cover the development costs. In the event that there is a clear demand for data curation and management training there is also a risk that the pool of trainers available to deliver courses will not be sufficient to meet this demand.

The recent *Riding the Wave* report[23] suggests that we should be educating "data scientists" and embedding aspects of both short-term data management and longer-term curation skills into all educational programs. However, can we guarantee that there is there a market for data scientists in disciplines outside of big science? Will students emerging with a specialism in data curation have enough knowledge in either the technical aspects of data management and the subject specific knowledge to be truly

---

[23] High Level Expert Group on Scientific Data *Riding the Wave*: How Europe can gain from the rising tide of scientific data report, October 2010: http://cordis.europa.eu/fp7/ict/e-infrastructure/docs/hlg-sdi-report.pdf (last accessed 03-26-2012).

effective? The Spanning the Boundaries workshop[24] highlighted that employers still tend to hire from traditional backgrounds and train new staff on institution-specific approaches. So, will those emerging with more broadly scoped data management and curation qualifications be any better off?

Rapidly Shifting Goalposts in Information Technology

While analogue data curation itself has a strong tradition and a solid body of expertise to build upon and has been embedded into educational programs, the shift to digital is more than a mere change of representation or data carrier. As entire processes become digital, the ability to curate these will require the development of an entirely new body of professional knowledge, building on entirely new foundations that are tightly linked to the very basic differences of digital information and the way information is processed digitally. While listing all of these differences is virtually impossible, some of the crucial distinctions that need to be addressed in information technology education include:

Formats

The type of material to be processed is changing from static data to complex IT objects and entire systems that contain active code, transformation routines, and dependencies that reach all the way to specific details of the processing chain from a sensor via a range of IT systems with different hardware/software combinations and the technical implications of different computing paradigms such as the cloud, Web services and others, to interpretation in a closed loop. Information technology graduates will need a solid understanding of these dependencies on a fundamental technical level to be able to address any challenges arising from preserving data, processes, and systems.

Volume

The immense volume of digital objects, systems and processes to be managed requires a completely different level of automation. As a consequence, many steps that can currently be handled manually by experts will have to be

---

[24] Workshop run as part of iPRES 2010, see
http://www.ifs.tuwien.ac.at/dp/ipres2010/workshops.html#ws1 (last accessed 03-26-2012).

automated, and thus ultimately implemented by technical systems if we want our solutions to scale. IT graduates will now need to be able to build scalable solutions rather than simply be able to develop short-term solutions. Equally, graduates must be capable of understanding security threats and developing means of protecting huge quantities of data.

Lack of Easy-to-Use Tools

The novelty of digital preservation at the level we are starting to see it now (i.e. preserving complex systems and processes rather than "just" PDFs or TIFF images) means that in many cases we do not even have available solid tool sets and procedures to train practitioners to manage them. We need to educate a large group of experts to help us develop the techniques that can then be used to train practitioners—while at the same time continuing to train practitioners to manage the less complex digital preservation settings that we have developed to date.

Lifecycle Management

Data management and curation will move from a largely ex-post activity, where an institution manages the data after its creation, to the operational systems, meaning that new IT infrastructure will need to be "preservation-ready." Preservation issues will need to be incorporated into the design and development process of such systems, rendering—in an ideal world—the actual curation invisible.

Opportunities for Alignment

There is no shortage of risks and challenges facing us as we attempt to better equip emerging graduates and existing professionals with up-to-date data management, curation, and preservation skills that they will need to perform well in their chosen professions. However, there are many opportunities that we can collectively seize to help overcome several of the challenges and risks described previously.

Defining Skill-sets and Facilitating Continuing Education

There is currently no consensus on the distinct range of skills, knowledge, behaviors, and attributes needed for different roles in data management and curation. However there have been several initiatives have been working to pin these down more concretely. Useful contributions to the discussion include Swan and Brown's study[25] for JISC of *The Skills, Role and Career Structure of Data Scientists and Curators*; Pryor and Donnelly's mapping of core skills identified at the November 2008 DCC/RIN Research Data Management Forum against the four roles described by Swan and Brown, namely data creators, data scientists, data managers, and data librarians; and the outputs from relevant curriculum development projects, notably the IMLS-funded projects at the University of Illinois at Urbana-Champaign and the University of North Carolina at Chapel Hill, reported and discussed at a December 2008 workshop of the International Data curation Education Action (IDEA) Working Group.[26] Additional evidence can be found in published reports from library practitioners already involved in data management and curation.[27]

The DPOE initiative in the US has engaged in a review of the curricula of the main continuing-education data management and curation programs in the US and has collaborated with experts to establish a set of core principles for training. Among the skills required are skills in science, technology, engineering, and mathematics (STEM). There have been challenges in attracting students with STEM backgrounds to data management and curation education or careers, although efforts are being made in this direction. Skill sets from the humanities and social sciences are better represented. The RIN Information Handling Working Group[28] are also active in this area and are using the Vitae

---

[25] Swan, A. and Brown, S. (2008) *The Skills, Role and Career Structure of Data Scientists and Curators: An Assessment of Current Practice and Future Needs*, Report to the JISC, Truro: Key Perspectives http://www.jisc.ac.uk/publications/documents/dataskillscareersfinalreport.aspx (last accessed 03-26-2012).

[26] Hank, C. and Davidson, J. (2009) "International Data curation Education Action (IDEA) Working Group: a report from the second workshop of the IDEA," *D-Lib Magazine*, 15 (3/4) http://www.dlib.org/dlib/march09/hank/03hank.html (last accessed 03-26-2012).

[27] Gabridge, T. (2009) "The last mile: liaison roles in curating science and engineering research data," *Research Libraries Issues*, 265, 15-21 http://www.arl.org/bm~doc/rli-265-gabridge.pdf; Garritano, J.R. and Carlson, J.R. (2009) "A subject librarian's guide to collaborating on e-science projects," *Issues in Science and Technology Librarianship*, 57 http://www.istl.org/09-spring/refereed2.html#15; Henty, M. (2008) "Developing the capability and skills to support e-research," *Ariadne*, 55 http://www.ariadne.ac.uk/issue55/henty/; Witt, M. (2008) "Institutional repositories and research data curation in a distributed environment," *Library Trends*, 57 (2), 191-201 (all last accessed 03-26-2012).

[28] See RIN Information Handling Working Group: http://www.rin.ac.uk/resources/consultation-responses/joint-response-vitae-consultation-draft-researcher-development-fram (last accessed 03-26-2012).

Researcher Developer Framework (RDF)[29]—noted above—as a means of agreeing information handling skills among researchers.

Data management and curation has also evolved into a discipline in its own right, and as such it has created a community of experts from different backgrounds collaborating to tackle the challenges. With this evolution into a well-formed discipline, interdisciplinary working has become a good and well-lived practice—however potentially at the cost of becoming closed within its own interdisciplinary circles. We need to be aware that we need more external expertise by groups who do not necessarily see themselves at all related to data management, curation, and preservation activity and who currently are neither part of this community nor do they know of its existence. Examples, specifically within the IT domain, include hardware engineers, software engineering, distributed systems, algorithms, IT security, enterprise architectures, and many others—the contributions and cooperation of all of these are essential if we want to mitigate the data management and curation challenge from the onset, and to solve the challenges that need to be managed on a continuous basis.

While there are a number of data management and curation programs and professional development courses on offer, there is no easy way for prospective students to find, compare, and select courses that meet their immediate needs and allow them to plan for career development. Course offerings are usually self-contained with little if any reference to courses offered by other training providers. Without any means of contextualizing courses it is difficult to disambiguate and benchmark training options. Recent attempts to develop and/or refine competencies frameworks and to define specific skills-sets are described below.

Seven Pillars Model

The SCONUL (Society of College, National and University Libraries) Seven Pillars Model[30] helps to define a pathway from basic library and IT skills through to complete information literacy and describes progressive stages ranging

---

[29] See Vitae Researcher Developer Framework (RDF):
http://www.vitae.ac.uk/policy-practice/165001/Consultation.html (last accessed 03-26-2012).
[30] See SCONUL Seven Pillars Model:
http://www.sconul.ac.uk/groups/information_literacy/seven_pillars.html (last accessed 03-26-2012).

from the novice to the expert. While the model has proved valuable as a planning tool among UK HEIs, the model developers felt that the model would benefit from additional details in data management aspects. A revision of the model was undertaken in during the first half of 2010 to incorporate additional data management elements.[31]

Researcher Development Framework (RDF)

In November 2009, Vitae released a draft of its Researcher Development Framework (RDF) for public consultation. The RDF is intended to be used as a "tool for planning, promoting and supporting the personal, professional and career development of researchers. It describes knowledge, skills, behaviours and personal qualities acquired by researchers and encourages researchers to aspire to excellence through development to a high level."[32] The RDF offers great potential for describing basic data management skills required at each stage of a researchers' career and for securing agreement on basic skill sets. However, while data management skills were implied throughout several sections of the draft RDF, they were not as explicit as they perhaps should have been. In November 2009, the Research Information Network (RIN) established an information handling working group[33] which developed a response to the draft RDF that included recommendations for more explicit data management skills at each of the RDF stages. Many of the WG's recommendations have since been incorporated into the revised RDF.[34] The working group has remained active and is working to improve the provision of information literacy education within UK HEI programmes. The working group includes members from relevant bodies including the Society for College, National and University Libraries (SCONUL), Research Libraries UK (RLUK), the Chartered

---

[31] See SCONUL Seven Pillars Model: Research Lens Model table of skills and attributes:
http://www.sconul.ac.uk/groups/information_literacy/sp/researchtable.jpg (last accessed 03-26-2012).

[32] See RIN Information Handling Working Group response to Vitae RDF:
http://www.rin.ac.uk/resources/consultation-responses/joint-response-vitae-consultation-draft-researcher-development-fram (last accessed 03-26-2012).

[33] See information about the working group: http://www.rin.ac.uk/mind-skills-gap (last accessed 03-26-2012).

[34] See Vitae Researcher Development Framework (RDF):
http://www.vitae.ac.uk/rdf (last accessed 03-26-2012).

Institute of Library and Information Professionals (CILIP), the Digital Curation Centre (DCC), the British Association for Information and Library Education and Research (BAILER), the Higher Education Academy (HEA), the UK Council for Graduate Education (UKCGE), and the Joint Information Systems Committee (JISC).

DaMSSI

Led by the Digital Curation Centre (DCC), this Data Management Skills Support Initiative (DaMSSI) aimed to facilitate the use of tools like SCONUL's Seven Pillars and Vitae's RDF to help researchers and their institutions to effectively plan data management skills development and training. Working with the *JISC 04/10: Managing Research Data programme: Promoting discipline-focused research data management skills*[35] projects, DaMSSI tested the effectiveness of the Seven Pillars Model and RDF for consistently mapping and describing data management skills and skills development paths in UK HEI postgraduate courses.

However, none of the efforts above goes far enough in defining the specific levels of skills, knowledge and understanding needed for particular roles. A prerequisite here is to reach some level of consensus on the different roles needed for effective data management. In the case of library and information professionals this means identifying the various positions or roles within libraries that should be involved in data management and curation, which could include, for example, institutional repository managers, cataloguers/metadata specialists, information literacy coordinators, and reference/subject/liaison librarians, rather than simply talking about "data librarians." We need to synthesize the work done to date, progress to more comprehensive and specific competency frameworks, then test the results in the field with practitioners in relevant roles.

---

[35] See JISC 04/10: Managing Research Data programme: Promoting discipline-focused research data management skills:
http://www.jisc.ac.uk/fundingopportunities/funding_calls/2010/03/410dataskills.aspx (last accessed 03-26-2012).

Improving Knowledge Transfer

There are many means of knowledge transfer, such as instruction (academic and experiential); research; exchange and dissemination of knowledge through professional networks, committee work, and publications and other methods of communication and outreach; identification and recruitment of needed expertise; and exposure to fresh perspectives (e.g., through new groups of interns). Formal knowledge transfer is currently happening almost exclusively at a training level, teaching practical skills on how to manage the simpler challenges in data management, curation, and preservation. Given the amount of work going on among the various stakeholders, it is essential that we better facilitate knowledge transfer between training providers and more importantly between disciplines. Presently, many professionals are expanding their knowledge of data curation and management through participation in funded research projects. This is often where the newest challenges are being faced and, while striving to come up with a solution, teams of experts evolve. Such partnerships and collaborations have been successfully employed by the Library of Congress, evident, for example, in the network of partners and relationships across the US and the globe that the Library has built and leveraged in DPOE and the National Digital Information Infrastructure and Preservation Program (NDIIPP) and other national digital programs. Acting collaboratively is especially important in order to traverse "new, uncharted waters," leverage diverse skill sets, and build on existing infrastructure. Coordination is also important, as are open sharing and transparency to the maximum degree possible in such endeavors as:

- Training opportunities;

- Workshops and other activities;

- A repository to share the results of and lessons learned from training; and

- Publications and other information products such as Webcasts, archived videos and survey results.

In addition to traditional methods of knowledge transfer, recently developed digital tools and applications should be harnessed, including social networking platforms.

Knowledge transfer opportunities often occur as an outgrowth of national and international meetings. There should also be regular opportunities to convene, including via teleconferences and Web conferences. However, in-person meetings that are too distant, too expensive, and/or too long can be obstacles for participants whose organizations are below a certain size or budget. In any respect possible, developing community is an important way to help people become invested in a goal or objective and to foster open sharing.

Engaging Employers and Professional Bodies

It is clear that we need to engage more with both professional bodies and prospective employers as we define curricula and develop training courses. Without their involvement, there is little chance that data management and curation skills will be recognized in the workplace or that productive professional development opportunities will be made available.

Ultimately, professional bodies should champion the cause of data management and curation. While the field has had some innovative individuals who have led high-profile projects, more needs to be done. This challenge may reflect the need for developing uniform sets of messages, procedures, and standards that can be communicated to professional bodies and, in turn, to members of professional bodies. Professional bodies could also offer materials, tutorials, and clearinghouses on data management and curation, free of charge or for a minimal cost-recovery fee. They might also provide venues for practical discussions, task forces and working groups.

Developing Accredited Trainers, Curriculum and Assessing Outcomes

As noted above, many professional development courses are offered by short-term research projects or initiatives. There is often little incentive for a professional to attend such courses as the provider is an unknown quantity. Instead, we need to engage more with professional bodies to enlist their help in promoting existing training courses on offer and—where appropriate—to cooperate on the development of accredited data management and curation training that reflects the distinctive expertise of practitioners in their fields. However, without having a solid understanding on what competences need to be taught, any accreditation currently would seem rather random.

Within the UK, the Chartered Institute of Library and Information Professionals (CILIP) accredits both educational programs and professional practitioners, who have to evidence their competence in relation to the CILIP *Body of Professional Knowledge*[36] to become chartered members of the institute. CILIP also plays a significant role in CPD, by offering formal revalidation of professional qualifications (which may in due course be replaced by a mandatory CPD scheme) and delivering a varied program of conferences, seminars, and workshops on professional issues through its extensive network of regional branches and special interest groups. CILIP's role in promoting and supporting the development of professional roles is exemplified by the range of external and on-site courses previously on teaching and learning, which made a significant contribution to the professionalization of the teaching role of librarians in relation to information literacy development. CILIP could potentially fulfill a similar role in promoting and supporting the more extensive involvement of library and information professionals in data management and curation. Professional bodies and potential employers may also have a role to play in developing and supporting paid internships.

Where Should We Be in Five Years?

Information Science Professionals' Perspective

Within five years, data management and curation should be regarded as mainstream activity for library and information professionals, to the extent that facilitating long-term access to data sets is accepted as part of their core business and managed alongside access to other key resources and services in the continually changing information universe of the digital world. Specialist posts (e.g. data librarians, data resources managers, or coordinators) or teams (e.g. data services teams, digital curation teams) could be used within libraries to support service development and embed data services in existing library functions, such as acquisitions, cataloguing, reference, liaison and education/training, in the same way that many libraries created specialist electronic resources posts and teams to manage the transition from the print-based to the hybrid print and electronic library, until e-resources became commonplace and were no longer regarded as a new specialist activity.

---

[36] CILIP (2004) *Body of Professional Knowledge,* London: Chartered Institute of Library and Information Professionals.

Data management and curation should similarly be included in the core curriculum of initial professional education programs in library and information science, incorporated into courses/modules/units covering subjects such as information resources, information literacy, knowledge organization, collection management, intellectual property, service development, research methods, and professional roles. In addition to the integration of data management and curation into generalist programs in librarianship and information management, we should have specialist provision with more in-depth technical content for practitioners interested in specializing in this area. It is not clear how extensive such provision should be, but it could take the form of one or more electives, maybe promoted as a specialist pathway. Similarly, it is not clear whether whole programs devoted specifically to data management and curation will be needed for library/information practitioners or for entrants to the field from other backgrounds, but these could be offered at the level of a postgraduate certificate, diploma or Masters, as both initial professional education and specialized CPD programs. Such offerings already exist (notably in the iSchools at the universities of Illinois, North Carolina and Michigan), but they need to be more widespread, especially outside the US. We should also be aiming to have an array of short courses and resources for self-paced learning available for practitioners whose initial education did not cover data management, for those who decide later to specialize in this area and for general professional updating.

Success could be judged by several different criteria, depending on the perspectives taken. A key question here is whether the goal is to make data management and curation core business for library and information professionals or to create a new professional field that could be seen as either a sub-profession within the information field or a hybrid profession located at the intersection of two or more professional disciplines (for example, library/information science, information technology/computer science and/or archives/records management) or combining information-related expertise with an academic discipline.

On the one hand, success could mean data management is seen as "business as usual" and *not* something novel or specialist; on the other hand, success could mean the establishment and recognition of a new professional career, whose maturity is evidenced by the existence of specialist positions at progressive levels of the management hierarchy; development of distinct communities of practice with their own dedicated professional networks and associations/formal bodies; and provision of specialist training courses and educational programs that are formally accredited and lead to recognized and valued qualifications.[37]

Information Technology Professionals' Perspective

One goal would be to have an accepted dual stream education scheme that is suitable to both educate experts on a foundational basis to develop the competences to develop solutions for the new data management, curation, and preservation challenges arising, as well as to train practitioners to obtain the skills to put existing know-how into practice.

Both will need to be based on extremely solid IT competences in order to understand the complexities of entire system processes. A measure of success of both the education and training activities in digital curation will be whether the experts emerging from these programs will find wide-spread acceptance in the domains where curation is currently not even being considered as a dominant topic, namely in the IT industry developing new architectures, computing principles and systems, and the industry where massive amounts of digital information (both data objects as well as entire business processes) will need to be curated or self-curating.

True success will have been reached when the concept of curation is so embedded as a standard non-functional requirement in any IT infrastructure that it would actually no longer be considered worth mentioning specifically—as a very far-reaching vision into the future.

Research Professionals' Perspective

Success would mean that data curation and management activity was seen simply as part of good research practice—a core part of any researcher's job and not something extra. Increasing funding body and research council requirements for evidence of data management planning as part of new grant proposals has led to some limited success in raising researchers' awareness of the importance of data management and curation. However, to avoid

---

[37] Corrall, S. (2008) "The emergence of hybrid professionals: new skills, roles and career options for the information professional." In: Turner, C. (ed.) *Online Information 2008 Proceedings*, pp.67-73. London: Incisive Media.

data management planning being viewed as a "tick-box" exercise by researchers, it will be increasingly important that peer reviewers are able to effectively assess data management plans that are submitted. Organizations such as the UKDA and DCC are currently developing guidelines to help reviewers assess data management plans fairly. Without strong evidence of potential rewards or demonstrable benefits for researchers undertaking data management and curation activities, it is highly unlikely that we will see any lasting success in this area.

Longer-term success could be measured by "invisible" curation where researchers simply make use of hardware and software that are capable of producing preservation-ready data. Until that time, success will depend on clear communication between all stakeholders. Researchers will need to be aware of their data management and curation responsibilities and be able to define their specific data management and curation requirements to both information technologists and information specialists. Researchers should understand the bigger picture and be able to make effective decisions about how they manage their data early on in the curation lifecycle so that longer-term curation, preservation and reuse is more easily facilitated.

Experienced Trainers' Perspective

A number of goals can be construed from progress on addressing the risks and challenges described earlier. Generally, it is hoped that the amount, depth, breadth, and flow of learning and knowledge in knowledge transfer and training in data management and curation will have expanded in five years' time across disciplinary, organizational, and national boundaries. Specifically, it is also hoped that:

1. There will be more data management and curation related internship programs offered. The concept of data management and curation training, including through internships, will have become more widespread and accepted and that data management and curation will be considered from the start in projects, grant designs, etc. Sustainability in training programs and employment will have become a reality, with budgets for opportunities that last for more than a year or two. The research base on internships will also have grown.

2. Metrics to evaluate data management and curation training and internships will have been further identified, developed, and utilized, with surveys and other data collection tools, to

study the alignment of and successes in educational and other knowledge-transfer efforts. Examples could include assessments of whether a given program or project raised the number of people skilled in aspects of data management and curation (data that can also be segmented in various ways, such as skill levels), student employment patterns, effectiveness ratings, costs over time, the number of cultural heritage institutions that have participated in data management and curation activities, and return on investment.

3. More standards, best practices, guidelines, and tools will have become available in data management and curation and internships in general. Expertise and collaboration, including on best practices, will be utilized not only across cultural-heritage fields and institutions, but from other fields (such as technology and business) where there is mutual interest and benefit. In addition to metrics, milestones will be important to incorporate into program designs, and reaching them will be key indicators of success. A consistent theme that underlies this paper is to start small, hopefully achieve some small successes, and from there build a cycle that will grow.

Recommended Areas for Alignment

Several actions could be progressed in the short term to address some of the challenges we are facing and to exploit the opportunities described above. Each of these recommendations depends upon cooperation—between disciplines, industry and at the international level—to foster any real and sustainable change in practice.

Develop Accredited Curriculum, Providers, and Metrics

As noted above, there are a number of continuing education courses incorporating aspects of data management, curation, and preservation currently on offer. Recent surveys have been carried out by DPOE[38] and DigCurV[39] to identify the number and range of training courses available across the US, Canada and EU. However, there is as yet no means of benchmarking these courses or their content. As such, it can be difficult to know who should be

---

[38] DPOE Needs Assessment Survey, 2010, http://www.digitalpreservation.gov/education/documents/DPOENeedsAssessment SurveyExecutiveSummary.pdf (last accessed 05-21-2012).

[39] DigCurV project training registry, http://www.digcur-education.org/eng/Training-opportunities (last accessed 05-21-2012).

attending these courses for maximum benefit and exactly what participants will be able to do in a practical sense upon completion. We need some way to classify training courses and to illustrate clear course objectives and outcomes for prospective participants.

The RIN Information Handling Working Group has developed a draft set of criteria that could enable course providers to self-certify and quality check their courses and help to address some of the challenges listed above.[40] The draft criteria includes elements drawn from teaching and learning resources criteria devised by other bodies including Vitae,[41] Jorum,[42] CILIP,[43] HEA,[44] and DELILA.[45] While the criteria are intended to assist with self-certification in the short-term, there is longer-term potential for an external body to use the criteria as a means of formal certification of training courses.

Key recommendation:

Foster cooperation between DPOE, DigCurV and RIN Information Handling Working Group to test the draft criteria using real-life courses identified via the training surveys. There may be potential for Knowledge Exchange partners to liaise with training providers at the EU level to help test and refine the criteria. An international workshop led by RIN and the DCC to bring together training providers to review and test the criteria would be a possibility in 2012.

Address Supply and Demand

As demand for data management, curation and preservation training increases amongst all stakeholders it will be vital that there is an adequate pool of qualified trainers capable of delivering high quality tuition. DigitalPreservationEurope (DPE) developed a

---

[40] Ongoing RIN work on defining draft "Criteria for describing and reviewing good practice in information literacy training" is being led by Stephane Goldstein, RIN
[41] See Vitae Database of Practice: http://www.vitae.ac.uk/policy-practice/34837/Database-of-practice.html (last accessed 03-26-2012).
[42] See Jorum Learning and Teaching Competition:
http://community.jorum.ac.uk/view.php?id=35 (last accessed 03-26-2012).
[43] CILIP CSG Information Literacy Group, Information Literacy Practitioner of the Year http://www.informationliteracy.org.uk/2010/12/csg-information-literacy-group-information-literacy-practitioner-of-the-year-nominations-sought/ (last accessed 03-26-2012).
[44] HEA evaluation of commercial online tutorial packages.
[45] DELILA criteria for evaluating information literacy and digital literacy open educational resources (OERs); these are drawn heavily from the original version of the above RIN criteria.

registry of trainers[46] to help identify individuals capable of contributing to and/or delivering data management, curation, and preservation training. While the list of experts is extensive and spans the globe, it is important to note that most of the individuals on the list are not full-time trainers. As such, there is a limit to the amount of training that they can realistically deliver. To avoid demand outstripping supply, we need to train up professional trainers, institutional support staff, and practitioners to deliver the courses where appropriate. The recent DPOE Baseline Workshop sponsored by the Library of Congress' Digital Preservation Outreach and Education (DPOE) Program aimed to develop a cohort of trainers capable of delivering curation and preservation training. Graduates of this pilot workshop were trained in six key aspects of digital preservation taught by leading experts in the field. A key component of the workshop was to guide the participants in developing and presenting their own workshops, which they will subsequently run in their own regions by the end of 2012. There is great potential for applying this approach to data management, curation and preservation in the UK, Europe and indeed worldwide.

Key recommendation:

Current training providers should evaluate the DPOE Baseline workshop approach and consider cooperating with DPOE to roll out this approach in other countries. The DCC sent a member of staff to take part in the pilot workshop as an observer and, as a result, is looking to work with DPOE to take this approach forward in the UK. The DCC will share details of the DPOE approach with fellow members of the RIN Information Handling Working Group and the Knowledge Exchange to see if there is potential for greater join-up at the EU level to run follow-on workshops in cooperation with DPOE. An initial meeting between DPOE, DCC and DigCurV to take this forward took place in October 2011 and follow-up meetings are planned.

Engage with Employers and Professional Bodies

Students need to know that participation in data management, curation, and preservation related education and training programs

---

[46] DigitalPreservationEurope (DPE) registry of trainers:
http://www.digitalpreservationeurope.eu/registries/trainers/ (last accessed 03-26-2012).

will help them to become graduates with the actionable skills that employers seek. Most training providers provide a list of learning outcomes as part of their course descriptions but little has been done so far to actually assess whether those who participate actually leave with the ability to fulfill those learning objectives. In addition to designing mechanisms to test knowledge, it requires time and effort on the part of trainers to assess coursework and examination results. As noted above, this may be problematic due to the fact that most data management and curation trainers have other responsibilities in addition to providing training. It can also be difficult to assess data management, curation, and preservation skills in the short term. A grasp of the key concepts may only emerge as students return to the workplace and start to implement what they have learned. Networks of trainers could possibly be set up to provide ongoing feedback in a distributed fashion. But, again securing trainers' time may be a challenge. Another option might be to emulate the approach taken by DigCCurr for its professional institute.[47] Students of the professional institute are reconvened after six-to-twelve months to share how they have implemented what they learned during the course in their workplace. This approach facilitates longer-term assessment of participants' skills and places fewer ongoing demands on trainers' time.

We must also seek to engage with employers and professional bodies to act as reviewers for current training offerings and associated learning objectives and either endorse these skills or identify gaps that need to be addressed. There are a number of current initiatives looking to engage with industry and professional bodies at the moment. For instance, DaMSSI has developed a series of career profiles to illustrate how data management and curation relates to the day-to-day activities for a small number of professions. These profiles may be of value in engaging with professional bodies and industry as they demonstrate in a tangible way why data management and curation skills are important. These profiles are a great starting point but we need to develop a larger pool of profiles for a greater range of professions. The EU-funded TIMBUS project has succeeded in engaging industry as core partners in their FP7 project. Training will be a key component of this project's work and the approach adopted by TIMBUS may be a useful model for others seeking to engage with industry in the development and delivery of training.

---

[47] See DigCCurr Institute: http://www.ils.unc.edu/digccurr/institute.html (last accessed 03-26-2012).

APARSEN, another FP7 funded project, is aiming to develop and deliver certified training. The results of both of these projects will be of interest as they progress over the coming years.

Key recommendations:

Current training providers should review their methods of assessing participants' knowledge and skills. In particular, providers should review the DigCCurr Professional Institute model.

Training providers may wish to develop and contribute to the DCC and RIN's collection of career profiles[48] using the DaMSSI template. The profiles help to highlight the baseline data management and curation skills that professionals in various disciplines need to carry out their daily work. These profiles may also serve as useful marketing tools for attracting prospective students and could be valuable for engaging with professional bodies and industry.

Group projects could be a useful way to assess skill levels. One possible exercise would be to have students collaborate on developing a data management plan for a sample data set resulting from a fictional project. This would work particularly well for courses that aim to attract participants from multiple disciplines, as it would provide an opportunity to hone communication skills and develop a shared solution to a specific problem. Another potential means of testing skills would be to have students develop experimental strategies that can be tested in the Planets Testbed and/or Plato tool. Plato allows users to measure the effectiveness of tools to preserve at-risk objects while the Testbed provides a controlled environment to carry out preservation experiments.[49] The EC-funded Planets project came to an end in 2010 but the tools are being maintained by the Open Planets Foundation (OPF). These approaches would be suitable for both professional development training and formal education courses and could be piloted by a number of the education ANADP panel members. The DCC will aim to pilot an assessed data management planning exercise as part

---

[48] DaMSSI career profiles collection, http://www.dcc.ac.uk/training/data-management-courses-and-training/career-profiles (last accessed 05-21-2012).
[49] See Planets project testbed: http://www.planets-project.eu/software/ (last accessed 03-26-2012).

of its DC101 training course by the end of 2012. iSchools may be an excellent place to pilot student group projects in a formal education setting.

Improve Cooperation in Defining Skill-sets

Recent government recommendations in the UK state that HEIs should be explicit about graduates' career prospects for all courses they offer. This is something that training providers should aspire to as well. There are a number of data management and curation related courses being offered around the globe. The DPOE course calendar[50] and Digital Curation Exchange (DCE) registry list just a few. However, without agreement on how to describe courses and their objectives it is very difficult for prospective students to be able to assess which courses are right for them—both with respect to their immediate needs and also to allow them to hone their data management and curation skills over their entire careers. We need to develop a coherent way to classify education and training options to facilitate effective comparison of offerings and to enable professional development planning.

Key recommendation:

One solution might be to make use of the existing DPOE pyramid, which classifies skills into three broad categories: executive, managerial, and practical. This approach could provide a logical framework to describe courses with minimal effort on the part of course providers and potentially great benefit for students. The DPOE pyramid also lends itself to the description of course materials for those wishing to undertake self-directed learning. For instance, there could be potential to retrospectively apply the DPOE pyramid classifications to materials deposited into JORUM and the DPE registry of training materials[51] to ease discovery by prospective students. We might also wish to consider making use of the DCC's curation lifecycle model as a means of describing specific data management and curation actions and roles. The information handling aspects of Vitae's RDF may offer a valuable progression map for career development. The

---

[50] See DPOE training calendar:
  http://www.digitalpreservation.gov/education/courses/index.html (last accessed 03-26-2012).
[51] See DigitalPreservationEurope (DPE) registry of training materials:
  http://www.digitalpreservationeurope.eu/registries/materials/ (last accessed 03-26-2012).

results of JISC and RIN funded-DaMSSI project may offer valuable insights into the potential value of the RDF for professional development planning. The EC-funded DigCurV project is currently undertaking course profiling work for EU data management, curation, and preservation courses. Current discussions between DPOE, DCC, and DigCurV staff may result in some pilot testing of the DPOE pyramid classifications on a corpora of EU courses. Other training providers should also consider the DPOE pyramid as a means of contextualizing course offerings. Ongoing discussions between RIN, DCC and DigCurV may also result in further testing of the RDF.

Provide Hands-On Experience

There is no substitute for hands-on, practical experience. In an ideal world, we would see curation and preservation professionals emerging from something akin to a teaching hospital. Internships and student placements are another great way to boost practical skills. These exchanges are also effective for feeding employers' needs back into course design. However as noted above, a number of elements need to be built into internships and placements to ensure that they are valuable for both the host and the participant. Potential hosts and interns/students often struggle to adequately pin down what it is they are aiming to get out of the experience. As a result, many internships and placements fail to live up to either party's expectations. Host institutions that do not get interns/students with the right skills for their particular needs may be reluctant to engage in future exchanges. Similarly, we do not want to send interns/students to host institutions where their skills will not be put to best use. Success depends upon well-defined work with clear expectations—for both parties—of what will result from the experience.

Finding a raft of suitable host institutions and candidates locally can be tough. In most cases interns and students will need to consider carrying out their placements in another city or even another country. While many students are keen to carry out work experience in another country there are often linguistic, financial, and legal barriers that limit the possibilities. Regional, national, and international structures to facilitate internships and exchanges would be beneficial to both host institutions and the candidates. It would provide access to a greater pool of host institutions and suitable candidates and enable more granular matching of students/interns' skills to hosts' needs.

Key recommendation:

DPOE has established a rigorous approach to its internship program. Hosts and candidates are carefully matched to ensure that maximum benefit is achieved for both parties. The proposed work is clearly described and concrete objectives for both parties are clearly spelled out. Those aiming to offer data management, curation and preservation related placements should review the DPOE approach and consider implementing a similarly robust approach. While DPOE hosts and candidates span the US, it would be beneficial to extend this pool internationally. The authors of this essay are keen to explore the potential of extending the DPOE approach to include European partners.

Conclusions

The risks associated with a lack of alignment between disciplines and nations in developing and delivering data management, curation, and preservation education and training are serious. Numerous challenges hinder our efforts to mitigate these risks. However, there are concrete actions that could be undertaken in the short to mid-term to improve the overall outlook. There are some degrees of overlap and some dependencies in the authors' list of recommendations. Agreement in the very short term on what practical actions should be prioritized and taken forward is needed. Several of the projects and initiatives mentioned in the recommendations section are already undertaking work in key areas and could be viewed as catalysts for action.

If the recommendations cited by the authors are taken forward collectively, we should—over the next five years—be able to make good progress in:

- Describing and comparing data management courses across disciplines and match skills across data curation lifecycle and the various roles;

- Communicating data management and curation requirements and activities across disciplines;

- Making use of established frameworks to help identify progression paths for skills development in a range of disciplines;

- Assessing and benchmarking data management, curation, and preservation skills in both recent graduates and professionals; and

- Engaging with professional bodies to endorse and accredit data management and curation skills.

Data management, curation, and preservation roles and associated skill sets will change over time. Improvements to infrastructure may eventually automate and effectively shield management, curation, and preservation processes from the majority of stakeholders. However, until that point in time we need professionals in all disciplines who are trained to undertake specific management and curation actions. These professionals should also be able to communicate effectively with other stakeholders in the lifecycle. However, we must always bear in mind that mindsets are as important as skill sets. Accordingly, we must endeavor to include elements of critical thinking and problem solving in education and training courses for all disciplines along with more practical data management and curation skills.

References

ALA. (2009). *Core Competences of Librarianship,* Washington, DC: American Library Association. http://www.ala.org/educationcareers/sites/ala.org.educatio ncareers/files/content/careers/corecomp/corecompetences/ finalcorecompstat09.pdf (last accessed 05-21-2012).

ALIA. (2005). *The Library and Information Sector: Core Knowledge Skills and Attributes,* rev. ed. Deakin: Australian Library and Information Association. http://www.alia.org.au/policies/core.knowledge.html (last accessed 05-21-2012).

APARSEN project, http://www.alliancepermanentaccess.org/index.php/aparse n/ (last accessed 05-21-2012).

ASIS&T. (2001). *ASIST Educational Guidelines,* Silver Spring, MD: American Society for Information Science and Technology. http://www.asis.org/Board/educational_guidelines.html (last accessed 05-21-2012).

CILIP. (2004). *Body of Professional Knowledge,* London: Chartered Institute of Library and Information Professionals. http://www.cilip.org.uk/sitecollectiondocuments/PDFs/qualificationschartership/BPK.pdf (last accessed 05-21-2012).

CILIP. (n.d.). *CILIP Accreditation: The Body of Professional Knowledge, A Guide for Course Designers,* London: Chartered Institute of Library and Information Professionals. http://www.cilip.org.uk/jobs-careers/qualifications/accreditation/bpk/Pages/default.aspx (last accessed 05-21-2012).

Corrall, S. (2008). "The emergence of hybrid professionals: new skills, roles and career options for the information professional." In: Turner, C. (ed.) *Online Information 2008 Proceedings,* pp. 67-73. London: Incisive Media.

DigCCurr Institute: http://ils.unc.edu/digccurr/institute.html (last accessed 03-26-2012).

DigCCurr II: Extending an International Digital Curation Curriculum to Doctoral Students and Practitioners http://www.ils.unc.edu/digccurr/aboutII.html (last accessed 03-26-2012).

DigCurV project: http://www.digcur-education.org (last accessed 03-26-2012).

Digital Curation Centre (DCC). (n.d.). Digital Curation Lifecycle Model. http://www.dcc.ac.uk/resources/curation-lifecycle-model (last accessed 05-21-2012).

Digital Curation Centre DC101 training materials: http://www.dcc.ac.uk/training/digital-curation-101 (last accessed 03-26-2012).

Digital Futures: http://www.digitalconsultancy.net/digifutures/ (last accessed 03-26-2012).

Digital Preservation Management (DPM) Workshops: http://www.dpworkshop.org (last accessed 03-26-2012).

Digital Preservation Outreach and Education (DPOE): http://www.digitalpreservation.gov/education/ (last accessed 03-26-2012).

Digital Preservation Training Programme (DPTP):

http://www.dptp.org/ (last accessed 03-26-2012).

Gabridge, T. (2009). "The last mile: liaison roles in curating science and engineering research data," *Research Libraries Issues,* 265, pp. 15-21. http://www.arl.org/bm~doc/rli-265-gabridge.pdf (last accessed 05-21-2012).

Garritano, J.R. and Carlson, J.R. (2009). "A subject librarian's guide to collaborating on e-science projects," *Issues in Science and Technology Librarianship,* 57. http://www.istl.org/09-spring/refereed2.html#15 (last accessed 05-21-2012).

Hank, C. and Davidson, J. (2009). "International Data curation Education Action (IDEA) Working Group: a report from the second workshop of the IDEA," *D-Lib Magazine,* 15 (3/4). http://www.dlib.org/dlib/march09/hank/03hank.html (last accessed 05-21-2012).

Henty, M. (2008). "Developing the capability and skills to support e-research," *Ariadne,* 55. http://www.ariadne.ac.uk/issue55/henty/ (last accessed 05-21-2012).

High Level Expert Group on Scientific Data. (2010). *Riding the Wave: How Europe can gain from the rising tide of scientific data* report. http://cordis.europa.eu/fp7/ict/e-infrastructure/docs/hlg-sdi-report.pdf (last accessed 05-21-2012).

Howe, D. *et al.* (2008). "Big data: the future of biocuration," *Nature,* 455 (7209), pp. 47-50. http://www.ncbi.nlm.nih.gov/pmc/articles/PMC2819144/ (last accessed 05-21-2012).

IFLA (2003). *Guidelines for Professional Library/Information Educational Programs,* 3rd rev. ed. The Hague: International Federation of Library Associations and Institutions. http://www.ifla.org/en/publications/guidelines-for-professional-libraryinformation-educational-programs-2000 (last accessed 05-21-2012).

Information Management and Preservation (IMP) programme at Humanities Advanced Technology and Information

Institute at the University of Glasgow.
http://www.gla.ac.uk/postgraduate/taught/informationman
agementpreservationdigitalarchivesrecordsmanagement/
(last accessed 05-21-2012).

JORUM: http://www.jorum.ac.uk (last accessed 03-26-2012).

Knowledge Exchange: http://www.knowledge-exchange.info/ (last
accessed 03-26-2012).

Lanier D, Henderson C. (1999). "Library residencies and
internships as indicators of success: evidence from three
programs." *Bulletin of the Medical Libraries Association.*
87(2):192-199.

Lewis, M. (2010). "Libraries and the management of research
data," in McKnight, S. (ed.), *Envisioning Future
Academic Library Services: Initiatives, Ideas and
Challenges,* pp. 145-168, Facet, London.

Library of Congress. (2010). Digital Preservation Outreach and
Education (DPOE) Training Needs Assessment Survey:
Executive Summary.
http://digitalpreservation.gov/education/documents/DPOE
NeedsAssessmentSurveyExecutiveSummary.pdf (last
accessed 05-21-2012).

Macdonald, S. and Martinez, L. (2005). "Supporting local data
users in the UK academic community," *Ariadne,* 44.
http://www.ariadne.ac.uk/issue44/martinez/ (last accessed
05-21-2012).

NSF. (n.d.) *Long-Lived Digital Data Collections: Enabling
Research and Education in the 21st Century.*
http://www.nsf.gov/pubs/2005/nsb0540/nsb0540_5.pdf
(last accessed 05-21-2012).

Open Planets Foundation: http://www.openplanetsfoundation.org/
(last accessed 03-26-2012).

Pryor, G. and Donnelly, M. (2009). "Skilling up to do data: whose
role, whose responsibility, whose career?" *International
Journal of Digital Curation,* 4 (2),158-170.
http://www.ijdc.net/index.php/ijdc/article/view/126 (last
accessed 05-21-2012).

Ray, J. (2009). "Sharks, digital curation, and the education of
information professionals," *Museum Management and*

Curatorship, 24 (94), 357-368.

SCONUL (2011a). *The Seven Pillars of Information Literacy: A Research Lens for Higher Education,* London: Society of College, National and University Libraries, Working Group on Information Literacy. http://www.sconul.ac.uk/groups/information_literacy/publ ications/researchlens.pdf (last accessed 05-21-2012).

SCONUL (2011b). *The Seven Pillars of Information Literacy: Core Model for Higher Education,* London: Society of College, National and University Libraries, Working Group on Information Literacy. http://www.sconul.ac.uk/groups/information_literacy/publ ications/coremodel.pdf (last accessed 05-21-2012).

Sides CH, Mrvica A. (2007). *Internships: Theory and Practice.* Amityville, NY: Baywood Publishing.

Swan, A. and Brown, S. (2008). *The Skills, Role and Career Structure of Data Scientists and Curators: An Assessment of Current Practice and Future Needs,* Report to the JISC, Truro: Key Perspectives. http://www.jisc.ac.uk/publications/documents/dataskillsca reersfinalreport.aspx (last accessed 05-21-2012).

TIMBUS project, http://timbusproject.net/ (last accessed 05-21-2012).

UK Data Archive: http://www.data-archive.ac.uk/ (last accessed 03-26-2012).

Vitae (2010). *Researcher Development Framework.* Cambridge: Vitae. http://www.vitae.ac.uk/rdf (accessed 05-21-2012).

Witt, M. (2008). "Institutional repositories and research data curation in a distributed environment," *Library Trends,* 57 (2), 191-201.

Conclusions

Clifford Lynch (Coalition for Networked Information)
Nancy Y. McGovern (Massachusetts Institute of Technology)

Introduction

The preceding six chapters discussed the accomplishments to date, the remaining challenges, and next steps pertaining to six core aspects of aligning national approaches to digital preservation—legal, organizational, standards, technical, economic, and education. The essays in the chapters build upon discussions that took place during the panels and breakout sessions of the ANADP conference in May 2011. Cliff Lynch closed the conference and now the volume with the following remarks that so effectively highlight important threads of the discussion, weave in broader trends from beyond the digital preservation community, and, identify a few potential gaps for consideration.

Closing Thoughts (Clifford Lynch)

What I'm going to try and do is conclude this very valuable conference with a bit of an opinionated synthesis. I will dwell a bit on some of the key things I heard and also reflect on some of the things that I was very surprised not to hear, some of the things we didn't talk about very much, which may be provocative fodder for future conversations.

Let me start with this term "alignment" that has been so central to many of our discussions here because I think it's a very important term. We have spoken about seeking to align national strategies; why do we want to do this? I think there are three motivations. One is that if we're working in the same general direction, it creates a set of opportunities for collaboration, for working together, for pooling resources. That's clearly desirable in areas like preservation where the demands are and probably always will be tremendously in excess of the resources that we can collectively bring to them. To the extent that we can deploy those limited resources more effectively through collaboration, "alignment" is obviously a winning approach.

A second, equally important reason for seeking alignment is not really so much about collaboration in *doing*—actually building systems, accessioning materials, preserving collections—but about establishing mutual support and shared learning. If we are aligned in our broad objectives and goals, we can learn from each other's efforts in a much more effective way. We can take ideas that come from one nation's work and adapt and re-apply them to another; that is again, I think, an important outcome and benefit of alignment.

The third benefit of successful alignment which I didn't hear nearly as much about, and I will be circling back to this several places in my summary, is if we align our strategies, I believe collectively we can make a more effective case for the importance of our preservation strategies to national governments, to other non-governmental funding agencies and really indeed to national and international society at large.

With a portfolio of aligned strategies, we can collectively speak more effectively about the importance of the work we do, and certainly that has come up in a background way again and again as we've spoken about economics, education, about legal issues and barriers. I think that this question of really clarifying the fundamental importance of digital preservation to maintaining the cultural and intellectual record, the memory of our nations and of the world, has got to be a central objective. We have a great challenge in educating both the broad public in our nations and the governments that represent these publics; to the extent that we can align strategies we can make that case better.

We laid out six axes of alignment—Legal, Organizational, Standards, Technical, Standards, Economic, and Education—which we talked about in detail. It is worth noting that they are not really orthogonal, that indeed these axes interrelate and interact in very complicated ways; they might almost be thought of as perspectives on the challenges of digital preservation.

I wanted to go through those six axes and make a few specific comments. Let's begin with the legal. I agree that the legal issues are becoming more and more dominant here. We really should look for opportunities to collaborate specifically on the legal issues. I was struck when I read the report *The New Renaissance* by the Comité des Sages (what a wonderful, wonderful name!) and then again when we talked about this report during the ANADP conference to address the necessity for thinking about legal barriers to the stewardship of cultural heritage, both internationally and as a collection of nations. Europeana, which was one of the developments that motivated the report, has been an excellent case study, though of course the focus here is really access rather than preservation; the real stewardship is done by the contributors to Europeana, I think.

The New Renaissance was so valuable because it was a collective effort: the recommendations were addressed not just to one nation but really consisted of broad principles intended to make sense across the European Union—and beyond. So what we had here was a group of smart people looking at the needs of a very large, complex multi-national project to make cultural heritage available, and trying to abstract out a set of principles and recommendations that could drive public policy and law-making in a number of different countries.

Can we come together to do something like that? Not necessarily to specifically collectively negotiate with the IP industries but really try to give a truly multi-national kind of view of what could help us move our work along? Having that conversation—and I'll link this up to a couple of other suggestions shortly—could be a tremendously importantly outcome of our deliberations at this meeting.

The organizational axis holds lessons for all of us, many of them around words and deeds. We have a lot of words here and we need to look honestly at the deeds as well. Some of the organizational alignment issues that showed up were collaboration around ongoing programs as opposed to projects. We are in fact now only in the early days in some nations of really moving from digital preservation as a project, or a series of projects, to digital preservation as a fundamental program that is one of the core activities of our memory organizations. I think we need to be conscious of that as we look at organizational issues.

Organizational things we did not talk about too much included strategies within nations—how you roll up from very local organizations in cities and towns to state or provincial organizations and then up to the national level, how you align efforts in this context. It's not neatly hierarchical—I'm thinking here also about the relative roles of institutions in specific sectors like universities that have a certain commitment to maintaining the scientific and scholarly record vs. the memory institutions at a national level that often have a much broader mandate that encompasses the cultural record. Clearly there's a lot of variation at the intra-national level from country to country there but this is an area that is going to become of increasing concern and needs focus.

The other organizational issue we largely ignored was the question of replication of material among organizations at whatever level or within whatever sector—how choices were made there, with what degree of autonomy those choices were made, and whether they were made by explicit agreements and declarations. The whole question of interdependence among organizations in preservation is a very central question, at every level, within nations and among nations; how this interdependence is negotiated and managed among a very large set of institutions in many countries is going to be very complex.

In the technical discussion there were some very valuable conversations about benchmarking and testing. We need to learn how to do these a lot better; we don't do them very well now. We've done them within some national efforts. As part of NDIIPP in the United States, I'm thinking of some test audits of trusted repositories, or some experimental ingest and export of materials from one repository to another for example, but we're never going to get enough scale unless we can do this across national efforts. Benchmarking will tie into economics. It will help us to understand where organizations are doing things cost-effectively. It may also help us to collectively evaluate commercial products and services that come into play.

There was a lot of rather glib talk about interoperability that came up in the technical discussions. I think we need to be quite rigorous here about what we mean by interoperability, what's interoperating with what and for what purpose and how broadly that interoperability is expected to occur; how much work we're going to put into specific instances of interoperability or just plain inter-system communication and interchange as opposed to the expectation of immediate interoperability that's characterized by electrical outlets, certain telecommunications, protocols, things like that. I think this is an important word and an important set of concepts, but it's a word we need to use much more judiciously and rigorously.

There are two words that I didn't hear in the technical discussions. I get very scared whenever I hear a lengthy discussion of technical issues in digital preservation that doesn't mention these two words. The first is *Monoculture*. There is a possibility, a danger, of doing too much alignment here. The reason for that is the second word that I didn't hear, which is *Hubris*. We need to acknowledge that we don't really know how to do long-term digital preservation. We're going to have a lot more confidence that we know what we're doing here about a hundred years from now as we look at what efforts actually brought data successfully a hundred years into the future. But in the relatively early stages of technologies like these, it's much easier to identify failures than long-term successes.

One always wants to be careful here to assume that there's not a simple magic bullet answer to the challenges of digital preservation and that a certain amount of diversity and redundancy in the system is actually a very valuable antidote to various kinds of mistakes we might make. When resources are very scarce, there's a great tendency to centralize, to standardize, to eliminate redundancy in the name of cost effectiveness. This can be very dangerous; it can produce systems that are very brittle and vulnerable, and that are subject to catastrophic failure.

There were two areas in the technical discussions that resurfaced repeatedly but I think were not sufficiently emphasized. I want to note these explicitly. The first was the bit storage layer— all of these efforts are going to need a commodity bit storage layer. These are starting to emerge from commercial services. We really need to focus some attention here on specific strategies about the bit layer, whether we want to trade it off among different national projects, or whether the right strategy is to go commercial—and if so, how do we evaluate those commercial services (and particularly their failure modes and behaviors, their resilience), how do we develop the standards we need so that we can unplug from one and plug into another in a fairly casual way. There's going to be a lot of money flowing in this direction and I think it's a common near-term opportunity where we need to spend some time.

The other area which I was really delighted to see featured in one of the presentations but that didn't get much coverage in the discussion was security and integrity. I'm terribly worried as we build up very visible instances of digital cultural heritage that these collections are going to become subject of attack in the same way that national libraries, museums, and similar cultural institutions have been subject to deliberate attack and destruction throughout history.

We need to be very thoughtful about our security and integrity and the many different ways that that ramifies out. Mind you, it's not simply denial of service attacks. For example, many of our archives contain embargoed collections where we're holding material until the people mentioned in them are no longer living or until a copyright expires or other kinds of trigger events. This is absolutely standard practice in archives.

Imagine the impact of having a major repository of this kind of material raided and having a Wikileaks type of dump of all of the embargoed collections in it. Think of what that would do to the confidence and the trust that people express in cultural memory organizations. Or imagine the deliberate and systematic modification or corruption of materials. The stakes here are substantial and we need to be mindful of this issue.

Let me move on to standards briefly. It's interesting that we see standards in so many different roles in digital preservation. One role of course is there are standards that really don't have anything to do with digital preservation directly but characterize the materials that we want to preserve—format and markup standards, for example. Digital preservation depends on literally hundreds of standards, many of which really we have no control over and come from outside. If we had any control over them, they wouldn't look the way they do in many cases.

We also have a thicket of what I characterize as analytical standards. These are not standards about interoperability, they are really best practices that organizations can use to try and self-evaluate. I worry that we have rushed some of this prematurely into the exalted status of standards rather than just saying "this is our current best thinking" and I think that this is a scenario where we may want to stress agility of re-standardization. At the same time, tying back to this question of interoperability, in those places where we need interoperability, we need standards and those two discussions go hand-in-hand.

On economics, there's a lot to say, but here, I just want to note a couple of things—one was the very important point about the distinction between investing in digitization and investing in digital preservation. These are two different activities (though digitization and the broader question of stewardship of both physical and digital materials are connected in deep, complex, and evolving ways) and digitization, because it has an immediate and visible payoff in terms of facilitating access, tends often to absorb money and then create resources that nobody has thought to fund the preservation of. This is an important issue that we need to all be wary of.

We didn't talk too much about scale but I think it's a very important question in economics. We certainly talked a lot about cost models and obviously as we try to budget for this work, understanding cost models better—which is something we will get a better understanding of collectively than individually—demands our attention.

We talked of course about sustainability. Sustainability is a real issue here, but there are cases, I think, where we need to simply take the position that these are public goods and that *is* the sustainability strategy: the public, through their government, pays to sustain materials using general public funds. Sustainability conversations often seem to be an effort to avoid saying that, but I think we need to remind ourselves sometimes it is okay to say that because it's true.

Linked to that issue, though, is the instability of public funding. We have alluded to the nightmare of the defunding of collections of digital materials in some of our conversations here. Actually, that's a nightmare we're going to have to think about harder and we're going to think about what to do about it— because there is massive disinvestment in cultural heritage in many parts of the globe.

The last point I make under economics—and this was touched upon but I think is something that perhaps requires a more intensive evaluation—is the connection between risk management for physical strategies on the one side and the costs that are incurred there, and the opportunity to digitize those collections and then protect the digital on the other as an economic trade off. Digitized versions of physical collections are a very special kind of insurance policy and that again is something that people are just beginning to realize.

Moving to education, there's not too much I can say about this at a high level. There was a very extended discussion of the need to redefine professional education and indeed the necessary expertise of professionals in this area. The one thing I would note is that a lot of these curricula and certifications and other developments are national in nature. So while it's wonderful to have an international discussion, for maximum impact, this discussion must get fed back into the national conversations that librarians and archivists and other players have on a national basis, and we shouldn't lose sight of that.

The other thing I wanted to say about education is that we focused almost entirely on the question of educating professionals in the field and training the next generation of professionals. There's a whole other piece of this that is about training people outside of the field, including indeed the general public. We talked a little bit about the Library of Congress DPOE program, but again, going back to this notion of making the case with the broad public about the importance of this work, I would note for example, the Library of Congress declared a national preservation week for the second year this year and actually used this as an opportunity to make outreach to the army of people who are showing up at their doorstep and the doorstep of public libraries all over America saying "What do I do with my digital photos so I don't lose them?," or "What do I do with movies that I'm making with my smartphone?."

There's a tremendous conversation to be had here, which will connect up with the whole notion not just of how we preserve heritage but ultimately what constitutes it. We should not miss that piece of conversation with the public. It's a very rich conversation actually, especially in the light of the rapidly occurring obsolescence being engineered in the consumer electronics field.

That in turn is starting to play out in the notion that books, which you used to be able to count on for a long time, are starting to look pretty ephemeral. Music, games, software, all of these are getting artificially enforced very brief lives now and this is something the public is starting to realize and wants to talk about.

So that's a very quick trip through the six axes that were identified and some of the highlights of the conversations from my perspective. Now, things I didn't hear about—there are a pair of idioms in English. One talks about "the elephant in the room," what this means is a major issue that everybody recognizes and agrees is there but nobody quite wants to talk about and everybody is sort of avoiding it by implication and maneuver.

There is a related idiom in English that talks about the "dead moose on the table"—this is a major issue that not only does everybody recognize without acknowledging or addressing, like the elephant, but the moose is dead and it's getting nasty because it's starting to smell. Everyone present knows we'll be forced to deal with the dead moose pretty soon.

We have a very large creature in the form of data-intensive scholarship, and a few more in other areas that I want to call to your attention. I leave it to you to decide which are elephants and which are dead moose—and how quickly we are going to be forced to deal with them.

Only one presentation here focused on e-science and e-scholarship and the data deluge that's coming out of these developments. This is centrally relevant to all facets of our work. There's a lot of money involved here, big investments. It's pushing technological developments. It's affecting funding patterns. It's transformative.

This is not an arena within which most national libraries have historically, or even in very recent times, been involved. Indeed while the strategies for dealing with this are in some cases at the national level (see the UK e-science programs for one example) they are most commonly centered around organizations—for example data archives—very distinct from the national library or similar long-established cultural memory organization. Some of the institutions that are being identified as responsible for stewardship of the "data deluge" are disciplinary and international, some of them are disciplinary and national, and yet others are institutional in nature—in this case putting the primary burden on the universities that house the scholars. All of those various assignments of responsibility are models that are being proposed and indeed actively deployed now for supporting e-science and the data stewardship requirements coming out of e-science.

This is not only driving technology and infrastructure support for scholarship, it's driving a growing segment of the IT-driven educational efforts, and, in fact, it looks to me like it's going to go even farther and become pervasive in our society, reshaping health care, investing, workforce development, intelligence, government and many other areas. There's going to be massive governmental and commercial infrastructure investment here in all sectors. We're seeing government and commercial players getting increasingly interested in things like data driven analytics—"big data" is the phrase of the year. There's a report that just came out from McKinsey global consulting about a week ago[1] about the big data

---

[1] McKinesy Global Institute, "Big Data: The Next Frontier for Innovation, Competition, and Productivity:" http://www.slideshare.net/fred.zimny/mckinsey-quarterlys-2011-report-the-challenge-and-opportunityof-big-data (last accessed 04-25-2012).

in the commercial sector and how exploiting this appropriately is going to really change business strategies. We need to be very cognizant of this and to talk much more explicitly about how this interacts with national strategies for digital preservation and where the policy and technical linkages belong, where infrastructure might be common and shared. We're going to need to think holistically about the digital preservation strategies at a national level as covering the full range of the cultural *and* scientific record.

There are two other areas I'd nominate as important creatures, living or dead, in our room. One is audio/visual materials as part of the intellectual and cultural record, and not necessarily digital ones. In fact, the worst problems here seem to be the ones that aren't digital, the ones that recap the history of audio and photographic and moving image capture technology throughout the late 19th and 20th centuries and actually comprise enormous, critically important swaths of our record of the 20th century in particular.

These unique, rare, critical and fragile culture records are nasty, they're expensive to deal with and often inextricably connected to playback mechanisms that rely on long-gone technologies, and in many cases they are literally decaying before our eyes. Their stewardship requires very specialized and scarce expertise. They are in many cases footnotes within the broader national preservation strategies, which still tend to privilege the written word over other forms within the overall cultural record. I think they deserve urgent and very focused attention and investment. There is a massive disaster happening here.

The second rapidly growing creature is the new born-digital content and really trying to understand the scope of that. We've gone to some of the obvious places—for example the surface Web—but there are tremendous amounts of digital data coming out of the government and business sectors, for example, and out of social networking, and out of any number of sources that we don't really have a good assessment about. There are inaccessible databases hidden behind Websites that formulate queries; these were once printed catalogs, schedules, and other documents that could be readily collected. We don't understand to what extent these constitute an essential part of the cultural record that we seek to preserve. And our means of accessioning much of this material into our memory organizations currently depends on *noblisse oblige* on the part of data producers; established mechanisms such as copyright deposit laws can and are being extended to broadcast media and to the surface Web but do not seem to have natural extensions to many other types of material, particularly those that are not publically accessible.

So with those identifications of creatures—elephants or moose—I'll conclude by suggesting that there are probably two additional axes (or convergences) that are of overriding importance when we talk about alignment. One is outreach, making the case, educating the public, educating the policy makers about the importance of digital preservation to the maintenance, management, and consistent presence of our cultural, scholarly, intellectual, and scientific record. That to me is an absolutely overriding priority that we need to continue to discuss. There is great strength and powerful vindication here if we can but harness and focus it.

The second line of convergence is archival scope, our institutional and national collecting and stewardship policies. What are we collecting and what are our strategies for prioritizing that and for obtaining it? This connects up to legal issues and institutional-level risk management questions directly linked to those legal fault lines, it connects up to public policy issues, but it encompasses everything from media to audio/visual material, and from e-science and e-scholarship to news. And how do we make decisions about what we must discard, and how long to keep it before we discard it, due to lack of resources—particularly when resources are so limited that it extraordinarily difficult to devise a rational decision-making framework.

Consider this as just one example, albeit a very well-selected and illuminating one. News has been a fundamental part of the public record in all nations. Newspapers are always important; but we know that news is completely changing its character. News isn't newspapers, it's a continuously updated set of databases, where early reports are often repeatedly superseded by more recent information; it's a system of social media interactions; it's increasingly dominated by visual media rather than text. The Library of Congress has convened several workshops in the last couple of years looking at some of the issues around the preserving of news, specifically.

I'm sure some of the other nations represented here have also looked at this because it's an obvious high priority issue. These are the kinds of areas where we should be talking together in some detail about our collecting and preserving policies. We should be discussing social media and how we set up the ways to obtain this, and what it means to preserve it; preservation of software; the whole notion of digital representations of the many facets of individual lives—all of these things fall under part of the discussion about collecting policy, and this is the place where there's collaboration, there's shared and mutual learning, there are connections to both the legal and the technical initiatives.

There are also deep connections to the organizational questions—for example, are you going to try and do this on a central basis for a nation or on a very distributed basis? And this becomes particularly important when one looks at phenomena like news, local history, personal papers, and family records, all of which are taking on a digital character. For some nations, it may be impractical to meet the challenges at the national level.

My time is up, and I must stop here. This is a fast and admittedly opinionated attempt to synthesize some of the conversations I've been fortunate to be part of during the Aligning National Approaches to Digital Preservation conference, and to sketch some of the thinking that they have led me to do about strategies for aligning our digital preservation strategies. It's my hope that these thoughts can contribute to setting the agenda for further discussions among the institutions represented here.

-Clifford Lynch, Coalition for Networked Information

Opportunities for Alignment

Each of this volume's essays identified opportunities for alignment that together provide a useful frame for further community discussion. The following summary brings the list of opportunities together for consideration from the opening keynotes, the chapters, and from Cliff's closing remarks.

Legal

- *Raise awareness about legal deposit* – To overcome resistance to legal deposit for digital material, the memory community needs to identify, articulate, and disseminate case studies demonstrating the benefits and impact of legal deposit to different stakeholder groups.

- *Pursue cooperative agreements* – As distributed preservation infrastructures and architectures become the predominant models, these activities need to be governed and implemented in a more certain and supportive legal environment, not just in terms of the agreements, but also in terms of the laws governing how content can be managed for preservation purposes.

- *Investigate collective licensing* – Preserving and providing access to digital material does not just take place at a national level, but current approaches to managing copyright tend to operate at this level. Extended collective licensing could help address issues of orphan works and cross-border access.

Organizational

- *Foster good practice* – Increasing the geographic spread of good practice for digital preservation and curation needs to include a more deliberate exchange of lessons learned and case studies documenting the use of emerging tools, workflows, and techniques across national and continental boundaries, including regions of the world that have not been well represented in the digital preservation field thus far.

- *Encourage collaboration* – Collaborations across institutions and nations should seek to extend the scope of content that is preserved by sustainable digital preservation programs.

- *Shift from projects to programs* – Digital preservation must move from project-driven activities to a core activity of memory organizations, worldwide.

Standards

- *Delineate interoperability standards* – "Interoperability" needs to be explored and defined along the whole chain of steps that form the lifecycle of an object—from its conception to its re-use through the process of preservation.

- *Express platform-agnostic digital preservation requirements* – Moving away from a repository-centric worldview allows concentration upon functional requirements that can be implemented in a variety of information systems that manage digital assets for the short to medium term.

- *Standardize requisite skill-sets* – Codes of practice that rely on clear requirements for skills and know-how should be better defined by setting standards for education and training courses in digital preservation.

- *Engage the users of standards* – The value of standards in digital preservation can best be demonstrated if we engage appropriate user communities in the discussion to determine relevancy, gaps in available standards, and roles in creating new standards

Technical

- *Develop evaluation protocols and benchmarking* – Common test data should be developed and made available to provide the means for evaluating and comparing technical benchmarks across solutions

- *Approach interoperability rigorously* – We must better understand the value of inter-system communication and interchange and weigh that against the value of immediate interoperability in the digital preservation realm.

Economic

- *Raise awareness about sustainable digital preservation* – Initiating a coordinated international campaign could help to make Library/Archive/Museum (LAM) directors and administrators (and the broader public) aware that long-term digital preservation is necessary and that it requires stable funding and a continuous allocation of resources.

- *Establish a digital preservation resource centre (DPRC)* – Provide decision-makers at LAMs with a single place for current information on various digital preservation solutions to enhance uptake and to foster a broader understanding of options.

- *Develop case studies* – Assemble and make available case studies of digital preservation costs in order to promote better and more comprehensive understandings of where costs accrue and where cost savings may be possible.

- *Define selection criteria* – Develop a matrix of selection criteria for digital preservation—in other words, a digital-preservation "triage chart"—to help build a common framework for digital content selection decisions.

- *Study and promote community-sourced solutions* – Identify viable, community-driven business models, particularly those that extend across national boundaries, and study how these models work and can be reapplied in other contexts.

- *Explore opportunities for public-private partnerships* – Identify ways to cooperate in mutually beneficial ways by standardizing the preservation needs of public-sector institutions and by creating conditions in which private companies can compete to meet those needs against an agreed-upon set of benchmarking criteria.

- *Define core services* – Identify key services, coordinate initiatives, promote common standards, implement policies and recommendations, and encourage the use of basic services for preservation networks to offer tested, universally applicable solutions for end-users and to stimulate competition among technology providers, which should in turn lead to lower prices.

- *Support research and development* – Support inter-institutional research and development across national borders to identify tools and services worldwide that yield the best return on investment.

Education

- *Develop an international certificate program* – Develop a common understanding of digital preservation concepts by developing an international certificate program in digital preservation.

- *Develop accredited curriculum, providers, and metrics* – Establish a means for benchmarking courses or their content and foster cooperation between international providers of education and training by using real-life courses to draft and refine metrics.

- *Address supply and demand for qualified trainers* – Develop an adequate pool of qualified trainers capable of delivering high quality training both within and beyond the cultural memory sector.

- *Engage with employers and professional bodies* – Rely upon employers and professional bodies to act as reviewers for current training offerings and associated learning objectives and either endorse these skills or identify gaps that need to be addressed.

- *Improve cooperation in defining skill-sets* – Develop a coherent way to classify education and training options to facilitate effective comparison of offerings and to enable professional development planning.

After emphasizing the benefits of alignment, Cliff Lynch noted a number of additional opportunities within each alignment aspect, observed gaps in the discussion, and proposed two areas for the convergence of the alignment aspects:

- *Develop a multi-national view on challenging issues* (legal) – building on the successes of the New Renaissance as an example, bring together problem solvers from a broad international pool.

- *Build on strategies within nations* (organizational) – align efforts intra-nationally and consider benefits of lateral collaborations at local and regional levels between nations.

- *Leverage interdependence between organizations* (organizational) – evaluate choices about replications at all levels to inform challenging negotiations about interdependence as the community aligns.

- *Link testing of software and implementation to economics* (technical) – the community can achieve economies of scale working cross-nationally on costly efforts like establishing operational benchmarks.

- *Avoid too much alignment* (technical)– multiple approaches are beneficial for technical development and the absence of diverse approaches can lead to a *monoculture* perspective that will be too limited.

- *Accept a long learning curve* (technical) – to avoid the damaging effects of *hubris*, accept that there is a long learning curve and that in a hundred years the community will really know about preserving over long periods of time.

- *Address the need for a commodity bit storage layer* (technical) – embrace the common near-term need for a well-managed bit layer as an opportunity for alignment and work together to evaluate options.

- *Protect against vulnerabilities of collections as examples of digital cultural heritage* (technical) – develop defenses against attacks to the security and integrity of cultural heritage collections that would jeopardize content as well as confidence and trust in repositories.

- *Monitor external standards* (standards) – be aware of the numerous standards pertaining to digital content that are developed beyond the influence of the digital preservation community.

- *Develop readiness for re-standardization* (standards) – prepare for interoperability that alignment might require and the need to adapt current thinking – or organizational standards – as practice evolves.

- *Distinguish between investing in digitization versus digital preservation* (economics) – understand in developing alignment collaborations that digitization is a short-term investment requiring long-term investment in digital preservation that is often not accounted for when content is selected to be digitized.

- *Benefit from a collective understanding of cost models* (economics) – it will be easier to develop a sound understanding of cost models collectively than individually.

- *Accept instances where the sustainability strategy identifies long-term collections as public goods* (economics) – the public through its government sustains digital materials by using general public funds, and international alignment may present opportunities to acknowledge that.

- *Prepare for disinvestment in cultural heritage* (economics) – related to public goods, work together on strategies to respond to massive disinvestment in cultural heritage globally due to economic challenges.

- *Balance costs of physical risk management strategies against opportunities of digitization* (economics) – understand the connection between the costs of risk-management strategies for physical collections and the opportunities to digitize and then protect the digital as an economic trade-off by recognizing the value of digitized content as a special kind of insurance for physical collections.

- *Confer about curricula internationally, then apply nationally* (education) – many curricula and certifications are national, so translate international outcomes into national action

- *Extend training to people outside the community, including the general public* (education) – address the growing needs of people who are preserving their own content as an opportunity to raise awareness more broadly through training and as a counterpoint to rapid commercial obsolescence.

- *Develop holistic strategies for data-intensive scholarship* (gap) – recognize the pervasive impact of data to develop national strategies that embrace the full range of the cultural and scientific record and that make policy and technical linkages to identify candidates for common and shared infrastructure.

- *Devise strategies to address the analog legacy in audio-visual portions of the cultural record* (gap) – address the costs and challenges of preserving fragile and at risk audio-visual resources (e.g., the need for specialized expertise, obsolete formats and media) that might benefit from cumulative effort

- *Extend strategies to new born-digital formats* (gap) – address content that is less familiar and may not be publicly accessible (e.g., data in government and business sectors, social media content, databases underlying Web content) to determine appropriate selection and accessioning approaches.

- *Engage in outreach efforts to make the case to the public and to policy makers* (convergence) – educate the public and policy makers to understand the importance of digital preservation for ensuring the consistent presence of our cultural, scholarly, intellectual, and scientific record.

- *Focus attention on the archival scope reflected in collecting and stewardship policies* (convergence) – enable effective decisions about selection and retention that encompass new and evolving content by evaluating institutional and national collecting and stewardship policies to consider shared collecting and preservation strategies.

Summary

The introduction to the volume provided some background on the emergence of the digital preservation community as context for the volume and introduced a model that might be used to identify milestones as the community takes its next steps towards alignment, incrementally and comprehensively. The six alignment chapters demonstrate both the need to come together to define common goals and objectives for the community to pursue globally and the benefits to be reaped by having an ongoing discussion of those issues. The intent of the conference and the volume was to contribute in some way to the next phase of community development for digital preservation and encourage international collaborations of all kinds. During the more than fifteen years since the release of the *Preserving Digital Information* report in 1996, the development and promulgation of community standards and practice has increased in measurable ways. There is every indication that the community's progress will continue, hopefully with greater frequency across national and domain borders.